S H A P I N G   A   N A T I O N

TWENTIETH-CENTURY AMERICAN ARCHITECTURE AND ITS MAKERS

SHAPING A NATION

Carter Wiseman

W. W. NORTON & COMPANY · NEW YORK · LONDON

For information about permission to reproduce selections from this book,
write to Permissions, W. W. Norton & Company, Inc., 500 Fifth Avenue,
New York, NY 10110.

The text of this book is composed in Electra with the display in Industria
    and Frutiger Ultra Black.
Composition by BTD
Manufacturing by South China Printing Ltd., Hong Kong

Book design by BTD / Robin Bentz and Mary A. Wirth

LIBRARY OF CONGRESS CATALOGING-IN-PUBLICATION DATA
Wiseman, Carter.
        Shaping a nation : twentieth-century American architecture and its makers /
Carter Wiseman.
            p. cm.
        Includes bibliographical references and index.
        ISBN 0-393-04564-1
    1. Architecture, Modern—20th century—United States. 2. Architecture—
United States. 3. Architects—United States—History—20th century. I. Title
NA712.W57   1998
720'.973'0904—dc21   97-9896
                                                                           CIP

W. W. Norton & Company, Inc., 500 Fifth Avenue, New York, N.Y. 10110
http://www.wwnorton.com

W. W. Norton & Company Ltd., 10 Coptic Street, London WC1A 1PU

2   3   4   5   6   7   8   9   0

TO E., E., O., AND D.

Contents

SHAPING A NATION

Introduction

This book begins in the past, but attempts to pass judgment on the present, a hazardous undertaking. Any number of architecture books that have attempted it over the years included all too many designers whose names and works promptly vanished from the collective memory.

My interest in American architecture began while I was in college, and intensified as a graduate student, but it took a different direction when I went into journalism. In beginning this book, I took comfort from a remark made by one of my first editors. Journalists, he said, are people who are willing to write "the first rough draft of history."

In attempting to write a new draft of the history of American architecture up to the present day, I should make my personal prejudices clear. I believe that serious architecture should be buildable, useful, and beautiful. Not that theory and fantasy don't have their places; but in the end, architecture in my view stands or falls by standing or falling, on aesthetic as well as functional terms.

Buildability and use are relatively easy to judge. Beauty is harder, largely because the criteria by which it is measured change over time. Today's success may be the object of tomorrow's ridicule.

I was reminded years ago by an architect of long experience that architects don't function as autonomously as they might like to think they do. Wittingly or not, they respond to the social and economic forces of their day. It is impossible to reinhabit a past age, but I have tried to make my aesthetic judgments by combining contemporary criteria and, where possible, a measure of hindsight, hoping to avoid the diversions of fashion at both ends of the spectrum.

For students of American architectural history, there is much in the early sections of this book that will be familiar. The material has been researched by legions of scholars (and journalists) over the years. My account draws upon the work of many of them, and I hope I have given adequate credit.

I have deliberately excluded most work done by Americans abroad, because, however American, they must design for different traditions and in physical contexts that are most often very different from our own. For much the same reason, I have not dealt extensively with foreign architects working in America, even though many of them have made welcome contributions to the American architectural fabric.

The emphasis on New York City and work by the graduates of a small number of architecture schools will no doubt provoke charges of Eastern elitism. For better *and* worse, however, most of the major issues in American architecture have been addressed at the grandest scale and with the greatest intensity in America's largest city. And many of the most influential practitioners—also for better and worse—have passed through a rather narrow educational channel marked by such schools as Columbia, Harvard, MIT, Princeton, and Yale. Nevertheless, I am well aware that as a native Manhattanite who attended three Eastern universities and has covered architecture for New York–based publications for twenty-five years, I am not immune to the influence of those experiences. The only solace in this conclusion is that, over time, the best work, wherever it originates, tends to percolate to the surface of the national—and eventually the Eastern—consciousness. It is rare that the historical process misses or permanently casts off truly great work.

I have attempted to highlight several major themes that seem to me important in American architectural history. One is the importance of historical publications as sources of inspiration for architects in a country with such a brief architectural history of its own. A second theme is the increasing separation of American architecture from the making of buildings. Since early in this century, American design schools have emphasized aesthetics and originality over construction and tradition. Even today, few American architects have had training comparable to that of the European master builders, and that lack has contributed to an architecture that often seems disembodied from both its artistic precedents and its physical context.

And then there is the American proclivity to approach art of any kind with a certain amount of suspicion, as something that is not practical, and is therefore quite possibly immoral. This impulse has been amplified over the nation's history by the conflict between partisans of the countryside, which has been cast as virtuous, and those of the city, a center of vice and corruption.

In the end, however, the most insistent theme of this book is the integrative ability of a diverse and constantly changing society that has become steadily more mature in its cultural judgments, while accommodating citizens from an ever-expanding list of origins.

Although the body of what I have written is about American architecture in the twentieth century, the themes I trace would be difficult to appreciate without at least a passing familiarity with their sources. Accordingly, the Prologue charts a rapid course from the 1620s to 1900. In the intervening years, this country changed from a small collection of colonies in a hostile natural environment to the world's dominant industrial nation, whose power flowed from its great cities. American architecture has reflected that evolution. No such transformation has occurred anywhere else, and there has been no cultural map for its explorers. Much was invented along the way, creating a variety that many have found confused, but can also be seen as uniquely comprehensive.

As a new century approaches, however, the profession of architecture as an art in the United States faces an uncertain future. The country's architectural leadership has become gradually more ingrown, distancing itself from the social and economic realities of the larger society. By isolating themselves from much of the public in the pursuit of power, publicity, or in theoretical flights of fancy, many of the country's best-known architects have come to be associated with arrogance, frivolity, and greed. As a result, architecture in America is in serious danger of becoming marginalized, if not irrelevant.

Fortunately, this country has always responded best to crises, and no doubt will in this case. There are already signs of a renewed commitment to the physical fabric of America's ailing cities and the revitalization of its suburbs. Most important, in the aftermath of a grossly commercial and narcissistic period in American design, there are signs of a heightened awareness that architecture can bring beauty to humble commissions along with the grand.

The Themes Take Form

The distinctly American architecture of the twentieth century was hardly a cultural inevitability. The buildings that are now taken for granted as integral parts of the nation's built environment—the Seagram Building in New York, the East Building of the National Gallery in Washington, the "Prairie" houses of the Midwest, the bungalows of Southern California—evolved from a remarkable variety of aesthetic and cultural sources, several of which might have become dominant had circumstances been different. The fact that so many architectural forms emerged with such power in the United States was a testament simultaneously to the energy of the growing nation, and to its unique ability to digest a multitude of influences reflecting the origins of its population and the lack of a cohesive architectural tradition. As with so much else in American culture, the nation's architecture has been a spectacular combination. To appreciate the stylistic elements and cultural themes that contributed to that confection, one must go back to days before the states were united, and even before the states themselves existed.

To the early English settlers of Colonial America, architecture, if the subject occurred to them at all, may have done so as an escapist reverie while they were hacking a habitation out of the wilderness. The impact of the environment of North America of the early seventeenth century on these ex-Europeans was daunting. Accustomed to milder climates in orderly lands, they encountered temperatures that swung from subzero during the winter months in New England to cloying, one hundred-plus-degree summers in Virginia; uncharted rocky, swampy, and otherwise inhospitable terrain; and native inhabitants who, despite the later lore of the Thanksgiving tradition, understandably resented the European intrusion and frequently did their bloodiest to reverse it.

Not surprisingly, the first Anglo-American dwellings were crude at best, not much better than holes hurriedly scooped in the ground and roofed with tree branches. The "English wigwam" of the 1620s (the colonists' version of an Indian original) was a slightly more advanced development, employing bent poles thatched with reeds or covered with bark. But such basic shelter could hardly be described as architecture.

As the settlers steadily subdued their environment, however, their habitations became more ambitious, and from the late seventeenth century onward they showed some signs of architectural aspiration.

This is the period most Americans call to mind when they think of original American architecture. However, the forms and building techniques were thoroughly derivative, largely attempts to recreate the brick and masonry buildings of late medieval Europe with the wood and brick of the new land. In New England, one of the best-known examples is the Parson Joseph Capen House (1683) in Topsfield, Massachusetts, a brooding, heavy-browed structure wrapped tightly in its clapboards against the weather, but embellished ever so chastely with carved pendants at the corners. Comparable survivors can still be found across New England and in such other Massachusetts towns as Deerfield,

Carter Wiseman

where a preserved door bearing the scars of Indian tomahawks serves as a grisly reminder of the non-meteorological threats that early Americans faced.

In the North, with its plentiful water power and thick forests, lumbering and manufacturing quickly took hold, creating a need for clustered structures to serve the activities of the mills. The local builders naturally turned to the layout of the traditional English village for their model. In the South, by contrast, the milder climate and an emerging agricultural economy based heavily on tobacco gave rise to more expansive—and mostly brick—architectural forms that led eventually to the spacious, isolated mansions on which the great plantations, with their clusters of outbuildings and slave quarters, were focused.

Although there was a vigorous architectural life in the native settlements of the Southwest, the buildings that would influence later architecture in the area were primarily the churches, missions, and other religious buildings erected by the earliest Spanish explorers. But with the growth of the Anglo-Protestant presence across the rest of the country, there was little enthusiasm for anything Catholic among those who

THE PARSON JOSEPH CAPEN HOUSE, *Topsfield, Massachusetts,* Anonymous, 1683. The medieval tradition in Colonial America.

were not of that faith. As a result, the Spanish tradition was relegated to a lesser place in the American architectural mainstream, and gradually faded as a significant influence, reappearing only much later as a revivalist style when sentimental or religious requirements called for a Spanish "look."

Since relatively few of the early Colonial clients and builders traveled back to Europe once they had arrived in America, most relied heavily for their inspiration on books, especially such English works as a popular translation of the *Four Books of Architecture*, by the Renaissance Italian architect Andrea Palladio, which first appeared in England in 1714 and was widely reprinted. Colen Campbell's *Vitruvius Britannicus*, also published in 1714, was another important source that promoted a formally correct interpretation of Italian Renaissance design, as was James Gibbs's *A Book of Architecture*, published in London in 1728.

As practical guides, these and other publications helped American builders adapt the predominantly stone, brick, and stucco forms of Europe to structures that could be executed in the materials most readily available in the colonies. But they also initiated what became something of an American architectural tradition of relying for inspiration on printed sources rather than actual buildings-in-the-round, especially because distances were so great and transportation so limited. Not surprisingly, this encouraged a sense that architecture was primarily two-dimensional, and that the original source could be considered more as a stylistic starting point than as a solution to an indigenous architectural problem with its own cultural context. The buildings of Europe that were documented in these books had been designed with native sensitivity to their history and surroundings, whether urban or rural. Lifting those published designs out of one context for use in an alien one offered no guarantee that the "fit" would be as successful. This characteristically American impulse to "mix and match" was later to have its worst incarnations as naive eclecticism, and its best as a knowing integration of the new country's own dramatically disparate cultural sources.

The capacity for assembling elements from a variety of styles and periods is a quality that affects American design to this day. But in the early years, it produced a remarkable overall uniformity of architecture throughout the colonies, if only because virtually all of the builders were working from a common set of texts, quoting details as they saw fit to embellish the most common structural types: individual dwellings, meetinghouses, churches, mills, and factories.

In New England, where the most durable image of Colonial America originated, the emerging architecture betrayed two other qualities that were to continue to influence it for decades to come. One was a deepset suspicion of aesthetic display, a sentiment based on the Puritan religious traditions that had drawn many colonists to America in the first place. Indeed, for many of the new Americans, high art was synonymous with the very excesses of the religious and state establishments of the "corrupt" Europe they had spurned.

The other quality was a no less moralistic dedication to utilitarian, no-nonsense buildings that would serve the purposes of a rapidly growing and increasingly industrial society. John Adams, while touring the architectural splendors of Paris on a diplomatic mission to France during the Revolutionary War, wrote to his wife Abigail: "I cannot help suspecting that the more elegance, the less virtue, in all times and countries." Or, as John Burchard and Albert Bush-Brown put it in their book, *The Architecture of America*, " . . . that in the worship of beauty there may be sin."[1]

Together, these instincts would create a peculiarly strong American architectural tradition of debate over not just the aesthetic quality of a given building, but also the "rightness" or "wrongness" of the inspiration behind it.

One of the earliest and still strongest expressions of the early American concern for the moral message transmitted by architecture was the work of Thomas Jefferson (1743–1826). Although he had never apprenticed to a master builder (the process that had for centuries served as architectural training), Jefferson was extraordinarily well-read and, unlike most of his peers, well-traveled. (He had been America's minister to France and spent five years there, during which he was mightily impressed by what he saw of the surviving Roman ruins, especially the Maison Carré at Nîmes, which he described as "one of the most beau-

---

[1] John Burchard and Albert Bush-Brown, *The Architecture of America* (Boston and Toronto: Little, Brown, 1961), p. 43.

THOMAS JEFFERSON

tiful, if not the most beautiful and precious morsel of architecture left us by antiquity."[2])

For Jefferson, architecture was the full physical expression of national purpose, and with the success of the Revolution, it became an essential part of his political program for the new United States. Indeed, each of his three major works—his own home at Monticello, the Virginia State Capitol, and the University of Virginia—embodied what Jefferson considered to be a fundamental element of the new American society: a free-standing farm, a seat of government, and a center of learning.

---

[2] See William H. Pierson, Jr., *American Buildings and Their Architects*, Vol. 1 (New York and Oxford: Oxford University Press, 1970, 1986), p. 296.

In all of his work, but especially in Monticello (see illustration on page 225), Jefferson asserted the role of the individual, and of the classical virtues, above all those of republican Rome as they had been interpreted by Andrea Palladio. The political associations were obvious: American architecture was to advocate independence and a return to the social and political verities that England had, in Jefferson's view, perverted, and in support of which the colonists had rebelled. Jefferson was outspoken in his condemnation of the buildings at Williamsburg, the first official seat of Colonial government, for their symbolic embodiment of English oppression, condemning the College of William and Mary, where he had been a student, as a "rude, misshapen" pile. But beyond that, he felt that the formal and aesthetic power of the Renaissance tradition in England had simply been exhausted by rote repetition.

The campus of the University of Virginia at Charlottesville, on which Jefferson worked from 1817 until his death, is thus both an architectural and a philosophical statement. Jefferson's concept of the university as an "academical village" also formed the basis for what became that uniquely American architectural phenomenon, the college campus.

To walk among Jefferson's buildings at the University of Virginia is to tread on sacred American architectural ground. Jefferson himself had persuaded the Commonwealth of Virginia to charter the institution, and he raised most of the money, designed the buildings, laid out the curriculum, and hired the faculty. Jefferson was in his seventies and

THE UNIVERSITY OF VIRGINIA, *Charlottesville, Virginia, Thomas Jefferson, 1826.* The Lawn is the heart of the architect's "academical village."

Carter Wiseman

eighties when he created the university, and it was the summation both of his philosophy and of his career. At the head of the composition he placed not a chapel or an administration building, as might have been the case in Europe, but a library, the source of learning essential to a fledgling nation. Reaching out from the library in two symmetrical arms he added pavilions to serve as classrooms and housing—but also as social and recreational gathering places—for both faculty and students. The arrangement had the added virtue of forcing all members of the community into regular contact, while educating the students about the classics; each pavilion embodied a variation on the classical orders, "to serve as specimens for the architectural lecturer." Down the middle was the Lawn, a great grass common to be shared by all. It originally opened out to an endless view westward—literally and symbolically toward the future of a country yet to be explored. (The view was grievously blocked in 1898 when the otherwise distinguished firm of McKim, Mead & White was commissioned to add a building at the western end of the Lawn.)

With the success of the revolutionary experiment, Jefferson's politically didactic aesthetic may have seemed less compelling to potential clients as a tangible example of political aspirations. In any case, it was virtually unique to him, and those in search of architectural guidance soon began to adopt a more purely formal mode of expression. No less than Europe, the new United States was susceptible to cycles of fashion. And with the work of Charles Bulfinch (1763–1844), the first native-born professional architect in the country, the nation veered from the architectural independence of Jefferson and began to rediscover its English sources. Shortly after graduating from Harvard College, in 1781, Bulfinch spent a year and a half traveling in England, France, and Italy. The experience gave him a considerable advantage over the other, mostly untraveled, builders of his day. His Massachusetts State House, completed in 1798, was the most ambitious public building undertaken in New England up to that time. Sited atop a low hill in Boston, its broad-shouldered mass was crowned by an imposing dome that proclaimed the importance of its function. Rendered in a provincial variation of contemporary London architecture, the building was a somewhat stiff and awkwardly proportioned structure, but it ranks with Jefferson's Virginia State Capitol (1789) as one of the most significant works of American architecture of its day.

Another of Jefferson's near contemporaries, the English-born Benjamin H. Latrobe (1764–1820), made a further contribution to the course of architecture in the new nation. America's first full-time architect, Latrobe arrived from England in 1796 equipped with professional training and considerable experience in both architecture and engineering. He relied less on architecture's political message than Jefferson had, and emphasized in particular an understanding of its structural requirements. "It is not the *ornament*, it is the *use* I want," he wrote.[3] This focus was most evident in Latrobe's finest building, St. Mary's Roman Catholic Cathedral, in Baltimore (1818). An earnest masonry composition of basic geometric forms, it showed a firm understanding of the requirements of a religious monument. Latrobe had consulted with Jefferson on the University of Virginia and was, at Jefferson's request, to spend ten years as surveyor of the public buildings of

**THE MASSACHU-
SETTS STATE
HOUSE**, *Boston,
Charles Bulfinch,
1798.* A provincial
variation on the
language of contemporary London.

---

[3] Quoted in Wayne Andrews, *Architecture, Ambition and Americans* (New York: The Free Press, 1964), p. 77.

the United States working on the completion of the Capitol in Washington. Nevertheless, Latrobe evidently felt sufficiently free from the older man's need to deliver one "right" architectural and political message that he offered his client two designs—one classical and one Gothic. The classical won out. But in offering a choice, Latrobe sowed the seeds of a historicism that was to flourish in American design from that point forward.

Although Latrobe had undergone formal training in architecture in England while still a young man, his successors relied heavily on books for their inspiration. Among these men were the early Grecophile Robert Mills (1781–1855), who had worked with both Jefferson and Latrobe before designing the Washington Monument; William Strickland (1788–1854), a former apprentice of Latrobe's; and Thomas U. Walter (1804–1887), who had worked for Strickland. Referring to the seminal English archeological text by James Stuart and Nicholas Revett, published in 1762, Strickland is said to have told his apprentices "that the student of architecture need go no further than the *Antiquities of Athens* as a basis for design."

But the local successors to the works of the English authors were beginning to reflect the fledgling nation's growing confidence in its own artistic potential. The most common texts for American builders of the time were by Asher Benjamin (1773–1845), the first American to produce books specifically intended as practical guides for construction. (He identified himself on his title page as an "architect-carpenter.") Benjamin's *Country Builder's Assistant* went through forty-seven editions between 1797 and 1856. And his *American Builder's Companion* of 1806 made a point—in both the title and the text—of asserting the country's independence in design. In one passage, Benjamin refers to "several European writers, who have given rules for their proportion" in the treatment of windows and rooms, yet concludes with some condescension that "I do not find it to answer in all cases."

At the beginning of the nineteenth century, American industrial prosperity was having a fundamental impact on the growth of the nation's architecture. An emerging middle class with an increasing amount of disposable income was creating markets for a different way of life. Money and leisure amplified the original freight role of the railroad, for example, giving rise to an entirely new American architectural opportunity—the passenger train station. Small shops gave way to department stores, which required storage and display areas on a scale previously unknown. And the spread of manufacturing made the utilitarian geometry of mills and factories a fundamental element of the contemporary American design vocabulary.

So, too, leisure and the steady domestication of the wilderness allowed city dwellers to seek a measure of relief from the increasingly oppressive urban centers, a trend that led to the spread of seaside resorts and country cottages. Tinged with a hint of the mythology surrounding the pioneer's wilderness cabin, these auxiliary settlements ultimately created that icon of the American dream, a house of one's own, on land of one's own—something virtually unknown in Europe except to farmers and the landed gentry. What had been a necessity imposed by the settlement of a vast land eventually became, in the form of the suburb, a symbol of the American way of life. This phenomenon created yet another enduring American architectural tension, that between the needs of the rural homeowner and the city dweller—a tension that would find its full expression decades later in the work of Frank Lloyd Wright.

Meanwhile, archeological expeditions in Europe and a resulting surge in scholarship on antiquity created a scientific basis for a renewed interest going back beyond Rome to the architecture of Greece. The publication in 1764 of *Die Geschichte der Kunst ders Alterthums*, by the German archeologist J. J. Winckelmann, provided for the first time an illustrated vision of ancient Greece as a culture of artists and architects as well as philosophers and writers. John Haviland's *The Builder's Assistant*, the first volume of which was published in 1818, introduced the American reader to the Greek architectural orders, and other writers, including the prolific Asher Benjamin, quickly added to the store of information. With the flowering of American democracy (at least among the non-slave population), the image of Greece as the birthplace of its political ideals—considered as yet untainted by Roman imperialism and corruption—created irresistible associations among architects and citizens alike. The result was a burst of interest in Greece which rapidly overtook the longstanding enthusiasm for the vision of republican Rome that had been passed down through Vitruvius to find its highest American incarnation in the work of Jefferson.

Characterized by a crisp, rational geometry and an eager fidelity to the original orders—Doric, Ionic, and Corinthian—the Greek Revival, as the architectural expression of the movement came to be known, spread so rapidly and thoroughly in the early decades of the nineteenth century that it became for all practical purposes the nation's first *national* style. Indeed, the Greek temple form was established for generations as a basic model for virtually every major American public building type, whether bank, church, college, or courthouse. Not the least of the style's appeal was that it spanned social and economic gaps even at the domestic level, providing as worthy a model for the humble New Englander's augmented saltbox as for the wealthy Virginian's plantation mansion. Where Jefferson's Palladian Romanism had represented the passion of an intellectual aristocrat, the Greek Revival communicated its democratic associations to a far wider audience.

Gone was Jefferson's focused didacticism, replaced by the first of many American romances with the exotic. To be sure, the purported link was to the democratic political and social Greek virtues, but the "look" was no less attractive to American eyes eager for a change from the utilitarian vernacular that had gone before, ungrounded as it was in any aesthetic ideology acceptable to the increasing ambitions of a new society.

Here again, the influence of books was critical. The most influential were by the architect and writer Minard Lafever (1798–1854), whose *The Modern Builder's Guide* of 1833 and *The Beauties of Modern Architecture* of 1835 provided plans and drawings of buildings that were easily constructed by ordinary carpenters, and went through several editions.

As American cities became increasingly congested, however, intellectuals and artists sought even more remote stylistic refuge. Many began to feel that the Greek tradition, for all its moral virtues, was too cold and rigid. Something more exuberant was needed to express the dynamism of the expanding nation. The result was yet another revolution of the American stylistic wheel, from the example of Athens to what was considered the more "emotionally authentic" example of the Gothic, with its rich tradition of sculpture, ornament, and questing after the sublime.

That development had begun as an outgrowth of the Picturesque movement in England, a movement that was a revolt against the restrictions of a long-dominant neoclassicism. One of the most vigorous advocates of the English Gothic Revival was the Victorian architect A. W. N. Pugin (1812–1852), who felt that architecture should be an art of the senses rather than of the intellect. But Pugin raised the debate over the styles to another plane, arguing that classicism, because of its pre-Christian associations, was essentially a pagan aesthetic, while the Gothic was rooted in Christian tradition. He further endorsed the Gothic for its lack of restrictive orders and greater overall design flexibility, which allowed the architect to create buildings that were more appropriate to their functions—and thus more "honest"—than the relatively rigid classical ideal.

Similar views were advanced by the English writer John Ruskin (1819–1900), whose books *The Seven Lamps of Architecture* (1849) and *The Stones of Venice* (1853) became required reading for most American architects of the day. Ruskin, who saw no need to pursue what he derided as a "new style of architecture," felt that the design of buildings and their ornament should be based on the forms and colors of nature: " . . . all most lovely forms and thoughts are directly taken from natural objects," he wrote. And for him, there were no nobler examples in architectural history from which to learn than those of the Venetian Gothic. The west front of St. Mark's, Ruskin declared, was "as lovely a dream as ever filled human imagination."

In America, such sentiments were furthered stylistically by the writings of Andrew Jackson Downing (1815–1852), a self-trained landscape architect and horticulturalist from New York's Hudson River Valley. In such works as *Cottage Residences* (1842) and *The Architecture of Country Houses* (1850), Downing, who liked to describe himself as a "rural architect," made the revolutionary leap from the monumental to the minimal, putting small but extravagantly ornamented Gothic "cottages" within the reach of thousands. "Domestic Architecture itself," wrote Downing, "which, amid the louder claims of civil and ecclesiastical art, has been too much neglected, seems to demand a higher consideration in a country where the ease of obtaining a house and land, and the ability of almost every industrious citizen to build his own house, constitute a distinctive feature of national prosperity."

From an aesthetic point of view, Downing felt strongly that what he called "irregular symmetry" was the main ingredient of fine design (he dismissed the fascination with Greek temples as a "disease"), especially in an American context where nature and political independence were symbolically inextricable. He described "Country Architecture" as something that is "not cramped in the manifestation, but develops itself freely, as a tree expands which is not crowded by neighbors in a forest, but grows in the unrestrained liberty of the open meadow."

Rising income and the growth of technology made it increasingly possible to address these urges at the domestic level. Fueled by the growth of the Picturesque movement in England, the upwardly mobile American embraced the Gothic with enthusiasm. Nowhere was this more apparent than in the alliance of Downing and his friend, Alexander Jackson Davis (1803–1892), who became the most influential American architect of his time. This writer-designer team enabled large segments of the American middle class to live a semblance of a life that only the gentry enjoyed in Europe.

In Davis, a New York City native who was as skilled a draftsman and watercolorist as he was an architect, Downing found the perfect collaborator to render his ideals in both printed and built form. An early advocate of the Greek Revival, Davis, with his early partner Ithiel Town, had created a number of elegant monuments in that style, and had proven adept at such other romanticizing modes as the Italianate, the Moorish, and the Egyptian. But he eventually tired of those, and, reflecting the growing popular fascination with the romantic possibilities of the American landscape, added to his repertory a flurry of asymmetrical and lavishly ornamented Gothic residences. His masterwork is Lyndhurst, in Tarrytown, New York, which he began in 1838 and added to in 1866.

Built by a former mayor of New York City (and originally known as Knoll, for its location on a hill above the Hudson River), Lyndhurst is a deceptively beautiful work, combining an eagerness for grandeur with an artist's sense of pictorial composition and balance. With its elegant tower and crenellated trim it might be mistaken for a diminutive castle or a church, but it has a deft domestic scale that has enshrined it as probably the best example of the Gothic Revival anywhere in America.

If Lyndhurst has become the symbol of Davis's highest achievement, his unexecuted designs had the more immediate and widespread impact on American architecture. In a series of portfolios entitled *Rural Residences* published in 1838, Davis provided designs for buildings ranging from the most humble farmhouses to Lyndhurst-like villas. Not only were the designs delights to eyes sated with Greek Revival architecture; they also could be easily and inexpensively built. Davis offered,

for example, plans for a three-bedroom "Farmer's House" that cost $1,500 to build, and a grand mansion that could be erected for $12,000 in stone, or $7,500 in wood. Moreover, most incorporated the thoroughly un-Gothic amenity of the porch, or veranda, an addition that provided substantial relief from the summer sun, but was also particularly suited to the outward-looking instincts of the American middle class. (There were, of course, no such structures in medieval Europe.)

Largely as a result of Davis's efforts, the expanding nation was rapidly sprinkled with sharply pointed gables, sinuous vergeboards, and assertive oriels. More important than the stylistic additions to the landscape, however, was the fact that in defining the aesthetically elevated "cottage" as a building type accessible to the common man, Davis—and Downing—had validated in architectural form what became a cherished symbol of American democracy. (In this, of course, they owed a considerable debt to Jefferson, who had always been a partisan of the land over the city as the proper setting for American life.)

The stylistic shift promulgated by Downing and Davis away from the neoclassical was abetted by the increasing size and economic diversity of the postrevolutionary population. And that led, predictably enough, to a steady fragmentation of the Colonial heritage as an architectural

LYNDHURST, *Tarrytown, New York, Alexander Jackson Davis, 1866.* A masterwork of Gothic romanticism.

expression of a homogeneous American culture. Inevitably, the process undermined the commitment to the classical as the unifying aesthetic it had been for Jefferson, and even Latrobe. Such architects as the English-born Richard Upjohn (1802–1878), creator of the neo-Gothic Trinity Church (1846) in New York City, and the American James Renwick (1818–1895), who designed the elegant Grace Church (1846) as well as the rather overblown St. Patrick's Cathedral (1879), also in New York, embraced the new diversity with an appropriately religious fervor. Unlike Upjohn, a loyal Anglophile, Renwick drew freely on sources in France and Germany as well as England. The point was not so much the national or denominational source as it was the purely aesthetic impact of the design. In fulfilling that, the period, location, and doctrinal association carried relatively little weight.

While the urban churches of Upjohn and Renwick remain their greatest monuments, their humbler but no less derivative designs for small towns provided the real measure of their influence. In those buildings one could detect the budding of yet another theme that continues to affect the American approach to architecture, a tension between a hunger for roots and authenticity—the resonance of medieval Europe—on the one hand, and an impulse to expand beyond them into uncharted ground on the other.

The architectural expression of these impulses was made increasingly easy with the coming together in the 1830s and 1840s of pre-cut lumber and machine-made nails to produce the "balloon frame." In simplest terms, the new technique did away with the traditional heavy timbers that had dominated wood construction since the late Middle Ages, replacing them with lightweight, standardized members that could be assembled easily, even by workers with little skill. Another technological innovation, the jigsaw, also contributed to the popularity of the Gothic, making it relatively easy to manufacture the sort of ornament that had previously required skilled carving. Such innovations enabled builders to indulge their tastes and imaginations in ways unimaginable in the days of masonry or medieval timber construction. And to a very large degree, the new flexibility began to drive the style it was intended to serve. Indeed, the display of structural virtuosity became something of a goal in itself, contributing to what the architectural historian Vincent J. Scully, Jr., has labeled with strikingly graphic accuracy the "Stick Style."

TRINITY CHURCH, *New York City, Richard Upjohn, 1846.* The goal was aesthetic impact over denominational accuracy.

The work of Downing, Davis, Upjohn, Renwick and the other Gothicists inevitably reheated the debate over what was morally correct in architecture. (Ruskin had declared that wood painted to look like stone constituted an architectural "deceit." He would have been horrified by the faux-marble of the Lyndhurst interior.) The debate was made more intense by the emergence of cast iron as a building material. One of its most creative advocates was James Bogardus (1800–1874), whose Laing Stores in New York City (1848) were assembled from prefabricated iron sections in the astonishingly short span of two months. Stunning as the achievement was, the ornament of this and other cast-iron works was made—and marketed—to look like stone, demonstrating that such otherwise innovative builders as Bogardus and his colleagues were still reluctant to embrace the new material for its own inherent aesthetic potential.

The growth of industry promoted by the Civil War produced some enormous personal fortunes, and many of the newly rich, in a drive to establish an instant cultural legitimacy appropriate to the scale of their material gains, encouraged a lively indulgence in stylistic borrowing. The movement was almost entirely divorced from any sort of aesthetic theory, let alone structural authenticity, and it was not without high-level precedent: Upjohn and Renwick had aped the buttresses of the thirteenth and fourteenth centuries, but their buildings were held up by iron, and their vaults were confected of lath and plaster rather than stone.

At the same time, the published designs of the English architect Richard Norman Shaw (1831–1912) were attracting widespread attention. Shaw's buildings were unapologetically sentimental, made of brick and embellished to evoke the cozy emotions associated with the life of the English country squire. In this sense, they departed from Ruskin's demand for "honest" expression of forms derived from nature. But then, the American version of the Gothic had long since abandoned any serious pretense of authenticity, and the way was now open to the free assemblage of details from a variety of styles for no more exalted a purpose than to create something the client liked.

But the traditional reliance of American clients on published sources was beginning to change; the emerging fortunes permitted their beneficiaries to travel as few Americans before them had been able to, and they came back from the Grand Tour—to Paris and Rome, Athens, and Venice—determined to celebrate their winnings by drawing upon the whole of European architectural precedent, even if it occasionally meant doing so in a single building.

These wealthy travelers gave architects like Richard Morris Hunt (1827–1895) enviably free rein, commissioning them to design some of the most lavish tributes to acquisitiveness the country had yet seen. Hunt was the first American to attend the Ecole des Beaux-Arts in Paris, where he remained for nine years. During that time, he was imbued with the school's principles of close attention to the classical orders, its fundamental belief in axial organization, and its firm reliance on symmetrical composition. He returned from France in 1855 to embellish America's most fashionable avenues and country estates with eclectic buildings that occasionally threatened to outshine the European examples on which they were based.

Under Hunt's leadership, Beaux-Arts rationalism came to dominate one portion of American design. His most famous works were residential, and included a host of mansions for the very rich (many of whom, in bursts of false modesty, insisted on calling them "cottages"). Hunt designed four of the most fabulous such buildings in Newport, Rhode Island, the most fashionable retreat of the 1880s and 1890s for the upper echelons of New York society. But the uncontested triumph of Hunt's luxurious if thoroughly derivative labors was Biltmore, in Asheville, North Carolina (1895), which was designed for George W. Vanderbilt. A pre-Disney fantasy of a Loire Valley château—at gargantuan scale—

RICHARD MORRIS HUNT

Brown Brothers

BILTMORE,
*Asheville, North
Carolina, Richard
Morris Hunt, 1895.
A touch of the Loire,
and the biggest
house in the land.*

Biltmore remains—with 255 rooms—the largest private house ever built in America (its foundation alone covers five acres).

Although Hunt's ebullient architecture was the main source of his fame, his efforts on the part of the architectural profession produced his most lasting legacy. At the time he returned from the Beaux-Arts, there were no architectural schools in the United States. By establishing an atelier of his own in New York along the lines of the Beaux-Arts system, Hunt laid the groundwork for virtually all American architectural training to follow. To his studio were attracted many young men who went on to shape the profession in the years to come, among them Henry Van Brunt, William Ware, George B. Post, and Frank Furness.

Hunt was twice elected president of the American Institute of Architects, which had been founded in 1857 by Richard Upjohn, and became the dominant organization in the profession. Among the laurels presented to him for his efforts were the first honorary doctoral degree granted to an architect by Harvard University, and the gold medal of the

Royal Institute of British Architects, the first ever won by an American. Whatever the lasting impact of his designs, Hunt was understandably dubbed by his contemporaries the "dean of American architecture."

One Hunt follower who saw no reason to be bound by the precepts of the Beaux-Arts was Frank Furness (1839–1912), who had apprenticed with Hunt from 1859 to 1861. Furness, a certified American original who won the Congressional Medal of Honor for heroism as a cavalryman in the Civil War, took Ruskin's call for the use of rich materials and the integration of ornament with structure to new heights in the Pennsylvania Academy of the Fine Arts in Philadelphia (1876). With an exterior that seemed to spew forth ornament from every available source and an interior embellished with a galaxy of gilt stars, it was an eclectic monument that defied stylistic categorization.

Unlike his mentor, who felt no compunction about relying on European precedent, Furness seemed determined to establish at last an architecture that was distinctly American. In this, he drew deeply on the teachings of his father's closest friend, Ralph Waldo Emerson, whose views on architecture included the statement in his 1837 essay, "The Young American," that "America is beginning to assert herself to the senses and to the imagination of her children, and Europe is receding to the same degree." Accordingly, while profiting from the stylistic devices of the classical, the Romanesque, and the Gothic that he had learned under Hunt, Furness abandoned any pretense of historical accuracy and recombined them in dazzling displays of compositional virtuosity. His library at the University of Pennsylvania (1891) is a riotous blend of decorative detail, but all of it in the service of a spatial concept that is both efficient for users and visually thrilling.

But Furness, whose practice was concentrated in Philadelphia, found few followers in the more influential artistic centers of New York and Boston, where an anti-Gothic reaction was taking hold, largely—and ironically—in response to the vogue for neoclassical architecture launched by the nation's Centennial celebration in Philadelphia in 1876. Unwilling to follow the shifting taste of both the public and the profession, Furness came increasingly to be regarded as a mannerist eccentric, and his work, for all its powerful individualism, gradually lost its allure.

Meanwhile, the influence of Furness's teacher continued to grow, and extended well beyond his own buildings and those of his followers.

FRANK FURNESS

In 1865, another of Hunt's students, William Ware (1832–1915), had set up the country's first professional architectural program, at the Massachusetts Institute of Technology. Ware went on to form a similar program at Columbia, in 1888. By 1900, there were schools of architecture at twelve other American universities, all of them based on the model of the Beaux-Arts as it had been interpreted by Hunt.

Not surprisingly, the emergence at this stage of architectural schools with such a shared heritage did much to codify the "correct" style of American architecture as the classical. But not all of America's most prominent designers followed their teachings. Like Hunt, Henry Hobson Richardson (1838–1886), was a former student at the Beaux-Arts. But he gradually strayed from the Ecole's path. In his work can be found a gradual stripping or "cleansing" of the more overtly picturesque Gothic, a process Richardson accomplished by turning yet further back in architectural history to the Romanesque (which was considered by Richardson to be less "tainted" by Catholicism), while simplifying the original forms and altering them for contemporary needs in muscular compositions of elemental stone masses. The earthy Romanesque was, in Richardson's view, better suited to the American qualities of straight-forwardness than the Gothic, and was also more adaptable to the many new building types required by the growing nation. (He once declared that "The things I want most to design are a grain elevator and the interior of a great river-steamboat.")

It is Richardson's Trinity Church in Boston (1877) that has left American architectural history with the term "Richardsonian Romanesque;"

THE PENNSYLVANIA ACADEMY OF THE FINE ARTS, *Philadelphia, Frank Furness, 1876.* An attempt at an all-American architecture.

The Pennsylvania Academy of the Fine Arts Archives

but several of his smaller buildings provide a clearer sense of his contributions to later American design. Two of his later private houses in particular show both the power of his imagination and the versatility with which he was able to use radically different materials. The Stoughton House, in Cambridge, Massachusetts (1883), is a masterful simplification of the clutter that characterized American domestic architecture at the time, and Richardson's use of shingles to wrap the building in a light and apparently seamless membrane elevated this once-humble cladding to an unprecedented level of elegance. In the more intensely urban setting of Chicago, Richardson proved no less adept at the residential scale using stone. The Glessner House (1887) ignored its château-style neighbors, turning an austere, rusticated facade to the street while opening the house to an interior courtyard. Without deliberately rebelling against European traditions, Richardson was pulling away from them as his elemental geometric awareness asserted itself ever more vigorously. At the same time, the architect paid

HENRY HOBSON
RICHARDSON

Corbis-Bettmann

careful attention to the client's desire for free-flowing space, opening up the traditionally cramped living areas of the standard American house in response to an increasingly less formal way of domestic life. The entrance hall expanded effortlessly into the parlor, which in turn opened out to the dining room, consolidating the interior spaces in a manner closely related to the simplified massing on the outside.

In his Crane Memorial Public Library, in Quincy, Massachusetts (1882), Richardson made one of his clearest statements of the sensitivity to exterior massing that was to give him his permanent place in the American architectural pantheon. The composition could not be simpler: a low rectangular block housing an entrance hall, a reading room,

TRINITY CHURCH, *Boston, H. H. Richardson, 1877.* The building that embodied the term "Richardsonian Romanesque."

Carter Wiseman

THE CRANE
MEMORIAL
LIBRARY,
*Quincy,
Massachusetts,*
H. H. Richardson,
1882. Massing,
more than style,
gives it its power.

and stacks in a single horizontal mass. But the articulation of those spaces on the exterior through the spare use of ornament and the precise but irregular rhythm of the door and window openings raises this building above any sort of stylistic limitations.

For his part, Richardson considered the Allegheny County Courthouse and Jail (1888) in Pittsburgh to be his greatest achievement. A brilliantly brooding complex of rusticated stone, it was a three-dimensional essay on the *gravitas* of the judicial process—and the grim result of criminal conviction. Yet in the interior—particularly the main staircase—Richardson showed an equal mastery of spatial relationships, flinging stairs and landings about with a skill that was at once Piranesian in its complexity and Mozartian in its agility.

For all Richardson's enthusiasm for the Pittsburgh buildings, however, architectural historians have been far more generous in their praise for his Marshall Field Wholesale Store (1887), in Chicago. Although demolished in 1930, the image that survives in photographs of this muscular block with its nonetheless graceful proportions has rightly become an icon of American architecture. The Greek temple had long since lost its applicability to the changing demands of American commercial life; neither its symbolic associations nor its limitations in form and scale were appropriate to the need for enormous spaces that responded to manufacturing's demands. The Marshall Field warehouse did more than any other building up to that time to recognize the new direction of American urban architecture, while ennobling it with an aesthetic treatment that was entirely appropriate to its function.

Largely for that reason, Richardson has been embraced by many Modernist scholars who saw in his attention to function and his simplification of form a precursor of that most quintessentially American architectural form, the skyscraper. But full claim to that title would have required a far more enthusiastic exploration of the steel and glass technologies that were already available to him. And Richardson showed little interest in their structural or artistic implications, remaining tied to a load-bearing tradition even as he advanced the concept of American steel-frame architecture.

The potential of the new materials was pursued with much greater vigor by the engineers of the day, most notably Washington Roebling and his son, John, the creators of the Brooklyn Bridge (1883). There was

MARSHALL FIELD WHOLESALE STORE, *Chicago, H. H. Richardson, 1887. Its muscular grace pointed American architecture in a new direction.*

Chicago Historical Society

more than technology involved, of course. In this structure as in no other in America one sees the simultaneous reach for the future and the past, and the embodiment of the schizophrenic but characteristically American impulse toward both the romantic and the technical, rootedness and unfettered expansionism. The graceful sweep of the span, supported by a gossamer web of steel cables, symbolized as nothing else before it the impulse to expand the national reach through invention. Yet the Gothicizing stone arches stood as reminders that, no less than Richardson, the Roeblings were reluctant to loose the reassuring bonds to the European past.

The celebrity accorded Richardson and the Roeblings in their day had much to do with the publication in the United States of the first professional architectural journals, which had begun to appear in the 1870s. Among the most prominent were the *New York Sketch-Book of Architecture*, which was first published in 1873, and the *American Architect and Building News*, which began its run in 1876. But apart from Richardson and his better imitators, and despite the tantalizing technological example presented by the Roeblings, the country, for better and worse, had yet to achieve an identifiable direction in design. The technological advances that were to lead to the skyscraper were being pursued vigorously enough, but as yet had to be integrated into architecture as an art. And following in the footsteps of Hunt, assorted classically oriented eclectics—most prominent among them Charles Follen McKim (1847–1909) and Stanford White (1835–1906)—were creating an increasingly conservative vogue for academic architecture. American architecture as the nineteenth century neared its close was actually becoming more varied as scholarship and technological advances provided steadily more stylistic sources and the means to exploit them. Depending on one's point of view, this reflected either a lack of vision or a celebration of the country's vitality.

A single event served both to provide a sense of purpose, and to sweep away, at least temporarily, the powerful example architects like Furness and Richardson had set for originality in American design. That event was the World's Columbian Exposition, held in Chicago in 1893. Conceived in observance of the four hundredth anniversary of the landing of Columbus in the New World in 1492 (construction delays forced postponement of the fair's opening by a year), the extravaganza was also intended to showcase the enormous power of the United States as a mature player on the world stage.

The site covered 633 acres on the shore of Lake Michigan just south of the Chicago city center, and was laid out by the landscape architect Frederick Law Olmsted (the designer, with Calvert Vaux, of New York City's Central Park). Oversight of its vast complex of buildings was put in the hands of Daniel H. Burnham (1846–1912), a Chicago architect to whom has been attributed one of the most resonant pronouncements in American architectural history: "Make no little plans, they have no magic to stir men's blood." (Scholars continue to debate Burnham's authorship, but the sentiment is apparently in character.)

To make the event appropriately representative of American architectural talent, the planning committee had assigned each of the major buildings to a different designer. (Hunt drew the Administration Building, which he topped with a gilded octagonal dome in full-fledged Beaux-Arts style.) But to give the overall undertaking coherence, the committee also required that all the buildings be designed in the classical style, with uniform cornice heights. And all were to be painted white.

WORLD'S COLUMBIAN EXPOSITION, *Chicago, Daniel Burnham, and others, 1893. Classicism used as symbolic language for American power.*

Corbis-Bettmann

**TRANSPORTATION
BUILDING**,
*Chicago, Adler &
Sullivan, 1893.*
It abided by the
rules, but provided
a taste of things
to come.

What came to be known accordingly as the "White City" included exhibits from around the globe, ranging from German artillery pieces and a full-size replica of an American battleship to a Ceylon Tea House and live Samoan warriors. By the time the fair closed in October 1893, it had drawn nearly 28 million visitors from the United States and abroad. So compelling was its scale, and so eager was most of the American population for the overwhelming sense of order offered by its architecture, that the exposition, as Talbot Hamlin has written, "fixed the taste of a people for a generation."[4]

By no means everyone was pleased, however. Louis Sullivan (1856–1924), a young Chicago architect who, with his partner Dankmar Adler (1844–1900), had reluctantly agreed to the fair organizers' design requirements in doing their celebrated Transportation

---

4 Talbot Hamlin, *Architecture Through the Ages* (New York: G. P. Putnam's Sons, 1940, 1953), p. 611.

Building (entered through the subversively gilded portal, the "Golden Door"), later concluded with most other progressive thinkers that the exposition had been a severe setback for the American architectural cause. Indeed, its overwhelming stylistic consistency turned Americans backward yet again to their European sources, diverting attention from their own creative potential and unique aesthetic opportunity.

The reasons for the fair's popularity were not hard to find. By virtue of its size alone, it had presented Americans with a reassuring image of cultural comprehensiveness and national self-confidence. The fact that so much of the world could be brought together in one place and housed in such impressive—if temporary—buildings was an unprecedented public relations achievement for the nation. Sullivan was not deterred by the fair's influence, however, and went on to pursue his own vision with such skill and artistry that he could rightly be judged by later generations to have forged the link between the historicist eclecticism of America in the late nineteenth century and what would come to be known in the twentieth as modern architecture.

The Lure of the Tall

f a single building type can — and should — be identified with twentieth-century American architecture, it is the skyscraper. Tall buildings were the stuff of the stories told by the legions of European
immigrants whose first glimpse of America was the southern tip of Manhattan Island, bristling with its forest of towers. Those buildings remain
a symbol of American corporate power. They are, after all, the way
Americans explain how high Superman can leap in a single bound.

For a study of twentieth-century American architecture, it would be
convenient if the first such building had been built precisely in 1900.

To locate the roots of the type, however, one must cast back a bit into the century before, when the idea of the tall building was only beginning to emerge, and was threatening architecture in the United States—and indeed the rest of the Western world—with profound change.

In an article for *Lippincott's Magazine* written in 1896 entitled "The Tall Office Building Artistically Considered," Louis Sullivan, arguably the most influential architect of his day, issued a challenge that would resonate through architectural history from that moment on. The tall office building, Sullivan declared, "must be tall, every inch of it tall. The force and power of altitude must be in it. It must be every inch a proud and soaring thing, rising in sheer exultation that from bottom to top it is a unit without a single dissenting line—that it is the new, the unexpected, the eloquent peroration of most bald, most sinister, most forbidding conditions."

Like so many architects before and after him, Sullivan was an energetic—if not always grammatical or especially coherent—writer, and he rejoiced in his own verbiage. In this passage he seized with remarkable accuracy upon not only the central architectural fact of his time, but also its spirit. The emergence of the tall building as an architectural type was an unprecedented opportunity, yet it was also somewhat frightening. Indeed, it was to sweep before it the very definition of the word "architecture" and establish the unchallenged power of American design for at least a century.

Of course, height had been an obsession with architects going back to the obelisks of ancient Egypt. But only with the coming of iron and steel as structural materials in the early nineteenth century were designers able to escape the inherent limitations of masonry and brick. As a rule of thumb for architects of those days, a one-story masonry building required a twelve-inch-thick wall, and the thickness at the base had to increase by four inches for each additional floor. Thus a stone building of sixteen stories required walls six feet thick at the base to support the load of the upper stories; at twenty stories, the walls at the base would have to be more than seven feet thick.

Thanks to the pursuit of metal technology—especially by bridgebuilders like John and Washington Roebling—the impulse to go ever higher could be indulged almost without limit, at least in theory. Metal beams could span great distances, and could also support increased loads with a minimum of bulk. Metal members freed the building's skin from its support role, permitting much larger windows, as well as much greater and more flexible interior spaces to meet the growing demand for offices and factories.

In fact, however, a serious obstacle remained to the exploitation of metal technology in building. Generally speaking, five flights of stairs was the maximum most people could be expected to climb, and it was virtually impossible to demand rent for space above that level. Thus, while it was technically possible to create much taller buildings, there was no practical use for the additional space. All that changed with the introduction of the passenger elevator.

Lifts and hoists of various types had existed for decades, but they were used primarily for hauling equipment and stores. In 1857, however, the first practical passenger elevator was installed in New York in the Haughwout Store, designed by John P. Gaynor, at Broadway and Broome Street. At a stroke, the tall building was flung open to those who were not alpinists.

The first office building to employ the new device was the Equitable Life Assurance Building, also in New York, designed by Gilman & Kendall and George B. Post and finished in 1870. Despite the new amenity, the building remained at the traditional limit of five stories. Driven by rising real estate prices, which obliged owners to squeeze ever greater square footage out of their sites, architects and engineers soon began to investigate the larger potential of the elevator. Prominent among those architects was the durable Richard Morris Hunt, who had ministered with such vigor and skill to the residential fantasies of the rich, but proved no less willing to embrace an office tower. His Tribune Building (1875), facing New York's City Hall Park, rose to a dizzying nine stories, and George Post's nearby Western Union Building (also 1875) outdid that at an even ten stories.

Thrilling as the prospect of increased height was to many architects, it was at the same time something of an artistic threat. While dazzlingly tall, the New York buildings designed by Post, Hunt, and their contemporaries were essentially smaller buildings living beyond their aesthetic means. The standard approach to the architecture of these increasingly tall structures was to make them look like amplified short ones. The Tribune Building culminated in a corbeled clocktower reminiscent of the Palazzo Vecchio in Florence, while the Western Union—which also in-

TRIBUNE BUILDING,
*New York City,
Richard Morris
Hunt, 1875.
A conflict of
decoration
and scale.*

cluded a clocktower—sprouted dormers and decoration worthy of the roof of a luscious country mansion. The result was a family of misshapen buildings whose ornament might have been appropriate to a Newport "cottage" used for vacations, but to some eyes was monstrously out of place at a greatly increased scale.

This dichotomy was natural enough, given the training of the architects. After all, many of the most prominent practitioners had studied in Europe, most at the Ecole des Beaux-Arts in Paris, where they had been steeped in neoclassical monuments. They and their colleagues were used to looking for precedents in architecture, and in their case precedents meant Europe. There had certainly been nothing in American architectural history to provide a competing set of forms.

Mindful of the conflict between height and the European architectural models on which they had been trained, many American architects of the day dealt with the problem by embracing the organizing principle of the classical column, with its three-part division into base, shaft, and capital. Thus the bottom few stories would be embellished with arches or multistory windows topped by a heavy cornice; the intermediate floors would be virtually identical; and the upper portion would be given a flamboyant culmination by adding a "hat" of some vaguely Gothic or Renaissance sort.

The form persisted for years, and while the height of buildings increased, the aesthetic treatment of them remained tethered to the teachings of the European monumental tradition. Although the results included some impressive objects—among them Daniel Burnham's Fuller (Flatiron) Building (1903), which employed the base-column-capital formula with powerful effect on a triangular New York City site—they more often verged on the silly. New York's Singer Building, finished in 1908 to the designs of Ernest Flagg, sported a bulbous mansard top capped by a classical lantern, looking like a buxom dowager at a Paris ball, while the Metropolitan Life Tower (1909), by Napoleon LeBrun & Sons, gave passers-by a taste of Venetian campaniles, but in such overscaled measure that it was bound to cause some architectural indigestion.

One should not be too harsh on the early New York skyscrapers. At their best, they were wonderfully romantic and entertaining, and at least one, the Woolworth Building, by Cass Gilbert (1859–1934), achieved truly aesthetic, as well as physical, heights. This 1913 landmark, which was the tallest building in the world at the time and was instantly dubbed the "cathedral of commerce" for its Gothic cladding, succeeded not just for its theatrical impact, but for the skill with which its architect handled its massing and proportions. The office block that constitutes the lower portion is seamlessly integrated through the use of slender terra-cotta piers with the tower, which soars to 792 feet. Together, the elements convey a formal resolution that removes it from its gaggle of competitors. The contrast with Singer is instructive: Singer depended for its impact on its ornament, without which the basic form

was unwieldy; Woolworth, on the other hand, could be stripped of its Gothic details and yet stand as a satisfying composition. Without the ornament, the Woolworth would be a very different building, but one senses that Gilbert had succeeded so well in his organization of the forms that he was almost ready to shed the cladding as unnecessary. He had, in the end, all but exhausted the ornamental tradition for the tall building of his day.

The Woolworth marked the highest expression of what might be called the early picturesque skyscraper, and for that reason has remained a classic of its kind. But its terminal quality hardly put an end to efforts to outdo it in opulence and ornamental complexity. What was missing from it and virtually all of its spiritual contemporaries before and after, however, was any underlying sense that height and the technology that made it possible created an opportunity for a fundamentally new form of expression, one that acknowledged the difference in kind between tall, metal-framed buildings and short ones held up by stone or brick. Although the earliest New York skyscrapers employed cast-iron columns in some cases (they all used cast-iron beams), the walls were still of load-bearing masonry. The later ones made increasing use of metal framing, but their architects chose not to express it in the exterior treatment of their buildings. Indeed, the Woolworth in this sense is no nobler than its lesser rivals, which made every effort to conceal what they were made of and how they were supported.

Although New York was late to grasp the fact, this aesthetic impasse had long since been broken by the fire that devastated Chicago in 1871. The disaster began with a small blaze that broke out at 9:00 P.M. on the

SINGER BUILDING, *New York City, Ernest Flagg, 1908.* An energetic building that overstated its case.

night of October 8 and spread until it engulfed virtually the entire city. By the time it was extinguished 48 hours later, the fire had consumed 18,000 buildings, killed nearly 300 people, and left 100,000 more homeless. The downtown area was leveled, and total property damage was estimated at what was then a staggering $200 million.

The disaster focused attention on the one remaining problem confronting the use of metal as a structural material: fireproofing. Exposed to concentrated heat in a fire, unprotected iron would, as numerous Chicago buildings had demonstrated, buckle and eventually collapse. In the early 1870s, however, engineers successfully experimented with a number of fireproofing techniques, including the use of hollow tile for subflooring and partitions, and the direct application of masonry and tile to exposed iron columns and beams.

The Chicago fire created a tremendous opportunity for the city. Most of the buildings that had been destroyed in the conflagration had been made of wood. The instant demand for new construction that would withstand such a calamity in the future forced builders and architects to come up with new techniques. Now that it was possible to use fire-proofed iron and steel in place of wood and masonry in a building's structure, owners and architects alike turned to the new materials with more than simply technical enthusiasm.

Economics, too, fueled the transition. Increasingly, modern business was demanding larger work spaces in which to house the armies of accountants, secretaries, and executives it was spawning. An office culture was now inextricably joined to that of the mill and the factory, and new and more flexible working environments were called for. In Chicago, that need intersected with the urgent necessity to rebuild on a massive scale, and together those forces concentrated attention on the center of Chicago's downtown business district, known as "the Loop" for the elevated railway tracks that encircled it.

Not surprisingly, real estate prices soared, creating even greater incentives to make maximum use of small sites than had been the case in New York. Within a year after the fire, prices for downtown Chicago lots had already surpassed the levels established before the fire, spurring developers to strive for the most square footage on each parcel. Between 1872 and 1879, some ten thousand building permits were issued by Chicago authorities. And over the decade of the 1880s prices for a quarter-acre of prime downtown real estate zoomed from $130,000 to $900,000. With metal construction technology now at hand, owners and architects naturally preferred to go up, rather than to spread out.

For all the pressures to move beyond the architectural traditions of the past, the leap probably could not have been made with such vigor anywhere else in the United States except Chicago—with or without a fire. Retaining much of its frontier spirit (Chicago was originally named Fort Dearborn), the city was especially attractive to entrepreneurs, adventurers, outcasts, and industrial buccaneers. Many of the men who "made it" in Chicago—the Armours and the Swifts among them—were industrialists who literally made things, and did so with a combination of brute force and all-American optimism. When the actress Sarah

Bernhardt visited Chicago at the turn of the century, she declared that in this city beat "the pulse of America." It has been called America's "Second City" (after New York), and the "Windy City" (after the fierce blasts off Lake Michigan), but the nickname that still catches its essence best is "the city of Big Shoulders."

By the time of the great fire, Chicago had become the hub of the largest system of inland waterways in the world, providing it with access by ship to the Great Lakes and the Gulf of Mexico. Its position astride a network of railway lines amounting to nearly 11,000 miles of track linked it to both the Atlantic and the Pacific coasts (the city's railway terminals handled an average of 350 trains every day). What in the 1830s had been a humble settlement with 100 inhabitants, a collection of rude dwellings, and one saloon had, 40 years later, achieved a population of nearly 300,000 people.

For all its wealth and energy, however, Chicago could not escape a feeling of cultural inferiority in its competition with New York, and manifested an almost compensatory determination to surpass its Eastern rival. Given Chicago's relative youth, the city should be given credit for substantial achievement in that effort. Contrary to much historical lore, Chicago in the middle of the nineteenth century had a vigorous cultural life of its own. The Chicago Historical Society was established in 1856, and by the time of the fire the city boasted 68 bookstores, or roughly one for every 4,400 inhabitants, and a large library became an essential part of the home of even the most philistine of industrialists. The Chicago Academy of Design, the precursor of the Chicago Art Institute, was founded in 1866. Nonetheless, Chicago's identity as a provincial city forced it to make comparisons to its Eastern competition, whose cultural elite persisted in dismissing the midwesterners as *arrivistes*.

In the realms of drama, music, and the plastic arts, there was considerable substance to the easterners' disdain, but in architecture New York's cultural "superiority" actually proved to be a fatal disadvantage in the competition for leadership. So wedded were most of the leading Eastern architects to the traditions of Europe that they simply could not see beyond the precedents on which they had been raised. And many of those who chose not to play by the traditional rules defected. Indeed, virtually all of the architects who eventually became associated with the "Chicago School" were Eastern refugees, most of them from New York or Boston, and they helped create a community that took a uniquely chauvinistic pride in the architecture that defined the city's reconstruction.

One of the most influential of the first-generation Chicago architects was Daniel Burnham. The man who was to become the master of ceremonies for the World's Columbian Exposition had been born in northern New York State, the grandson of a Congregational minister and the son of a wholesale druggist who moved to Chicago to improve on a record of business failures. Young Burnham had hoped to make his way as a merchant, and briefly tried mining before turning to architecture in 1872 at the age of twenty-six, joining the local firm of Carter, Drake

DANIEL BURNHAM

Brown Brothers

& Wight. There he met John Wellborn Root, who had been trained in part by James Renwick, the architect of Grace Church and St. Patrick's Cathedral in New York City. Burnham and Root went into business for themselves in 1873. Despite Root's talent for design and Burnham's drive, the firm got off to a shaky start, but it eventually flourished, as did Burnham's ambition. The portly and rather pompous Burnham (who was widely known as "Uncle Dan") is quoted as having declared to Louis Sullivan at one point, "My idea is to work up a big business, to handle big things, deal with big businessmen, and to build up a big organization, for you can't handle big things unless you have an organization."

The firm's accomplishments ranged from the unexceptional ten-story Montauk Building of 1882, to the hefty block known as the Rookery (1888), with its airily elegant iron-and-glass dome hovering above a three-story light court. But the most memorable of their early works was without doubt the Monadnock Building. Completed in 1891, it rose sixteen stories on the southwest corner of Jackson and Dearborn, and with its slope-sided base and unembellished facade it presented a crisply sober—almost ominous—shape to the city around it. In fact the most distinguishing aspect of this building was not its form, which looks remarkably "modern" in retrospect, but the fact that it was built in conventional masonry fashion. Indeed, the reason the building's walls were so much thicker at the base—seventy-two inches—was that otherwise it could not have supported the rest of the structure. Although their colleagues were already experimenting with metal, Burnham and Root remained tied to stone, in much the way Richardson had been in his later buildings. And like Richardson in his houses, these two architects pushed masonry just about as far as it could go in a tall building (and to accommodate the great weight, developed an innovative foundation system that replaced the traditional pyramid of stone with a leaner platform of concrete). The Monadnock remains the tallest building ever constructed with brick walls. From that point onward, height would have to be achieved by accepting the new materials.

The architect who did that with the earliest and greatest ingenuity was William Le Baron Jenney (1832–1907), who has traditionally been considered the founder of the Chicago School of architecture. Also an easterner (he was a native of Fairhaven, Massachusetts), Jenney had been educated as an engineer at the Ecole Centrale des Arts et Manu-

Chicago Historical Society

THE MONADNOCK

BUILDING,
*Chicago, Burnham
& Root, 1891;
Holabird
& Roche, 1893.*
A unique example
of technological
transition.

factures in Paris, where he became familiar with the innovative French research being conducted in metal-framed and fireproofed commercial and exhibition buildings. During the Civil War, Jenney became a major in General William Tecumseh Sherman's corps of engineers, studying the mechanics of bridge building and the structural properties of iron. A proud man, who could exasperate those who worked for him, Jenney insisted after his discharge on being addressed by his military rank.

Corbis-Bettmann

The "major'" arrived in Chicago in 1867 and set up an architectural office the next year. His first significant work was the Leiter Building, a five-story structure completed in 1879 and expanded by two stories in 1888. It was nothing to speak of as a work of high design, but in his skillful combination of wooden floor beams and cast-iron columns, Jenney was beginning to probe the possibilities of an all-metal frame. It was his nine-story Home Insurance Building, completed in 1885, that brought to Chicago the most fundamental element of skyscraper constuction: an entirely metal structure from which the external cladding could be hung in "curtain" fashion. The Home Insurance Building was no more alluring to look at than the Leiter, but it set a new standard for structure. Clearly, there was no longer any reason to use masonry as anything more than a skin.

THE HOME INSURANCE BUILDING, *Chicago, William Le Baron Jenney, 1885.* The all-metal structure set a new standard for tall buildings.

In the end, though, Jenney's contribution to the progress of the tall building was amost entirely in the realm of construction rather than in aesthetics. (His justly famous Manhattan Building of 1890 is a landmark more for the innovative system of wind-bracing Jenney developed than for its looks.) His architecture bears the mark of an earnest intelligence animated by the solving of technical problems, but unfired by the challenge of form. Critical as they were to the history of design, most of Jenney's buildings remained blocky and ill-proportioned and were marred by an awkward overlay of ornament. He himself seems to have tired of the pursuit of a new aesthetic to match his technical achievements after solving the problems posed by the Home Insurance Building. Although his so-called Second Leiter Building (1891) was a substantial achievement, it had scant grace and gave no useful direction to those followers in search of a high-rise architecture that aspired to more than function.

Nonetheless, the training Jenney provided to his younger employees gave those with a taste for the *art* of design a firm grounding in the necessities of construction. In this sense, like Hunt before him, Jenney's influence was communicated by more than his architecture. At one point, his staff included Martin Roche and William Holabird, who later joined forces to make substantial—if workmanlike—contributions of their own to the Chicago portfolio. Among their finest work was the 1893 addition to Burnham and Root's Monadnock Building, an addition that adhered to the original's form, but was constructed on a steel frame, providing in one building a striking transition from the methods of the past to those of the future.

Another Jenney alumnus was Daniel Burnham, who by 1891 was working on his own following the premature death of his partner, and quickly recognized his former employer's technical achievements. But Burnham was able to augment them with a measure of aesthetic sensibility. His fourteen-story Reliance Building, completed in 1895, showed that he was not at all trapped by the masonry tradition that he and John Root had brought to such noble heights in the Monadnock Building only four years earlier. Making full use of metal framing, Burnham created a minimalist cage whose openings he filled with an elegant version of what came to be known as the "Chicago window"—a wide fixed pane of glass flanked by two narrower ones that could be opened for ventilation. (More than two-thirds of the surface of the street facade was glass.)

Library of Congress

Even today, the Reliance stands out as a graceful and knowledgeable expression of its own structural realities and the artistic uses to which they could be put.

But after the Reliance, Burnham, too, let slip the thread of innovation he had been holding. Having immersed himself in the planning for the World's Columbian Exposition, he chose to spend his later days pursuing the monumental opportunities that the extravaganza threw open to him, creating in 1909 the vast Plan of Chicago, a neo-Baroque scheme for his city that compared favorably with Baron Haussmann's plan for Paris (but included no skyscrapers), and leaving to others the challenge of integrating art and the new technology. The man who accomplished that with nothing less than historic impact was another former Jenney employee: Louis Sullivan.

Sullivan had been born in Boston, where his father taught dancing, and at the age of sixteen enrolled at the Massachusetts Institute of Technology to study architecture. The architecture program—the first in the nation—had only recently been established, by William Ware in 1868, and its curriculum was based closely on that of the Ecole des Beaux-Arts in Paris. Even as a boy, Sullivan had shown little patience with traditional schooling, and, dismissing MIT as "but a pale reflection of the Beaux-Arts," he left at the end of his first year. Evidently feeling that he needed some hands-on experience before tackling the real thing, he spent that summer in Philadelphia, where, on the advice of Richard Morris Hunt (to whom he may have had an introduction from William Ware at MIT), he soon found himself working for the redoubtable Frank Furness.

At the time, Furness was at the height of his powers, and Sullivan was suitably impressed, not just by the energetically creative architecture coming out of the Furness office (the Pennsylvania Academy of the Fine Arts was then under construction), but also by his employer's single-minded stylistic irreverence and his skill as a draftsman.

That skill was especially apparent in Furness's treatment of ornament, for which he had derived a highly personal and ornate system based on contemporary French and English designs. Judging from the spectacularly inventive ornament Sullivan himself was to develop as a mature architect, one can only assume that the example set by Furness had an especially strong impact.

In retrospect, Sullivan seems to have had an unerring sense of just where to go for the most useful training in his art. After a year with Furness, who was hit hard by a financial panic, Sullivan went on to Chicago to join his parents and his brother, Albert, who had moved there from Boston, and took a job in the offices of William Le Baron Jenney. (Lore has it that the rather cocky Sullivan, in seeking a satisfactory office, roamed Chicago's streets looking for a building that interested him. He singled out Jenney's Portland Block, and promptly offered the firm his services.) This, too, proved to be a brief interlude, but it could only have been an enlightening one. Having come from the aggressively artistic

Corbis-Bettmann

Furness office to Jenney's hard-core, engineering-based environment, Sullivan was absorbing the most powerful work being done in the country at that time. But he evidently felt that what the United States had to offer—even at the feet of the likes of Furness and Jenney—was still not sufficient, and that he needed to test architectural education at the source. In July 1874 Sullivan boarded a boat for Europe, and that fall, just nine years after Henry Hobson Richardson had left, Sullivan himself prepared to enter the Ecole des Beaux-Arts to study with the best architectural faculty Europe had to offer.

To prepare himself for the Ecole examinations, Sullivan engaged tutors in French and mathematics. The mathematics tutor, a man named

Clopet, made a profound and long-lasting impression on the aspirant by insisting on solutions that, as Sullivan recalled them with appropriate typographical emphasis later in his autobiography, were "*so broad as to admit of* NO EXCEPTION!!" Sullivan's own biographers have, with reason, suggested that the appeal of this all-embracing declaration launched his later search for a comparably definitive pronouncement on architecture, culminating in his oft-quoted (and just as often misinterpreted) declaration in his 1896 essay on tall buildings that "form ever follows function, and this is the law."

Despite the wisdom dispensed by Clopet and his colleagues, the Ecole struck Sullivan as suffering from a "residuum of artificiality," and exercised no more hold over him than had Furness or Jenney. (However, he never lost the attraction he acquired in Paris for suits of the most elegant cut.) After spending the winter of 1874–75 in Paris, Sullivan set out for Italy, where on a visit to the Sistine Chapel he was apparently overwhelmed by the power of Michelangelo's frescoes. Persuaded that he might follow the example of an artist he called "the first mighty man of Courage . . . the first mighty craftsman," Sullivan returned to Chicago. There, he briefly found work with a friend he had met in Jenney's office during his earlier Chicago days, John Edelmann, who was by then on his own designing a synagogue, and (perhaps on the strength of the new man's description of the Sistine Chapel) put Sullivan to work designing the frescoes.

Edelmann eventually rejoined a firm for which he had worked some years before and introduced Sullivan to one of the partners, a German immigrant named Dankmar Adler, who was twelve years older than Sullivan and already an established architect and engineer known for respectable residential and commercial work. (He was especially admired for his acoustical engineering.) Adler took Sullivan on, giving him assignments that were at first those of an office helper and draftsman, but his greater talents quickly became apparent; within a year, the relative newcomer was offered a one-third partnership in the firm, and a year later he was elevated to the rank of full partner. Under the new arrangement, Adler retained responsibility for the engineering and business sides of the operation; Sullivan took over design.

The work produced by Adler and Sullivan during their first decade together was hardly extraordinary. It included conventionally eclectic residences for well-off Chicagoans eager to display their prosperity in Queen

Anne mansions, as well as a number of office and warehouse buildings of no particular distinction, either artistically or technologically.

At the time, of course, the most progressive American architect was still Richardson, and Sullivan, who had grown up in Boston and followed Richardson to Paris, was intensely aware of the older architect's example. That example was made even more insistent with the open-

ing, in 1887 (a year after Richardson's death), of the Marshall Field Wholesale Store in Chicago. Writing years later in his collection of essays entitled *Kindergarten Chats*, Sullivan described Richardson's building in anthropomorphic terms: "Here is a man for you to look at. A man that walks on two legs instead of four . . . broad, vigorous and with a whelm of energy—an entire male." Just how much the Richardson legacy meant to Sullivan became clear in 1888–89 with the design of the Walker Warehouse, a foursquare utilitarian building that, despite its taut neoclassical garb, revealed a heavy debt to Richardson's massing. But Marshall Field's full impact emerged soon afterwards, when Sullivan and Adler were in the midst of designing the Auditorium Building.

The site for the Auditorium, which was begun in 1886 and completed in 1890, covered a half-block on Michigan Avenue, an area roughly the size of Richardson's site for the Marshall Field Wholesale Store. From the start, it was to include, as the name proclaimed, an auditorium, but also space for offices, a hotel, and a restaurant. The early schemes for the building included a tower with a mansard roof and a frosting of the sort of Queen Anne and Romanesque ornament the firm had used before. But as Sullivan came to appreciate the underlying simplicity of Richardson's form (and as the client pushed for economies), he gradually peeled away the trimmings, leaving a sturdy ten-story block from which sprang a seven-story tower. The organization of the facade elements owed much to Richardson: The bottom floor was pierced by squat arches trimmed in rusticated stone, while the middle stories were linked by four-story pilasters culminating in arches, and the top three stories were articulated by smaller windows grouped in pairs and threes. The tower loomed above them in neo-Renaissance fashion, providing, in addition to a dramatic focus for the composition, new offices for the firm of Adler & Sullivan.

At first glance, the Auditorium might be taken merely as a work of compositional homage to Richardson, but the overall effect is entirely different. Sullivan's treatment had little of Richardon's boldness, relying more on surface embellishment than mass to convey its impact. The legacy of Richardson's fondness for massive forms marked the Auditorium as a building of the past, but its comparatively lighter facade—a mere surface over a metal frame—betrayed a desire to break free and rise higher.

With the availability of the steel frame—to which Jenney, Burham, and others were already devoting much attention—Sullivan could make good on the challenge Richardson had chosen to avoid. And with the Wainwright Building in St. Louis, completed in 1891, Sullivan launched American architecture on a course toward aesthetic and technological dominance for decades to come. In the Wainwright, Sullivan (who later declared that the basic scheme for the building had been worked out "literally in three minutes") dispensed with the neoclassical details (although not the base-shaft-capital organization) on which he had relied so heavily in the Auditorium and the Walker Warehouse, and allowed the new building's structure to express itself (almost) unconcealed on the facade.

In his 1896 essay, Sullivan declared that the frame must be "the true basis of the artistic development of the exterior." In fact, though, the vertical elements that gave the Wainwright its feeling of vertical thrust were only partially expressions of the underlying steel cage. There were twice as many piers as there were structural columns behind them, leading

THE AUDITORIUM BUILDING, *Chicago, Adler & Sullivan, 1890.* An homage to Richardson that looked forward as well as back in time.

some later critics to attack the architect for "faking" his facade. And in this they renewed the argument that had raged with such peculiarly American intensity through the Greek and Gothic Revival periods over what was "honest" architecture. Of course, if Sullivan had been more literal-minded about his use of piers, his building would have lost much of the visual impact his solution provided (it was accentuated by recessing the spandrel panels between the columns), and in that sense the architect was certainly striving for effect over fact. On the other hand, the essential quality of the overall design is the expression of the vertical properties of its frame, and by embracing *that* fact, Sullivan could be seen as being absolutely "true" to the idea of the Wainwright.

The argument is related to the one over which building deserves the title of the first true skyscraper. If the inclusion of a passenger elevator is used as the sole criterion, then Hunt's Tribune Building would probably take the prize. If the standard is the use of a fireproofed metal cage structure, the winner must be Jenney for his Home Insurance Building. But what has come to be known as the skyscraper has always had more to do with the sense of height than the facts of construction, and if the *spirit* of the building is the issue, then Sullivan's St. Louis entry is the clear champion. Whether or not it was a "pure" expression of structural form, it was a summation of all the other requirements; but most important, in it the architect marshaled all of these devices to convey the *feeling* of height.

Sullivan refined that feeling in his Guaranty (later Prudential) Building in Buffalo, completed in 1896. Here, over a clearly articulated base, he attenuated the piers (but still used twice as many as were necessary to express the vertical steel members), finished them neatly at the top with arches, and provided a sort of architectural "full stop" above each with a small circular window. The midsection, which has a lean, Renaissance lightness, was topped by a heavy cornice that restrains the building's dramatic upward thrust from appearing to go on indefinitely. Bold achievement that it was, the Guaranty also documented one of the major unresolved issues facing contemporary architects of tall buildings. Sullivan could not devise an effective transition between the base and the midsection, leaving one to sit upon the other in an almost literally disembodied fashion.

Nonetheless, in almost every other way, Sullivan had, with the Wainwright and the Guaranty, loosed the bonds inherited from Richardson.

THE GUARANTY
(PRUDENTIAL)
BUILDING,
*Buffalo, New York,
Adler & Sullivan,
1896.* A combination
of structure and
ornament that served
an "emotional"
function.

He had faced the potential of steel-frame construction, and mastered it. He had rejected the stylistic conventions of the past—whether those of the Ecole, of Frank Furness, or even of Richardson—and he had triumphed where such Chicago colleagues as Jenney and Burnham had hesitated, in giving full artistic expression to a revolutionary technology. And it is that achievement that seems to be embodied in the deathless declaration about form ever following function.

Those few words have caused tremendous problems for many of Sullivan's chroniclers, particularly those of a doctrinaire Modernist persuasion, who have never been quite able to deal with his enduring devotion to ornament. It was the one area in which Sullivan appeared tied to tradition. Although most of the overtly classical details had vanished from his work shortly after the Auditorium, the fascination Sullivan conceived in Furness's office with designs based on natural forms remained with him. In the Wainwright, he filled the panels separating the vertical piers with a richly varied series of floral patterns. In the Guaranty, he extended the ornament to the surface of the piers themselves. In his Schlesinger & Mayer Department Store (later the Carson Pirie Scott), in Chicago, of 1904, Sullivan turned his concern for structural clarity from the vertical to the horizontal, creating a building so spare in its organization that it seemed a preview of Modernist developments forty years later (although the site and size of the building seemed stronger motives for the shape than any devotion to pre-Modern horizontality). But at the entrance he produced a thicket of metal ornament so intricate and delicate that it seemed almost to shudder in the gusts of Chicago's famous wind. Significantly, scholars who saw a proto-Modernist in Sullivan always preferred photographs of the building that emphasize its horizontality, while obscuring the ornament that the architect felt was such an important part of the whole.

Unlike some of his later critics, Sullivan did not see a conflict between his search for structural truth and his devotion to ornament. On the contrary, he saw them as inextricable, and said so many times. In fact, his definition of the "function" that the "form ever follows" included the demand of the eye for uplifting diversion, and of the heart for inspiration. Emotion was to be served by architecture no less than the need for shelter and mechanical efficiency. Nor was his system of ornament in any qualitative way inferior to his overall spatial and compositional sense. At its best, it was sublimely beautiful. But just as Richardson's dedication to historicism seemed to be steadily eroded by the insistent pull of his geometry, Sullivan's ornament seemed increasingly irrelevant to the industrially based architecture that was developing in his own hands. Despite his commitment to nature, the sculptural forms of the buildings themselves were beginning to take over the most powerful visual role, leaving the ornament in an increasingly subservient position.

The dichotomy became clearer as Sullivan was forced to husband his architectural resources. Worsening economic times and growing family demands persuaded Dankmar Adler to leave the partnership in 1895 for work as an executive at an elevator company. His sortie in search of more money failed, but when he decided to return to architecture, Sullivan would not have him. Evidently angered by Adler's departure, Sullivan chose to shun his former partner, and subsequently went out of his way to minimize Adler's contributions to their work together. (In late 1895, Sullivan published the plans for the Guaranty Building, but left Adler's name off them.) The absence of Adler's sturdy talents became steadily more apparent, and combined with the poor business climate, it contributed to a dramatic falloff in Sullivan's production. Between 1880 and 1895, the two men had produced more than a hundred buildings together. In his remaining thirty years, Sullivan would produce a mere twenty.

Prominent among them was the Bayard Building on New York's Bleecker Street, completed in 1898. It was Sullivan's first major commission since Adler's departure, and, despite his renown, it was to be the only building he designed for New York City. Crowded by a host of banal commercial buildings, it is hard to appreciate the elegance of the Bayard—or Condict, as it became known after a later owner. But even from the cramped perspective of a narrow New York street, the lightness and elegance of the facade organization is immediately evident to a determined observer. Departing from the rhythm he established in the Wainwright and Guaranty buildings by using piers of equal width, Sullivan in the Condict alternated the major piers with thin ones, linking them at the cornice with arches and oculus windows topped by reliefs of winged maidens. For those who would describe Sullivan as a proto-functionalist, this building is especially hard to accommodate. But coming in the wake of his leaner and better-known office buildings, it can only be seen as a more mature work. And since it is so frankly lyrical in its decoration, it would seem to be an indication that ornament—no matter how much it seemed to conflict with functionality—was becoming more than ever an integral part of his design vocabulary.

That direction was confirmed by a series of small banks Sullivan designed for several Midwestern cities in the first years of the new century. To be sure, these were not the commissions of his choice. The combination of an ailing economy, the loss of Adler and his business and engineering skills, and an almost self-destructive insistence on getting his own way despite his clients' wishes, had reduced the great man to accepting almost any work that came along.

The banks could not have been simpler as programs or as forms. All were essentially squat rectangular boxes housing banking rooms and public spaces. But their exterior embellishment took Sullivan's fascination with ornament to new heights. Indeed, the decoration in some cases threatened to overwhelm the underlying architecture, particularly in the banks for Grinnell, Iowa, and Sidney, Ohio, where the eruptions of terra-cotta foliage and pure geometry might as well have been freestanding panels. (They evoke simultaneously the "false fronts" of Western frontier towns and the sort of signage that Robert Venturi would describe decades later in his discussions of the "decorated shed.")

But these late works, for all their jewel-like intensity, had limited impact beyond the shrinking circle of Sullivan's loyalists. The World's Columbian Exposition had been an instant sensation with the overwhelming majority of those who saw it, and many of the visitors went away with visions of a new American architecture made not of structurally authoritative office buildings and banks that looked like "strongboxes," as Sullivan described his own buildings, but of neo-Gothic office towers and banks that looked like Roman temples. The "White City" so dazzled the audience for architecture that those practitioners willing to embrace its message — Charles McKim, Cass Gilbert, and the changeable Daniel Burnham — became arbiters of taste for nearly half a century.

Sullivan, of course, would have none of it. Although the innovative Transportation Building he and Adler had designed for the fair had attracted international attention (models of it were exhibited in Paris and Moscow), the American public was clearly more interested in the instant "authenticity" of architectural fantasies, and Sullivan grew increasingly embittered by the eagerness of his colleagues to provide them. He mocked the most powerful practitioners of the day — McKim, George Post, and Burnham — who, not surprisingly, shut him out of the New York and Chicago architectural societies that were such a fertile source of commissions. Sullivan railed at the architectural establishment as it expressed itself through the American Institute of Architects, and grew ever more vitriolic in his criticism of what he saw as aesthetic backsliding. In a speech to young architects at the Chicago Architectural Club on May 30, 1899, Sullivan declared: "You will realize, in due time, as your lives develop and expand and you become richer in experience, that a fraudulent and surreptitious use of historical documents, however cleverly plagiarized, however neatly re-packed, however shrewdly intrigued, will constitute and will be held to be a betrayal of trust." And in June 1900, he described the current architecture of steel frames hidden under classical cloaks to a meeting of the Architectural League of America as "the offspring of an illegitimate commerce with the mongrel types of the past."

Although Sullivan concentrated his attacks on the architectural establishment, he might almost be seen as trying to sublimate a frustration within his own artistic being. While his skyscrapers pointed directly toward an aesthetic defined by materials and technology, his poetic nature could not abandon the pull toward nature and its expression in ornament. It is as if the original suspicion of beauty harbored by the Puritan founders and the conflicting lure of the romantic as seen in the works of Andrew Jackson Downing and Alexander Jackson Davis had taken up residence in the same soul—with an almost inevitably disastrous effect. Without dipping deeply into psychology, one might characterize Sullivan's dualistic impulses as a sort of artistic schizophrenia. And the almost evangelical fervor with which he condemned his colleagues might be seen as an expression of the frustration he himself evidently felt at his inability to resolve the conflicting demands of the elemental and the decorative.

As his personal fortunes diminished, Sullivan became steadily more reclusive, moving to humble quarters in a Chicago hotel. His marriage, in 1899 at the age of forty-two, had never taken hold, and ended officially in 1916 when his wife, from whom he had been separated for years, formally divorced him. A brief resurgence of the old energy brought some young architects into his office, but the work did not sustain them, and they were forced to move on, leaving Sullivan—always quick to take a departure as a betrayal—even more embittered. Before long, he was reduced to having his meals at his club paid for by friends; his once extensive library of architectural works had shrunk to a few volumes, which he stored in his bathroom. A special indignity was visited on him when the owners of the Carson Pirie Scott store decided to add to the building, and hired Daniel Burnham to do the job. Sullivan could take cold comfort in the fact that Burnham decided temporarily to leash his enthusiasm for the classical and virtually copied the original (extending it by several bays and thus ironically amplifying the building's later appeal to Modernists).

In 1920, Sullivan was evicted from the two-room office in the Auditorium to which he had already been forced to retreat from his once grand quarters on the top floor of the tower. His health declined with his fortunes, and on April 14, 1924, at the age of sixty-seven, he died of kidney and heart problems.

Widespread recognition of Sullivan's fundamental contributions to architecture would have to wait until the arrival of Modernism in the 1930s and 1940s, when it became increasingly clear that Sullivan, as no other architect—European or American—had been the first to bring art and technology into something approaching a symbiotic union. But even as he slid into temporary eclipse, Sullivan's influence was being perpetuated by one of his former employees.

Sullivan had hired Frank Lloyd Wright early in 1888 during work on the Auditorium Building, and the two developed an intensely personal and professional relationship. Wright eventually became foreman of the thirty designers in the office, but, in classic Sullivan fashion, the relationship ended abruptly when the older man discovered that Wright had been moonlighting. Nonetheless, Wright remained devoted to Sullivan, and, as his mentor's career declined, was one of the few to stand by him, writing frequently to cheer Sullivan up and enclosing the occasional check to help cover the rent.

But if Sullivan's example endured through Wright, it was in spirit rather than in the building type that had made Sullivan for a time America's most prominent architect. At first, Wright had little use for tall buildings. He was, however, devoted to the private house in both its formal and philosophical dimensions. While the skyscraper phenomenon was pursued with varying degrees of success by others of Sullivan's heirs, Wright was to catch the crest of a wave in residential design and create a revolution of his own at the domestic scale.

Domestic Diversity

o other figure so dominates the American architectural landscape as that of Frank Lloyd Wright. Best known as the designer
of the low-slung "Prairie" houses of the Midwest, the sublimely
romantic Pennsylvania retreat called Fallingwater, and the spiraling
Guggenheim Museum in New York City, Wright has assumed larger-
than-life proportions, both as an artist and as an individual. Born in
1867 (although he later claimed the date to be 1869), he lived to the
age of ninety-two, and was producing major works of art virtually until
the end. A congenital contrarian, he battled the architectural estab-

FRANK
LLOYD
WRIGHT,
1915

lishment wherever he met it, and he did so with a unique flair for personal and professional publicity. Surely no other American architect of his or any other generation has been able to get away with anything like his public peccadillos, his flowing capes, and his outrageous pronouncements on his own genius, the mediocrity of his fellow architects, and the aesthetic timidity of society at large.

Wright played a prominent role in the creation of his image, writing and rewriting his thoroughly extraordinary history with a hagiographer's zeal. Over his long career he produced scores of books and articles, and was the subject of hundreds of others by high-minded academics and gossip columnists alike. Through them all, Wright strove to convince the public that he had sprung fully formed upon the architectural stage, cleansing it of past excesses and endowing it with an entirely new vision.

That promotional process continued to his last years, but it began with the residential work that followed his abrupt departure from Louis Sullivan's office, work that established him as by far the dominant member of what came to be known as the Prairie School. "The old architecture, so far as its grammar went, began literally to disappear," Wright wrote approvingly of his early work in the first edition of his autobiography, published in 1932. "As if by magic new architectural effects came to life—effects genuinely new in the whole cycle of architecture. . . ."

Despite such claims, Wright was hardly alone in doing innovative work as the century turned. And although the fascination with his architecture (and his persona) seems only to expand with succeeding generations, the work itself, at least in the beginning, was not in every case much more remarkable than what was being done by a number of other architects. Particularly in California, the Eurocentric conventions of the East were being questioned in response to changing social conditions and a dramatically different climate. Neither the Californians nor Wright would have been possible without the preexisting examples of American residential architecture. No matter what the architectural innovators of the early twentieth century might say about the uniqueness of their work, they followed firmly in the footsteps of such men as Asher Benjamin and Andrew Jackson Downing, as well as the anonymous carpenters who raised the Parson Capen House on that hillock in northern Massachusetts.

Nor were their sources all historical. Americans who could afford to build their own homes still relied heavily on what could be found in catalogues. The successors to pattern books like Downing's *Cottage Residences* were such publications as *Palliser's Modern Homes* (1883) and *The Radford American Homes*, which began publication just after the turn of the century and provided a rich menu of residential inspiration ranging from the vaguely Gothic to the no less vaguely Anglo-Colonial. In 1906, a pair of brothers in Bay City, Michigan, founded the Aladdin Company, which produced a catalogue that offered pre-cut manufactured homes for less than $300, and two years later Sears, Roebuck and Company brought out its *Book of Modern Homes and Building Plans*, which included twenty-two balloon-frame house designs. (By 1940, the company had sold close to 100,000 houses to customers throughout the United States.) Virtually all of these buildings had at least a minimum of architectural pretension. The 1912 catalogue for Montgomery Ward & Co. offered models described as "Elizabethan," "Swiss Cottage," "Bungalow," and "Southern Colonial."[1]

If these buildings fell well short of high design, they should not be altogether spurned. They were, as their evocative titles suggested, responses to what Americans wanted in their homes—not merely shelter, but also something that conjured up a way of life, and a sense of history. In authentic American fashion, they were as much about aspirations as they were about protection from the elements.

Another source for the architects who embraced the domestic agenda was the increasing flow of publications through their offices, especially *American Architect and Building News*. Its pages displayed richly rendered images of lavish country houses, some perched like fairy-tale castles on rocky ocean promontories, others spreading out across their owners' vast estates for distances that must have kept the household staffs in peak physical condition answering the calls of the weekend guests. Regardless of style—whether Queen Anne, Dutch Revival, or mock-Colonial—most of these buildings were by definition vigorously anti-urban, evoking at once the characteristic American profligacy with land and—at least for the wealthy—the ability to afford summers off with plenty of servants.

In addition to such sources, Wright and his contemporaries had access to developments beyond America's shores, mostly through the British architectural magazines—which published the contemporary work of Richard Norman Shaw, Charles Rennie Mackintosh, and C. F. A. Voysey and were found in the better architectural offices. Gustav Stickley, like Wright another Wisconsin native and the chief proponent of the Arts and Crafts movement in America, began to publish his *Craftsman* magazine in 1901, providing architects and potential clients with a glimpse of the handiwork tradition that had already reestablished itself so firmly in England. At the heart of this movement was a feeling that industry and the machine had debased design and that only a return to the basics of artisanship could reform it. The whole-

---

[1] See Robert Schweitzer and Michael W. R. Davis, *America's Favorite Homes* (Detroit: Wayne State University Press, 1990), p. 69.

sale rejection of the machine had never sat well with most Americans, fascinated as they were by technological progress and gadgetry. But many clearly felt that something had been lost in the embrace of a mechanistic society. The result was a compensatory eagerness for the handmade, the weathered, the "organic." For them, Stickley's publication of quaint country houses and handmade furniture was deeply reassuring.

Yet another family of publications should be included in recreating the domestic design context of the turn of the century. The role of women in American society had been changing steadily since the end of the Civil War, and the publishing world was adjusting accordingly. The year 1896 saw the debut of *House Beautiful*, the first of what was to become a large group of "homemaker" magazines. Like those that followed, *House Beautiful*, which was published in Chicago, showed an avid interest in design, and in fact published the first two articles ever written about Wright (in 1897 and 1899). Such publications gave the wives of industrialists considerable authority when it came to selecting architects for their homes (although not their office buildings). In an age when burgeoning wealth and the resulting surge in social and cultural ambition created a need for country houses as symbols of success and status, that authority could have far-reaching consequences.[2]

Although most American architects and clients alike still looked to Europe for inspiration, other sources began to make inroads by the fourth quarter of the nineteenth century. And for those with an open mind, the Japanese Pavilion at the 1876 Centennial in Philadelphia, which was published in an issue of *American Architect and Building News*, provided the first glimpse of a compellingly different architectural imagery. The strongest impression was made by the building's free-flowing interior spaces, articulated only by movable partitions. Many of those who saw it were also taken with the elemental sense of shelter conveyed by the broad overhanging eaves, and the appealing textures of the hand-wrought wooden structural members. Not the least of the allure of this building was its formal clarity, which must have been a revelation to architects wearying of the disorderly complexity of many conventional American residences. The impact of Japanese architecture

---

[2] See H. Allen Brooks, *The Prairie School: Frank Lloyd Wright and His Midwest Contemporaries* (New York: W. W. Norton, 1972), p. 24.

THE HO-O-DEN, *anonymous, World's Columbian Exposition, Chicago, 1893.* For many American architects, their first glimpse of Japanese design.

became even stronger less than two decades later with the construction of the Ho-o-Den, a half-scale reproduction of a famous Japanese pavilion, at the World's Columbian Exposition in Chicago.

One of the leading architects who undoubtedly knew of the 1876 Japanese exhibition was Bruce Price (1845–1903), whose William Kent House in Tuxedo Park, New York (1885), with its flowing interior spaces and bold exterior massing, went well beyond the vocabulary of the merely picturesque that had characterized so much earlier domestic work. Even more influential were the early residences designed by McKim, Mead & White. This extraordinary architecture firm, which at its peak was the largest in the world, received close to a thousand commissions between 1870 and 1920. It was ultimately best known for its urban monuments—such as the Boston Public Library (1895), and Madison Square Garden (1891) and Pennsylvania Station (1911) in New York City. But some of its most creative work was done at the domestic scale. Both Charles Follen McKim and Stanford White had worked in Richardson's office, absorbing his affection for historical allusion and clear massing, and both took part in the design of Boston's Trinity Church. But in partnership with William Rutherford Mead (1846–1928), with whom they joined as a firm in 1879, they struck out on a course of their own, embracing and amplifying the most progressive work of the day, to which Richardson had contributed heavily, especially in his Stoughton House in Cambridge and his Watts Sherman House in Newport, Rhode Island (1876), setting the stage for the new firm's own distinctive brand of academically based eclecticism.

McKim, Mead & White's Newport Casino (1880), not primarily a gambling establishment but a social club, reflected the leisurely lifestyle to which it was dedicated and displayed an easy way with spaces and a mastery of the flexible potential of shingles as a cladding. The William Low House (1887), in Bristol, Rhode Island, displayed an ar-

WILLIAM RUTHERFORD MEAD, CHARLES FOLLEN MCKIM, AND STANFORD WHITE

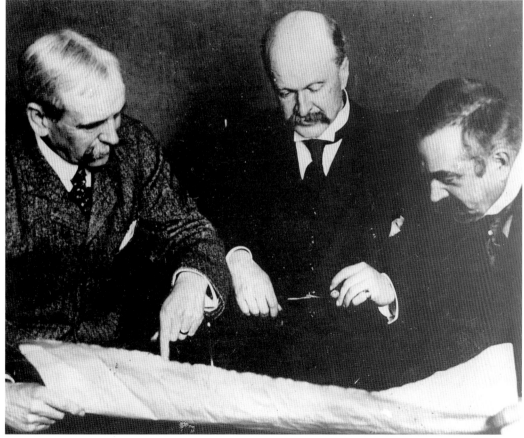

AP/Wide World Photos

Newport Historical Society

THE NEWPORT CASINO, *McKim, Mead & White, Newport, Rhode Island, 1880. An easy way with spaces and masses.*

resting sense of abstract form, with its all-inclusive gable that took Price's example a step further to the domination of the entire structure. This striking abstract use of geometry was radical at the time, and seemed to sum up the motto of the young firm, *"Vogue la Galère"* ("Let's Chance It"). But it was not a direction the architects were inclined to follow. As their practice grew, the partners turned increasingly to urban buildings, and in the process assumed a tighter, more historically correct stance appropriate to the changed setting. While the later buildings—and especially the institutional work—set a lofty standard for visual delight and urban sensibility, the tantalizing ebullience of McKim, Mead & White's resort architecture gradually ebbed, to be replaced by an elegant sobriety.

What most distinguished the best residential designs of Price, McKim, Mead & White, and their like-minded colleagues from their predecessors was greater sophistication about the integration of historical precedent. Stylistic liftings were no longer used for their associative effect alone, but rearranged into composites that met the aesthetic standards of resolved works of architecture. And architecture, as these practitioners understood it, included the other arts as well. Thus McKim, Mead & White frequently called upon the most distinguished painters and sculptors of the day—men like the sculptor Augustus Saint-Gaudens and the painter John LaFarge—not just to embellish their buildings, but also to collaborate in their conception.

A sensitivity to the other arts played an important role in the career of another prominent architect of the Eastern establishment, one who was eventually to come into direct conflict with Wright. Charles Adams Platt (1861–1933) started his career as an etcher, but expanded into landscape architecture, and finally into architecture itself, becoming perhaps his day's most sought-after designer of mansions for the wealthy. A genteel sort, who conducted much of his business at the better social clubs in New York and Boston, Platt became a master at country houses (and, later, town houses) that resonated with historical references and radiated a certifiable good taste. If his architecture was less than bold, it was precisely tuned to the needs of a ruling elite. Platt represented an earnest restraint that reflected a general calming of the late nineteenth-century exuberance in the use of historical styles. He was most comfortable in the Italian Renaissance, the French eighteenth century, and

THE WILLIAM LOW HOUSE, *McKim, Mead & White, Bristol, Rhode Island, 1887.* The abstract form was a bold gesture for its day.

the Georgian modes, and could be relied upon to produce a building that would do credit to a client whose money had freed him from the youthful vulgarity of the previous century.

Easterners like Platt, McKim, Mead, and White were understandably partial to European precedent. But just as Chicago's buccaneering spirit had contributed to the creative freedom that gave rise to the best in skyscraper thinking, the freewheeling atmosphere of America's "last frontier," the Far West, must be seen as critical to the residential architecture that flourished with such vigor for a brief period in California. Prominent among the Californians was a pair of brothers, Charles Sumner Greene (1868–1957) and Henry Mather Greene (1870–1954). Born in the Cincinnati suburb of Brighton, Ohio, both brothers were sent to a manual training school in St. Louis (the first in the country), where they developed skills as craftsmen according to a curriculum based on the teachings of the English Arts and Crafts advocate William Morris. They went from there to the Massachusetts Institute of Technology for their architectural training, imbibing the Beaux-Arts principles that had earlier influenced Hunt and Richardson. Henry Greene later moved on to the Boston firm of Shepley, Rutan & Coolidge, which had inherited Richardson's practice and continued to work in his style. The brothers might have remained in Boston but for a trip in 1893 to Pasadena to visit their parents.

During their visit, the Greenes were struck by the simplicity and environmental appropriateness of the local vernacular architecture, which included aged Spanish missions as well as humble dwellings that drew on the style of the bungalows built by the British in India, a style well suited to the California heat. After being invited to design a residence for a friend of their father's, they decided to stay on.

The Greenes' early work focused on the then-standard selection of Colonial and Queen Anne, but in the mid-1890s it began to change, and in the first years of the new century the brothers were designing buildings with personalities of their own. Most were rather simple vacation homes for wealthy clients. The Greenes were heavily influenced by the Craftsman movement, so much so that they often took part personally in the finishing of the wooden details that became so much a part of their characteristic works. They were also clearly fond of the intricate woodwork of Swiss vernacular architecture, even if the only chalets they had ever seen were in books. Beyond that, the Greenes, like

CHARLES AND HENRY GREENE

their Eastern contemporaries, were intrigued by the Japanese design they had seen at the World's Columbian Exposition, which they had visited on their way west.

Perhaps most important in distinguishing what the Greenes did from the work of their contemporaries to the east was the local climate. Their sweeping overhangs were designed not merely to make a formal statement, but also to shade the occupants from the year-round sun. The deep porches were intended not only as aesthetic gestures, but also as practical spaces to sleep during the steamy California nights.

The house Greene and Greene designed for David B. Gamble in Pasadena, completed in 1908, is the highest expression of the brothers' ideals. Built for one of the partners in the Procter & Gamble empire, it was a sumptuous residence, every detail of which was designed and executed with an almost palpable love of the materials—primarily wood of the richest varieties—and a sympathy for the leisurely way of life that the house was to serve. The interior paneling was mahogany, and joints were secured with wooden pegs, their exposed surfaces hand-rubbed to a rich luster. Clad in dark shingles, its expansive roof stretching well out from the walls, and its overall mass leavened by the staccato rhythm of the exposed beam ends, the Gamble House exuded welcome and security.

Rotch Visual Collec

**THE DAVID GAMBLE
HOUSE**, *Greene &
Greene, Pasadena,
California, 1908.*
Its design suited the
climate as much as
the architects.

However, the building also betrayed a certain philosophical un-steadiness. By 1908, such indulgence in craftsmanship had become pro-hibitively expensive, even for the wealthy (a fact that contributed to the decline of the Greene partnership), and in an age of emerging tech-nologies it seemed retrograde to more progressive eyes. The architects were clearly entranced by the formal possibilities of their expansive de-sign, but they seemed too tethered to the ideal of coziness to pursue ab-stract ends. Here is a building about a credo—craftsmanship—but without much architectural courage. From the rather conventional or-ganization of its interior spaces to its lustrous details, the Gamble House gazes longingly backward in time.

Much harder to categorize is the work of another transplanted east-erner, Bernard R. Maybeck (1862–1957). The son of a master wood-carver in New York City, Maybeck studied at the Beaux-Arts in Paris and worked briefly in New York and Kansas City before settling in San Fran-cisco in 1890. There, he designed a wide variety of picturesque eclec-tic buildings, including the First Church of Christ, Scientist, in Berkeley (1910). But he also did a substantial number of private houses. Like the Greenes, Maybeck was entranced by the easygoing lifestyle of California, and also like them, he took a cue from the outdoors in his use of natural materials, particularly wood and stone. Unlike the

Greene brothers, however, Maybeck never limited himself to a particular building type—or style. He seems to have had no firm design philosophy, drawing with equal enthusiasm on English half-timbered precedents and the masonry tradition of the Mediterranean. He made much of his distaste for the turreted excesses of the Queen Anne style, yet frequently outdid them with sorties into the Middle Ages. Maybeck's

BERNARD MAYBECK

Jacomena Maybeck

best-loved work is the unashamedly neoclassical rotunda for the Palace of Fine Arts at the Panama-Pacific Exposition of 1915 in San Francisco. (Built as a temporary structure, it gradually deteriorated, but was reconstructed by popular demand in the 1960s.)

Maybeck was the quintessential renegade, a man fascinated by the choices available to him and determined to exploit them, yet without the ideological underpinnings with which to give them much coherence. He insisted on making many of his drawings without triangle or T-square, believing that inspiration should be allowed to flow unfettered by even the most basic of architectural tools. A mystic who enjoyed dressing in a red velvet robe and a crocheted tam-o'-shanter, Maybeck declared that an architect's duty was to design for the "man in the street. He's the person you have to please, for he's the one who'll buy the building after the owner sells it."[3] He was also fond of declaring that "the sewer is the background of any plan."[4]

Yet for all his bizarre behavior, Maybeck embodied a special freedom of thought that is characteristically American. And although his work spawned virtually no legacy of architectural followers, it endeared itself sufficiently to the professional imagination that the American Institute of Architects in 1951 conferred upon him its gold medal (albeit six years before his death, at the age of ninety-five), and an Institute poll taken in 1991 listed him ninth among the ten best architects in American history.

If Maybeck was a phenomenon unto himself, he was not alone among the architectural experimentalists in the California of his day. Ernest Coxhead (1863–1933) was a native of Eastbourne, England, who set up a practice first in Los Angeles and then in San Francisco, where he created some intriguing houses in the Arts and Crafts tradition. Willis Polk (1867–1924) arrived in San Francisco in 1889, having worked in New York and Kansas City, and did much to further the academic ideas of McKim, Mead & White, while making the occasional foray into neomedieval residences that have become known, improbably enough, as rustic city houses.[5] After the earthquake and fire that de-

---

[3] Esther McCoy, *Five California Architects* (New York: Reinhold, 1960), p. 4.
[4] Ibid., p. 6.
[5] Richard Longstreth, *On the Edge of the World: Four Architects in San Francisco at the Turn of the Century* (New York: Architectural History Foundation; Cambridge, MA: The MIT Press, 1983), p. 112.

stroyed much of San Francisco in 1906, Polk briefly became head of Daniel Burnham's West Coast office and exploited the situation by concentrating on the sort of urban classicism to which Burnham himself had turned.

Polk worked for a time with another Eastern immigrant, A. Page Brown (1859–1896), who had served in the McKim, Mead & White office before moving in 1889 to San Francisco to set up his own practice (in which Maybeck also played a brief role). Brown became a leading exponent of academic eclecticism in the fashion of his former New York employers, providing his socially prominent clients with a taste of Eastern elegance in hefty homes of mostly classical and Georgian inspiration. He was strongly aided in this by his chief draftsman, A. C. Schweinfurth (1864–1900), who later developed a more independent streak and strove to create a regional style based on California's early pueblo and mission architecture. He was not limited to those sources, however, and created some shingled buildings of striking geometric simplicity.

All of these architects reflected a simultaneous appreciation of, and rebellion against, the European tradition as expressed in the training of the Beaux-Arts and its American followers. Although they were eager to embrace the aesthetic accomplishments of the past, they were acutely aware that American life—particularly in California—had created entirely different architectural needs. There were few precedents in Europe for the wealthy *arriviste*'s summer retreat (the Loire château and the English country house were expressions of a totally different culture), nor was there anything to compare with the emerging phenomenon of the American suburb. And while these architects were sensitive to their lack of formal training, they also exploited the freedom it provided for the recombination of stylistic precedents in unorthodox ways.

The appeal of the Hispanic tradition made an especially strong impact on Irving Gill (1870–1936). Another striking exemplar of the variety of architecture that flourished in California, largely out of sight of the mainstream Eastern architectural press, Gill was born in Syracuse, New York, the son of a building contractor, and, having decided to become an architect and wanting to apprentice with the best, went to Chicago to work as a draftsman. He worked first in the office of Joseph Lyman Silsbee (1845–1913), and then, in 1890, with Adler and Sullivan while they were designing the Transportation Building for the

THE FIRST
CHURCH OF
CHRIST,
SCIENTIST,
Bernard Maybeck,
Berkeley, California,
1910.
A picturesque
aesthetic that defied
categories.

World's Fair. (Wright, who had also worked for Silsbee, and was just two years older than Gill, was already a prominent member of the team.) Gill remained with Adler and Sullivan for only two years before health problems forced him to move to San Diego, which even then was known for its restorative climate. In an article he later wrote for *The Craftsman*, Gill said, "The west has an opportunity unparalleled in the history of the world, for it is the newest white page turned for registration."[6] Gill was particularly taken by the architecture of the old Spanish missions: simple geometric forms clad in whitewashed adobe. He found them "a most expressive medium of retaining tradition, history and romance, with their long, low lines, graceful arcades, tile roofs, bell towers, arched doorways, and walled gardens."[7] But he was not so seduced by the romance of the local historical buildings that he chose to copy them. After a period during which he designed some rather conventional Craftsman houses, Gill set out on a distinctly original course. He brought the appreciation he had learned in the Sullivan office for new materials to bear on what had proved itself a climatically appropriate design vocabulary, using reinforced concrete (a material then in its infancy) in place of stone or adobe, and steel in place of wood for structural members. (He also came up with some remarkably farsighted devices, including one that automatically hosed down automobiles parked in the garage, and a garbage disposal system that carried waste directly to a basement incinerator.)

In his appreciation of modern materials and his interest in simplified form, Gill would appear to have paralleled developments in Europe at the time (especially the work of the Austrian Adolf Loos). But while Gill followed contemporary architecture abroad through various publications, there is little to suggest a direct influence. His inspiration was a fundamentally original one, grounded in the physical and social facts of his surroundings. In this, Gill may actually have been aided by his lack of formal training (he had not gone beyond high school); there was, to be sure, no overlay of Beaux-Arts orthodoxy to abandon.

There was another way in which Gill's sensibilities seemed similar to those of some of his European contemporaries: He was deeply committed to using architecture to benefit the poor, working intently on designs for low-income housing. Here, too, he employed the latest technology, borrowing from a local army barracks project a system for prefabricating concrete slab walls that could be erected on a site with minimum expense. Gill said late in his career that his favorite design was for a low-income complex he had designed in Sierra Madre.

From an aesthetic point of view, the finest example of Gill's work was

[6] *The Craftsman*, vol. 30, (May 1916), p. 141.
[7] Ibid.

the Dodge House, built between 1914 and 1916 in Los Angeles. Here, the clean, cubic forms are assembled with an assured compositional ease, reflecting a free-flowing floor plan that was linked to the outdoors by porches adjoining each of the bedrooms. In this building, Gill's forms were fundamentally responses to region and climate, and thus differed from those of the European Modernists, who based theirs to a much greater degree on an ideology of artistic innovation, and opposition to the past. Their devotion to formal simplicity derived from a metaphor for the machine, while Gill's was deeply rooted in tradition, but *facilitated* by modern technology and entirely appropriate to the hot, dry conditions of the local environment.

The limited impact of the diverse work of the Californians on the rest of the country should probably be attributed to the fact that the West Coast was still considered provincial by the Eastern architectural establishment, which controlled most of the architectural press. This might be said as well of the Midwest. But the Californians also had no one of Frank Lloyd Wright's genius or charisma. And when it came to talent, Wright was not about to let his languish in the heartland.

Wright's father, William Cary Wright, was a music teacher who—after wanderings that took him to several states—had moved to Lone Rock, Wisconsin, with his wife and three children in the early 1860s. To supplement their income, they shared their house with several boarders, one of whom was a young schoolteacher named Anna Lloyd Jones. Anna came from a strong-minded Welsh Unitarian family whose patriarch, feeling that "his outspoken liberality" had offended "conservative popular opinion," concluded that America would provide "a hope and a haven." The family, which rejoiced in the motto "Truth Against the World," eventually settled in the rolling farmland near Madison in the 1840s (and continued to worship in Welsh). After William's wife died, in 1864, he married Anna, and went on to become an ordained Baptist minister. Their son Frank was born on June 8, 1867, in Richland Center, where William had become pastor of the local Baptist church.

According to Wright's flowery account in *An Autobiography*, his mother was determined even before his birth that he would become an architect. The choice of profession seems especially odd because then, even more than today, it was financially risky, and it was hardly consistent with the stern religiosity of the family's background. The son's colorful version of events also includes the claim that his mother decorated his room with pictures clipped from magazines of the great English cathedrals to encourage him in the career path she had chosen for him.

A sojourn in the Boston suburb of Weymouth, where his father had been offered a preaching job, evidently exposed Anna to the thinking of the New England romantic writers and transcendentalist philosophers, including Whittier, Lowell, Longfellow, and Emerson. (Emerson's declaration in his essay "Self Reliance" that "Whosoever would be a man must be a nonconformist" would become a motto for Wright.) And it is an article of Wright lore that Anna, having seen a set of creative playthings at the 1876 Centennial Exhibition in Philadelphia, purchased them for her son and set about raising him according to the progressive "Kindergarten" principles espoused by their creator, the German educational philosopher Friedrich Froebel. (Wright was nine years old in the year his mother bought the Froebel toys, suggesting that, like the tale of the cathedral prints in the nursery, the role of Froebel's

THE DODGE HOUSE, *Irving Gill, Los Angeles, 1916.* An original inspiration grounded in physical and social facts.

teachings was later amplified by the architect and his followers to suggest that his creative success was inevitable.)

Upon their return to Wisconsin, the family consigned the young Wright to a stay on an uncle's farm, telling him that "Work is an adventure that makes strong men and finishes weak ones." The intimate involvement with nature he experienced on the farm made a lasting impression on Wright. "Farm-days had left their mark on him in a self-confidence in his own strength called courage," Wright later wrote of himself. "Something in the nature of an inner experience had come to him that was to make a sense of this supremacy of interior order like a religion to him." But at the same time he rebelled against the drudgery, and found more of the same in school.

Like Sullivan, Wright had little patience with institutions. He left high school during his senior year, but was accepted at the University of Wisconsin as a special student in civil engineering. This, too, proved a short tour, lasting less than two years. During that time, however, Wright also worked in the office of the dean, who was a professional builder, and acquired a measure of practical experience, augmenting it by reading Ruskin's *Seven Lamps of Architecture*, which had been given to him by his aunts. The relationship between Wright's mother and father had by then deteriorated from their earlier, happier, days, and in 1885 his father abruptly left the family, never to be heard from again.

Two years later, Wright, too, decided to abandon the homestead, and, without ever having seen an electric light, set out for the modern hurly-burly of Chicago. His first job, like Irving Gill's, was with J. L. Silsbee. Before leaving Syracuse, Silsbee had been steeped in the romantic carpentry of the local suburban architecture, and is generally credited with having introduced it to the Chicago area. The fact that Wright sought Silsbee out as an employer was not coincidental, as he had done extensive work for the Wright family, designing a church for one of Wright's uncles. One of the unexpected advantages of the office for Wright was Silsbee's extensive collection of Japanese prints, which probably gave Wright his first exposure to Japanese art.

Whatever Silsbee's attractions, they were evidently not sufficient to hold the young Wright, who was frustrated with the conventional nature of what the office was designing—a "combination of gable, turret, and hip with broad porches quietly domestic and gracefully picturesque," as he described it. In 1888, having heard of an opening at the firm of Adler & Sullivan, Wright paid the partners a visit and was hired, on the strength of his drawings, at a salary of $25 a week. Brief though his formal training may have been, Wright was already a skilled drafts- man, and his arrival caused some dissension among his new colleagues. To establish his credentials with some particularly envious members of Sullivan's staff, Wright suffered through a brawl that left him with sev- eral cuts in the back, but he quickly established himself as Sullivan's leading assistant, eventually overseeing a force of some thirty employ- ees. By his own account, Wright became "a good pencil in the master's hand," while pursuing his education with such office texts on architec- ture as Viollet-le-Duc's *Habitations of Man in All Ages* and Owen Jones's *Grammar of Ornament*.

At the time Wright joined them, Adler and Sullivan were already im- mersed in the design of the Auditorium Building. This was the com- mission that put Sullivan on the architectural map, and the excitement of being involved in designing the largest structure in what was arguably the most vibrant city in the land can only be imagined. As is often the case in any apprenticeship, the best time to serve it is when the masters are at their creative peak, and although greater buildings were to flow from the Adler & Sullivan office, none would generate the sort of in- novation and energy spawned by the Auditorium.

Although Wright at first served primarily as a draftsman in the office, he also became something of a personal confidant to the senior de- signer. When the Auditorium was completed, the firm moved its own offices to the top floor of the tower, which provided breathtaking views of Lake Michigan and the surrounding city. According to Wright, he spent many nights contemplating those prospects as Sullivan—whom the younger man came to call his *Lieber Meister*, or "beloved master"— perorated about architecture and life. (Wright provides no explanation of why he used German, a language he did not speak, to describe his mentor; it may have been a gesture to Adler or to the large German- speaking population of Chicago at the time. He said in his autobiogra- phy that "I have always loved Germany.") Not that Wright was altogether slavish. He later recalled Sullivan as "an absorbed ego- centric," and an "incorrigible romanticist" who indulged in "sentimen- tality," a serious failing to the Unitarian Wright.

As the office relationship developed, Wright became steadily more involved in residential design. Sullivan himself was not much interested in houses, but Wright quickly showed a talent for them, and eagerly took on most of whatever domestic work came into the firm. It began with some unexceptional structures for Sullivan himself, who had bought land for a summer retreat in Ocean Springs, Mississippi, and wanted to put up a small house and some outbuildings. More ambitious was the crisply geometric Charnley House in Chicago, completed in 1891. Although this was officially Sullivan's building, Wright always claimed it as his own, and its strongly horizontal planes and surprisingly spare ornament suggest that he was justified in doing so. The Harlan House, also completed in 1891, is even more intriguing as a glimpse of what Wright was capable of on his own. Its hip roof extended well beyond the walls, and its interior organization hinted at the centrifugal plans Wright exploited later. Whatever the extent of Wright's involvement in the Charnley and Harlan commissions and the others that came his way while still in Sullivan's office, the experience provided him with a body of knowledge that would serve him well as the country's most innovative designer of private homes.

But the domestic work Wright did while with Sullivan was not—despite Wright's later claims to the contrary—at first glance always outstanding. The English Colonial vocabulary he used for the George Blossom House (1892) in Chicago, while interesting in its details, is as proper and polite as anything done by McKim, Mead & White and calls to mind especially their H. A. C. Taylor House in Newport, built only six years earlier. To earn extra money, Wright began to design the occasional building on his own time, and these "bootleg" houses, as he called them, proved fully responsive to his clients' wishes for Queen Anne profiles and Tudor detail.

The first strong indication that Wright was willing to depart from these conventions emerged in the design of his own house, in the Chicago suburb of Oak Park (known to its detractors as "Saints' Rest" because of its numerous churches and the absence of saloons). Having become engaged in 1889 to Catherine Tobin, a nineteen-year-old neighbor he had met at a church social, Wright was eager to have a place of his own; and despite the short amount of time he had served in Sullivan's office, he secured a five-year contract with the extraordinary provision that he could draw against his future earnings to build it. The original structure (to which Wright added substantially in later years by creating a studio for himself and his employees) was distinguished primarily by its dominant gable, a feature he may have borrowed from publications of Bruce Price's work in Tuxedo Park. The other striking aspect of the building was its unusual interior spaces. The rooms were allowed to flow into one another, the spaces articulated by thin partitions rather than traditional solid walls, and unified visually by horizontal moldings that extended uninterrupted from one room to the next. Both of these devices recall the spatial system of traditional Japanese architecture; although if that was indeed the inspiration, it had to have come from the prints in Silsbee's office, since Sullivan had no apparent interest in Japan, and Wright could not have seen a Japanese building in the round until the exposition of 1893.

When Sullivan discovered that his trusted acolyte was doing work on the side apart from his own house, he called Wright on the carpet for an explanation of what Sullivan—characteristically—considered a personal betrayal. Wright—also characteristically—saw nothing wrong in his extracurricular activities, and said so, bringing the conversation to an abrupt and stormy end. Wright walked out, and soon thereafter began sharing office space with Cecil Corwin, a friend from Silsbee's office who had also decided to try his own wings. For more than seventeen years following the rift between Sullivan and Wright, there was no contact at all between these two brilliant and equally unyielding spirits.

Wright's architectural moonlighting had established him as a talented domestic architect in the eyes of local clients, and in short order he had a commission from William H. Winslow for a house in River Forest, a Chicago suburb adjacent to Oak Park. In this building (1894) one can see themes emerging that became fundamental to virtually all of what became known as the "Prairie" houses: a low horizontal profile; the division of the facade into bands; a massive central chimney; a hip roof with deep overhangs; and no attics or basements, which Wright declared "unwholesome."

The Winslow House made a major impact on the Chicago architectural community, and especially on Daniel Burnham. In the wake of the 1893 exposition, Burnham was prospering, and he was looking for someone who could eventually relieve him of his senior design role while he attended to the bigger business and city-planning matters. When Burnham saw the Winslow House, he concluded that Wright was the man, and offered to pay for a six-year stay in Europe that would have included schooling at the Ecole des Beaux-Arts and a two-year visit to Rome, as well as support for Wright's family while he was abroad. Wright made a point of telling people later in life that he had turned the offer down flat, no doubt to further his claim on the image of the genius who could do without conventional training, especially training in what he already considered a decadent European tradition. "I have seen the men come home from there all one type," he told one of Burnham's friends at the time, "no matter how much they were individuals when they went."

In expanding on his reasons for turning down Burnham's offer, Wright in his autobiography drew on more than architectural precedent. He also placed himself directly in the line of those American moralist-architects from Jefferson to Downing who felt that their art had as much to do with idealism as it did with form and space. The houses Wright found around him as a young architect had, in his words, "no sense of Unity at all nor any such sense of Space as should belong to a free man among a free people in a free country." By contrast, he was

HOME AND STUDIO, *Frank Lloyd Wright, Oak Park, Illinois, 1891.* Derivative, to be sure, but with a touch of genius.

Hedrich Blessing

Carter Wiseman

proposing "a new simplicity," something "organic" that "might be seen producing significant character in the harmonious order we call nature." What became the most identifiable formal characteristic of Wright's houses—the relentless horizontality of their organization—was something he went to great lengths to explain as a philosophical statement: "I had an idea that the horizontal planes in buildings, those planes parallel to earth, identify themselves with the ground—making the building belong to the ground." Returning to the subject later in the book, he says: "This parallel plane I called, from the beginning—the plane of the third dimension. The term came naturally enough: really a spiritual interpretation of the dimension." Still later, he declares that "the very word 'organic' itself, means that nothing is of value except as it is naturally related to the whole in the direction of some living purpose."

Wright repeatedly sought to base his aesthetic manipulations on metaphysical concepts. Jefferson had done the same thing, as had Downing, Davis, Sullivan, and virtually every other thoughtful architect before him. Nor was Wright to be the last. (To cite only one of the more prominent Modernist examples, the Swiss-French architect Le Corbusier in the late 1940s developed an entire proportional system, called the "Modulor," which was intended to link his own architecture to a tradition stretching back to the Golden Section of classical times.) The very concept of the "Prairie" house can be seen as an attempt at

THE WINSLOW HOUSE, *Frank Lloyd Wright, River Forest, Illinois, 1894.* The emerging themes of the "Prairie" house.

packaging an artistic impulse. After all, many of the design elements these houses contained were derived at least in part from the architecture of a country—Japan—in which there are no prairies. And while Wright insisted on their inextricable ties to the Midwestern landscape, he built one of the best Prairie houses—the Darwin Martin House (1904)—in Buffalo, New York. Like so many other artists, and especially architects, Wright was creating a retrospective overlay of reason in order to elevate what was essentially intuitive to the level of the deliberate. He was making a theory to fit his own extraordinary facts.

Some scholars have suggested that Wright's most assertive architectural devices—such as his massive but basically superfluous fireplaces, and the oppressively low and narrow passageways leading into his houses—had even deeper roots. The dominance of the hearth, some have argued, represents a symbolic compensation for the unstable family life Wright suffered as a child; the restricted hallways, which often open into enormous, brightly lit living rooms, have even been interpreted as representations of the birth canal. Wright's colorful autobiography and his even more colorful embellishments of it invite such speculation, but speculation it should remain. A blazing fire beneath a stone mantel is a cozy sight regardless of the architect's—or the critic's—upbringing. Likewise, the progression from a small dark space to a large and well-lit one is an ancient theatrical technique that requires no special psychological insight for its effect. As Freud himself is said to have quipped, there are times when a cigar is really only a cigar.

On the other hand, one should not entirely dismiss the imprint of Wright's background on his art. Any family that chooses as its motto "Truth Against the World" might be expected to produce an occasional rebel. (As a young man, Wright changed the middle name he had been given at birth—Lincoln—to Lloyd, apparently in solidarity with his nonconformist Welsh forebears.) Should that rebel become an architect, he might be expected to contest the contemporary conventions. Nor should one minimize the imprinting effect of Wright's native landscape on his work. The area of Wisconsin in which he grew up is composed of rolling hills leading to vast flatlands that stretch to the horizon. Roads and railroad tracks make few turns. The straight line and the horizontal plane are the dominant elements in the natural composition. And on exposed hillsides the native limestone emerges in layers that might well have contributed to Wright's affection for the thin "Roman" bricks that became such a part of his palette. Had Wright grown up in the Appalachians, the Rockies, or on the California coast, one can imagine him producing a very different if no less powerful repertory of forms.

Whatever the architectural or subconscious sources that were most important to Wright at the time, his future direction was laid out most forcefully not in a finished building, but in a proposal published in the February 1901 edition of the *Ladies' Home Journal*. Wright described it as a "Home in a Prairie Town," thus affixing a label to what became his most recognizable building type. The published project, which was soon followed by a dazzling series of constructed buildings (some forty in Oak Park and the neighboring Chicago suburbs alone), displayed most of the elements of what lay ahead. At the center was the massive chimney anchoring a roughly cruciform plan. The interior spaces were arranged in a fluid fashion, with little trace of the familiar Queen Anne "box" system of distinct rooms. The roofline was long and low, supported on a few masonry piers and appearing to hover over strips of windows that asserted themselves where walls would have been expected. The open planning of the interiors became even more free following a visit Wright and his wife made to Japan in 1905 in the company of Mr. and Mrs. Ward Willets of Highland Park, for whom Wright had designed a house.

Like the Greene brothers, Wright had almost certainly seen the Japanese exhibit at the 1893 fair in Chicago (although he later insisted that he had not). In any case, Japanese design had become increasingly well known in the United States through prints and publications, and Wright had clearly absorbed its message of free-flowing interior spaces and long, horizontal masses, as well as the interpenetration of interior and exterior. But in his buildings of the next few years, he blended the spatial freedom of the Japanese interior with an American sense of attachment to the land. Unlike so many Modernist buildings, which seem to want to levitate, Wright's houses hug the earth, reaching out in pinwheel plans, their foundations expressed with sturdy platforms of stone set into the ground, and whole compositions executed in muted earth tones and surrounded with plantings. Wright's combination of horizontality and rootedness can be seen as a unique expression of the recurrent American conflict between wanting to expand to new horizons, while at the same time establishing some sense of permanence. Never before or since has an architect so fully and empathetically embraced this fundamental American dualism toward the idea of the home.

However fundamental such instincts may have been, not every potential client in 1890s Chicago was eager to risk abandoning architectural conventions to have them expressed in his own dwelling. But for those bold (and wealthy) enough, Wright proved a master salesman, sweet-talking the balky into a vision of the future, assuring them all the while of their aesthetic superiority. It was not unlike the performance Wright put on for his grocer and the other merchants with whom he pushed his credit well beyond the normal limits. "It was my misfortune that everybody was willing to trust me." Wright commented with sly modesty. "I don't know why they were willing, either, because I don't imagine my appearance or my way of life would appeal to a business man any more than my buildings appealed to the local bankers a little later on." (To this day, fund-raising for the restoration of Wright's Wisconsin buildings is hampered by resentment among some potential donors with long memories of Wright's cavalier attitude toward his debts.)

One client who needed no persuasion on Wright's behalf was Frederick C. Robie, a prosperous twenty-seven-year-old manufacturer. Himself a thoroughly unconventional man (his main occupation was making bicycles and sewing machines, but he also designed an experimental automobile called the "Robie Cycle Car"), Robie had a growing family, and wanted a house where his children would have plenty of room to play without being exposed to traffic. His Hyde Park site, adjacent to the campus of the University of Chicago, was a narrow one, but Robie also wanted ample natural lighting and a view of the neighborhood that would prevent the neighbors from looking in.

Wright's design became the most enduring example of his early domestic work (eventually contributing at least in part to the "split-level" suburban houses of the 1950s). The Robie House, begun in 1908 and finished in 1910, was a masterpiece of interlocking spaces and dynamic asymmetry. Forced by the location to organize his building along a single axis, Wright exploited the necessary and produced a building of almost literally moving power. The characteristic hip roof is here extended to unprecedented proportions. It is supported by piers that are separated by long bands of windows; the conventional wall has simply vanished. By concealing the entrance, Wright added to the sense of privacy Robie sought, but in so doing the architect also freed himself from having to accommodate the design of the facade to a compositional element—the front door—from which most residential facades had always evolved. The delicate exterior composition of layered planes and compelling horizontals keeps the eye in constant motion, while inside the building is suffused with a luminous glow produced in part by patterns of colored glass in the windows.

Although it is now considered an icon of modern architecture, the Robie House subjected its client to considerable derision at the time of its completion. Mocking what they saw as a resemblance to nautical superstructures, some German-speaking neighbors dubbed it the "*Dampfer*," or steamer; others referred to it as the "battleship." And although the Robie family was apparently pleased with it (late in life the client declared it "the most ideal place in the world"), one can only wonder how they accommodated their daily activities to the maze of cramped secondary rooms and the bowling alley-like space in which Wright combined the living and dining rooms. Grand as they were as compositional elements, these spaces posed a challenge to Wright's purported devotion to domesticity. As in so many Wright buildings, domestic and otherwise, this one creates the uncomfortable feeling that the users have been pressed into the service of a spatial autocrat, genius though he may have been.

The need to control extended to virtually every aspect of this and all of Wright's subsequent houses. He insisted on designing all the furniture and further insisted that the clients dispose of their old furnishings before moving in. If he happened to visit one of his houses after completion and discover that his own creations had been removed, he would demand that they be replaced—and according to his original scheme, which was almost always beautiful if not easy to live with. "Very few of the houses, therefore, were anything but painful to me after the clients moved in and, helplessly, dragged the horrors of the Old Order along after them," Wright lamented in his autobiography. Since his own furniture, however pleasing aesthetically, was often hard on the human frame, one can understand the clients' disloyalty; even Wright was capable of some self-mockery on the subject, confessing that "I have been black and blue in some spot, somewhere, almost all my life from too intimate contact with my own early furniture."

But if Wright was unflinching in his demands about space and its

THE ROBIE HOUSE, *Frank Lloyd Wright, Hyde Park, Illinois, 1910.* The horizontal thrust created a signature for Wright's architecture.

embellishment, he was radically open-minded about other matters. Unlike Richardson, who had shied away from the aesthetic exploitation of steel and glass, and the Greene brothers, who so loved the hand-wrought dimension of the Ruskinian tradition, Wright shared with Gill an openness to new materials and techniques, which he embraced without hesitation. The Robie House, to cite only one of the more prominent examples, incorporated the most up-to-date electric lighting system, telephones, burglar and fire alarms, and even a precursor of central vacuum cleaning. Glass, tile, and metal were used in innovative ways throughout, with dramatic effect on the design itself. Indeed, the cantilevered portions of the roof, without which the building could never have achieved its visual impact, would have been impossible without steel beams to support them.

Wright's experimentation with materials extended well beyond his residential commissions. The 1904 Larkin Company Administration Building in Buffalo (see illustration on page 230) included built-in metal furniture, the first wall-hung toilets, and an unprecedented air-conditioning system. Wright rejoiced in calling the Larkin an example of the "genuine and constructive affirmation of the new Order of the

Machine Age." The building he designed for the Oak Park Unitarian congregation, Unity Temple (1906), was constructed of poured reinforced concrete, a material whose plasticity was exploited by Wright to create a seminally sculptural monument. Nonetheless its interior spaces are some of the most magically sensitive ever designed.

Not surprisingly, Wright's sorties into new technologies produced some problems. With the passage of time, many of his cantilevers began to sag. His shallow hip roofs, however appropriate visually to the flatlands of the Midwest, were hardly suited to the area's brutal winter weather: They held the snow and helped launched Wright's reputation as an architect whose roofs always leaked. Even the walls suffered from his innovations. To amplify the horizontal thrust of the Robie House, Wright had his workmen rake out the horizontal beds of mortar between the rows of bricks, while leaving the mortar in the vertical joints flush with the surface. The result was a subtle pattern of parallel shadow lines that swept across the building's facade, adding to its visual power. Unfortunately, the recessed mortar also retained water, which froze in winter, and eventually weakened the rest of the brickwork.

Working with new techniques and materials also involved unpredictable costs. Added to Wright's habit of altering a design well into the construction phase, his experiments frequently drove the bills for his work well beyond the original estimates. One of the more dramatic examples was a Unitarian church in Madison, Wisconsin, which he predicted would cost $60,000; the final bill was $213,487.61.

Many of Wright's clients were content to accept leaky roofs and cost overruns as the price of inhabiting a work of art. But others were not so generous. Wright was under almost constant assault from one client or another for exceeding his allowance or falling short on structural details. The architect usually responded with a combination of charm and shaded truth, but he could lapse into almost unbelievable high-handedness. A tale that has become a standard part of Wright lore describes a client calling the architect in the middle of a dinner party to complain that rain was dripping on his head from a leak in the (brand-new) roof. Wright is reported to have advised the malcontent to move his chair. Attacked many times for such breezy disregard for practical matters, Wright declared defiantly that "Early in life I had to choose between honest arrogance and hypocritical humility. I chose honest arrogance."

The impact of Wright's arrogance and self-absorption was not lim-

UNITY TEMPLE,
*Frank Lloyd Wright,
Oak Park, Illinois,
1906.* The concrete
shell housed a
magical space.

ited to his clients. By 1909, his marriage to Catherine Tobin had soured, and Wright had less and less contact with his six children. Much as he apparently loved them, he was not, according to his own analysis, cut out for fatherhood. "I didn't feel it," he wrote. Increasingly, what he did feel was a passion for a Mrs. Edwin (Mamah) Cheney, the wife of a client for whom he had built a small house in Oak Park. In October 1909, Wright hurriedly wrapped up his business affairs, collecting fees and selling many of the Japanese prints he had been collecting over the years, and took a train for New York. He was joined there by Mrs. Cheney, and together they boarded a ship for Europe, going first to Berlin, and then on to Fiesole, outside Florence.

There was more to the Berlin portion of the trip than mere escapism. Some months earlier, Wright had received a visit from one Kuno Francke, a German-born visting lecturer in aesthetics at Harvard, who had taken an interest in Wright's work. Not long afterward—and possibly as a result of Francke's efforts—the architect was invited by the Berlin publisher Ernst Wasmuth to prepare a monograph on his architecture. Doing so hardly required a total abandonment of Wright's office and family, but the excuse evidently suited the architect's emotional and artistic needs. The fact that it concealed a personal upheaval uncannily like the one his father had gone through in abandoning his own family was something Wright never mentioned publicly.

With Wright's flight to Europe, the cadre of followers he had assembled at his studio in Oak Park had little to do but complete the existing commissions. This they did under the direction of a German-born architect named Herman von Holst, a designer of no particular distinction to whom Wright—for no convincing reason that he ever offered—turned over the entire practice on the strength of a recent introduction. There seem few better examples of "*Après moi, le déluge.*" In 1910, the Wright studio closed, and the best of the employees, including Walter Burley Griffin and Marion Mahony, Wright's chief draftsman for more than a decade and the person who gave the renderings of his buildings much of their graphic power, departed to fend for themselves.

They and such other Chicago architects as William Purcell, George Elmslie, and George Maher—all of whom had subscribed in differing degrees to Wright's Prairie aesthetic—continued to pursue the ideas that Wright had set in motion. Some created powerful works worthy of independent praise. Purcell and Elmslie, who went into partnership, produced at least one landmark building, the shiplike Bradley Bungalow (1912), in Woods Hole, Massachusetts. But none could come close to matching the power of Wright himself, and with his dynamic personality absent from the center of the stage, the rest of the cast gradually faded into relative obscurity.

There was more to the eclipse of the Prairie phenomenon than Wright's departure. By 1910, the vigorous individualism that had so animated the Chicago of the late nineteenth century—the self-consciously independent entrepreneurial spirit that characterized the early businessmen like Robie, and to which Wright had given architectural form—began to recede with the "maturing" of the local society. Midwesterners who once had taken pride in their status as renegades and tough-minded industrial pioneers began to sense that their youthful philistinism was no longer appropriate to their more established position as citizens of a world city.

Their reaction, which was similar to that of their counterparts in California, was to seek membership in a more "grown-up" aesthetic. Its architectural attributes were buildings that spoke of learning and travel, stability and respectability. Having spurned such values in the days of expansion and enterprise, they came to embrace them during a time of increasing international uncertainty—soon to be aggravated by the Great War—and the end of a society in which it was acceptable, even admirable, to flaunt one's own roughhewn ways. To the vogue for neoclassicism launched by the 1893 Chicago fair was added a nostalgic fervor for the Colonial, which emitted messages of American straightforwardness in the face of European perfidy, not to mention solidarity with England against the assault of the "Hun." A more tangible blow fell in 1913 with the coming of the graduated income tax, which cut deeply into the fortunes that had fueled the market for grand domesticity.

There is no better example of the shift in sensibility—or the ascendance of the role of women in making architectural decisions—than the fate of Wright's 1907 design for the Lake Forest residence of Harold McCormick.[8] The heir to a fortune built on agricultural equipment, McCormick had hired Wright to design an enormous house for a site overlooking Lake Michigan. Wright obliged, with a sprawling complex of pavilions linked by covered verandas and galleries that seemed to constitute a village in themselves. But Mrs. McCormick evidently would have none of it, fearing perhaps that her social life might suffer from living according to Wright's spatial dicta. The job was abruptly transferred to Charles Platt, whose elegant essays in country classicism had made him such a bankable servant of aspiring East Coast wealth. Platt produced for the McCormicks a comfortable but thoroughly unexceptional U-shaped Italian Renaissance palazzo. The loss of the McCormick commission was a severe blow to Wright personally and professionally, and it can be argued that the death sentence of the Prairie School was pronounced at that moment.

Not long afterward, however, Wright's influence began to assert itself beyond the confines of the United States. The Wasmuth Portfolio—entitled *Ausgeführte Bauten und Entwürfe von Frank Lloyd Wright*, or *Executed Buildings and Projects*—appeared in 1911, and had a powerful effect on a number of the leading progressive European architects who

---

[8] See Brooks, op. cit., p. 23.

saw it. Struggling to shake off the very neoclassical tradition that so attracted the American *nouveaux riches* of the McCormick variety, some of the pioneers of what became Modernism in Germany, Austria, France, and the Netherlands saw in Wright's clean lines and simplified forms a beacon of reform. Indeed, one need only compare the work of the Dutch *De Stijl* movement with Unity Temple to see how closely some Europeans were reading Wright's message of planar manipulation and spatial exuberance.

Needless to say, the context of Wright's architecture was totally absent from the portfolio: no leafy suburban streetscapes like the ones in Oak Park or Lake Forest, or gritty Buffalo industrial neighborhoods like the one surrounding the Larkin Building. The portfolio was pure Wright as Wright himself surely wished it to be, and rendered by the romantically evocative hands of draftsmen who worshipped the tech-

THE BRADLEY BUNGALOW, *Purcell & Elmslie, Woods Hole, Massachusetts, 1912.* The lines are Wrightian, the feeling is not.

niques of the Japanese printmaker. (To make the drawings seem even more "modern" than they were, Wright had them redone, deemphasizing or eliminating many of the original decorative details such as the ornamental art glass.) Little wonder that these exotic but disembodied forms should fascinate a culture that had grown weary of the rote repetition of Beaux-Arts orthodoxy. It could not have hurt that the author of these forms fulfilled the fondest European fantasy of the American, that of the pioneer and rebel—an architectural "cowboy" who had turned down a chance to study at the Beaux-Arts. So much the better that Wright confounded another stereotype of the American, however rebellious, as a philistine. On the strength of the Wasmuth Portfolio and the images that were reproduced from it in other publications, it was abundantly clear that this particular American was an architectural genius.

Of course, the Beaux-Arts orthodoxy against which Wright and the progressive Europeans were rebelling represented the very cultural authority to which America as a nation was then being drawn in its proto-imperial stage of evolution, and to which, in fairness, it was entitled. Wright and his fellow domestic innovators on the West Coast had simply appeared a bit early for all but a small segment of the American architectural clientele, and a period of time would have to pass before a new generation, having itself tired of the neoclassical message, would again turn to Europe for guidance. As Wright was later bitterly to observe, his own contribution to European Modernism would find few chroniclers among his own countrymen, fixed as they had been for more than two centuries on the idea that high quality had to be imported.

When Wright returned with Mamah to the United States in 1910, it was to widespread opprobrium. In social mores as in aesthetics, infidelity was something for which Americans had far less tolerance than Europeans. The newspapers hounded him as a traitor to the very idea of family that his hearth-centered homes were supposed to represent. In fact, however, family in the idealistic American sense had never played the role in Wright's architecture he would have had the readers of his autobiography believe. If Wright was indeed an apostle of the ideal of family, then it was not the Oak Park version, but one more closely resembling a medieval court. Wright, as his subsequent career confirmed, was only truly happy when he was in total control not just of his designs but also of the people around him.

To reestablish that control—and to protect himself and his paramour from the prying of his creditors and other tormentors—Wright set about planning a retreat on land given to him by his mother in Hillside, near Spring Green, Wisconsin, in what the family, in a tribute to their Welsh forebears, called the "valley of the God-Almighty Joneses." It was a sprawling, intricate complex dug into a bluff and named "Taliesin," Wright's translation of the Welsh for "Shining Brow," in honor of a bard of ancient times. In its splendid isolation, Taliesin (see illustration on page 187) was intended to be self-sustaining, and it inevitably recalled Jefferson's Monticello, an architectural symbol of the American pioneer staking his claim to the frontier. But this was no testament to the primacy of the intellect, reason, and history. This was no didactic model for a nation of shared values and common purpose. Taliesin was more the citadel of the autocratic separatist, a refuge in which an absolute ruler could surround himself with vassals. There Wright hunkered down, sealed off, he hoped, from the pettiness of contemporary society and free to pursue his genius in a setting of his own making. He was defiant as ever, telling the *Chicago Tribune* that "I think when a man has displayed some spiritual power, has given concrete evidence of his ability to see and to feel the higher and better things of life, we ought to go slow in deciding he has acted badly."[9]

Some of Wright's critics have attempted to diminish his artistic importance by focusing on his many failings, whether practical or social. But one should not lose sight of the fact that, through it all, he remained committed to a consistent body of architectural ideas. And alluring as the psychological interpretations of his inspiration may be, it is the formal and conceptual legacy that fully illuminated those ideas. So insistent were some of these—the integration of each part with the whole, the interrelationship of architecture with the landscape, the obligation to remain true to a formal scheme throughout a given design—that they should properly be viewed as an ideology. If this was not exactly Louis Sullivan's search for a "rule that admits no exception," it was not unrelated. The "organic" dimension of Wright's architecture had less to do

[9] *Chicago Tribune*, December 26, 1911.

with nature than it did with an intellectual concept of oneness based upon the integration of disparate sources to create an entirely new synthesis.

It is that synthetic legacy upon which the Europeans seized, and which was to return with them to America more than two decades later, albeit mightily transformed. When it did, Wright would again emerge to do battle with what had become a new orthodoxy. But before he made his comeback, he would have to wait out the triumph of the old.

Eclecticism and
the Uses of the Past

In a book on American architecture originally published in 1947, a leading historian and critic concluded that "At first glance, the period from 1900 to 1933 appears to be an esthetic wasteland: and a closer scrutiny of the individual buildings of the period does little to correct that first impression."[1]

That view was all but universally held until at least the mid-1960s.

---

[1] James Marston Fitch, *American Building: The Historical Forces That Shaped It.* 2nd ed. (Boston: Houghton, Mifflin, 1966), p. 228.

(The passage quoted above survived to the 1975 edition of the book in which it appeared.) In the late 1930s, architects who had dominated the coverage in the leading architectural journals—men such as Wilson Eyre (1858–1944), Charles Z. Klauder (1872–1938), and Horace Trumbauer (1869–1938)—suddenly vanished from the historical scene as if they had been rendered "un-persons" by some faceless Stalinist censor. One searches in vain in most major architectural surveys written since that time for any extensive mention of such once powerful designers.[2]

The reason for their absence, of course, was the arrival in America in the early 1930s of European Modernism, whose advocates mounted a propaganda campaign of such fervor against what had gone before that even the mention of historical precedent could doom an architect's prospects for success. Modernism as it was translated for American consumption meant, in simplest terms, the banishment of ornament and the elimination of architectural history. Architecture based on historical precedent was pronounced derivative, inauthentic, and, ultimately, dishonest, primarily because—in the view of the new orthodoxy—it failed to acknowledge advances in materials (primarily glass and steel) and construction technology. Henceforth, architecture was to embrace the social and structural realities of the twentieth century. In the eyes of the new generation, that meant buildings were to adhere to a "machine" aesthetic that expressed itself primarily in planar geometry, flat roofs, strip windows, and a total absence of decoration in the traditional sense.

But the concept of a "wasteland" redeemed by ideological "cleansing" was manifestly unfair. In fact, the period between Frank Lloyd Wright's departure for Germany and the arrival of Modernism in the United States can be considered the most diversely creative of American architectural eras. To be sure, most of the buildings of the time were derivative, and many were not worth serious critical attention. But the best of them—making allowance for their social setting and stylistic mantles—were the equal of any later works when judged by the funda-

---

2 Notable exceptions are Leland Roth, *A Concise History of American Architecture* (New York: Harper & Row, 1979), which devotes a full chapter to the eclectics during the period between 1915 and 1940, and Walter C. Kidney, *The Architecture of Choice* (New York: George Braziller, 1974).

mental architectural standards: siting, attention to function, proportion, use of materials, manipulation of space, and execution of detail. One need only think of the sublimely solemn Gothic forms of Saint Thomas Episcopal Church, by Cram, Goodhue & Ferguson on New York's Fifth Avenue (1913); McKim, Mead & White's now demolished Pennsylvania Station (1910), also in New York, with its soaring waiting room; or Henry Bacon's crisply Grecian Lincoln Memorial in Washington (1922), to realize that first-rate architecture in America did not stop with Sullivan and restart with the arrival of the European Modernists at American architectural schools in the 1930s.

For all the importance assigned to Frank Lloyd Wright by later historians, the impact of his early work at the time he created it was decidedly limited, and its reception was by no means all favorable. Indeed, many critics of the day seemed puzzled about just how to handle such a renegade talent, so dramatically different were his buildings (and those of his Prairie School colleagues) from what anyone else was designing. The photographs of Taliesin in an *Architectural Record* article on Midwestern residences published in September 1915 seem strikingly out of place—and time—alongside those of the comfortable Georgian and Tudor mansions displayed on the surrounding pages. By 1925, despite the artistic success of his Wisconsin retreat, Wright had been all but forgotten by the architectural mainstream in the United States.

What most Americans wanted in architecture in the first decades of the century was what they wanted in virtually every other sphere: stability. Those longings were compounded by the onset of the World War I, which deepened Americans' desire to avoid the turbulence of European entanglements, political and otherwise. By and large, those longings, at least in the realm of architecture, were well satisfied by the better designers of the day, who were sharply attuned to their clients' wishes and entertained no theoretical agenda beyond creating comfortable environments that were appropriate to their settings and—by the lights of the time—beautiful to look at.

Most of these architects belonged to what amounted to an artistic and social elite. Centered in New York and Boston, it was a small and homogeneous group, many of whose members were independently wealthy and had graduated from Harvard, Yale, or perhaps the Massachusetts Institute of Technology. A growing number had also attended the Ecole des Beaux-Arts in Paris, where they were steeped in the French formal concepts of unity, harmony, balance, and repose, and indoctrinated in the primacy of tradition over originality, at least as it is understood today. Those who had not been abroad were likely to have apprenticed in one of a few prominent firms. Much of their business was conducted under shrouds of cigar smoke and accompanied by the clink of whiskey glasses in a few gentlemen's clubs with clients who were likely to be college classmates or family friends.

The pattern of their professional lives had been set most forcefully by the firm of McKim, Mead & White. After showing such dazzling creativity in buildings like the Low House and the Newport Casino, the partners pioneered what came to be known as the Renaissance Revival with an embrace of semischolarly accuracy and discipline in a series of sober civic monuments. McKim, Mead & White's elegant designs for the Villard Houses in New York (1885) and the Boston Public Library (1895) had extended their reputation well before the turn of the century as the dominant firm in creating grand urban buildings. Their work was unfailingly tasteful and historically correct, and their vigorous participation in the 1893 Columbian Exposition in Chicago had sealed their reputation as nothing less than the nation's leading architectural firm.

McKim, Mead, White, and their colleagues were people who cared deeply about the architectural vocabulary they were using. They understood the history of architecture, and the context of the styles in which they worked, and they had been schooled—whether at the Ecole or as apprentices in firms dominated by the Ecole system—in the precise rendering of ornament and details by arduous drawing from plaster casts. But they were no mere copyists. "Copying," wrote Thomas Hastings (1860–1929), who with his partner John Carrère(1858–1911) designed the majestic Beaux-Arts New York Public Library (1911), "destroys progress in art, and all spontaneity. . . . To build a French Louis XII or Francis I or Louis XIV house, or to make an Italian cinquecento design, is indisputably not modern architecture."[3]

Increasingly, "modern" architecture for this generation of American designers had come to mean the knowing selection and reintegration

---

[3] See Wayne Andrews, *Architecture, Ambition and Americans* (New York: The Free Press, 1964), p. 200.

of historical elements into a synthesis they deemed appropriate to contemporary American life. And American life was changing. The country was settling into a period of consolidation, of post-frontier confidence, even complacency. By 1918, the dislocations of war in Europe had been accompanied by America's triumph on the world stage as a savior of Western civilization, and the conquerors were eager to consolidate their gains. Yet the first major involvement of the United States in European affairs had also exposed many Americans— particularly those who had served with the military in France—to the products of modernity, whether in the trenches of Château Thierry or the salons of Paris. Along with a firsthand experience of European history and culture came a powerful awareness that the war had ended an era. Those Americans who marveled at the riches of the past displayed at Chartres and Fontainebleau could not hide from the implications for the future of the airplane and the machine gun.

Well before the Great War, the art of architecture in America was already in a state of flux. A sense of the transitional nature of the times for architects in the closing moments of American innocence emerges from two commentaries appearing just a year apart. The distinguished critic Montgomery Schuyler, writing in 1912 on the publication of Wright's Wasmuth portfolio and the relationship of Wright's work to Sullivan's, declared: " . . . it is hard to see how an unprejudiced inquirer can deny that such designers as Mr. Sullivan and Mr. Wright have the root of the matter, and that their works are of good hope, in contrast with the rehandling and rehashing of admired historical forms in which there is no future nor any possibility of progress."[4]

A year later, John Galen Howard, the founder (in 1903) of the school of architecture at the University of California, and a stalwart Beaux-Arts alumnus who had worked for McKim, Mead & White, wrote of the current architectural developments across the Atlantic, which already included the lean geometric forms of such Modernist pioneers as Walter Gropius and the Austrian Adolf Loos: "Europe is tired of saying and doing the same old things, and bursts with desire to get on; America dis-

---

[4] Montgomery Schuyler, "An Architectural Pioneer—Review of the Portfolios Containing the Works of Frank Lloyd Wright." *Architectural Record* (April 1912) p. 435.

trusts and hates more and more the crudities and anxieties of revolt and yearns for the halcyon peace of establishment."[5]

For the moment, at least, Howard's analysis prevailed. In the search for that "halcyon peace," Sullivan and Wright were confined to the sidelines of American architectural life, while the traditionalists brought their talents to bear on the task of giving architectural shape to the nation's increasingly powerful institutions.

Primary among those institutions were churches, which still served as symbolic as well as religious statements of the country's values. The enormous success of Richardson's Trinity Church in Boston had spawned an entire generation of vaguely Romanesque imitations, sweeping the work of such early Gothicists as Richard Upjohn from their path. But few of Richardson's followers had even a trace of the integrative power and subtlety of the original. Architects soon began to realize that the style had for all practical purposes become the property of Richardson alone, and was destined to deteriorate with his passing. Without apology, congregations turned again to the Gothic, which was judged by many Americans to offer more design flexibility and a more spiritually uplifting model for church buildings than the brooding forms of the Richardsonian Romanesque. The man who more than any other provided the link between the Gothic Revival of the 1860s and 1870s and the renewed interest in the style was Henry Vaughan (1845–1917), an English architect who had immigrated to the United States in 1881.

Simply being English gave Vaughan a special credibility among Americans eager for an "authentic" brand of Gothic to refresh the tradition overwhelmed by Richardson, and he dutifully provided a remarkable series of buildings that would have done the English countryside proud. Among his most successful were the chapels for two New England preparatory schools, Groton and St. Paul's, which were serenely elegant essays in high Anglicanism. An example of Vaughan's ability to adapt that tradition is the interior of his 1898 Christ Church in New Haven, Connecticut, where the architect used exposed brick as the primary material for the interior walls, at once departing from the standard (and more expensive) stone, yet preserving its durable feel with

---

[5] John Galen Howard, "The Outlook and Inlook Architectural." *Architectural Record* (December 1913) p. 542. ·

a remarkable warmth. The success of these buildings led to Vaughan's selection, in 1906, as architect of the National Cathedral in Washington, D.C., which he designed in collaboration with his English mentor, George F. Bodley (1827–1907). The selection was a symbolic gesture that confirmed the persistent proclivity of American officialdom for an unimpeachable — rather than innovative — set of architectural credentials.

The result of the collaboration between Vaughan and Bodley — the sixth largest cathedral in the world when it was completed in 1990 — is a spectacularly anachronistic structure. Impressive in almost every respect except its fundamental inauthenticity, it remains handsome but drained of creative blood by its dependence on the past. Intended at the outset to be a shrine that would serve no specific denomination, the building lacks even the revivalist religious fervor that animated the churches of other, denominational architects. But given the original goals set for the building, it must be judged a programmatic success.

While Vaughan's own architectural contributions to the American church scene were substantial, his greatest influence was indirect, manifesting itself in the impact he had on the man who became identified with the latest resurgence of neo-Gothic architecture in America, Ralph Adams Cram (1863–1942). Entranced by Vaughan's lyrical forms, and well aware that Richardson had all but consumed the possibilities of the Romanesque for American purposes, the devoutly Anglican Cram embraced the Gothic with an almost apostolic fervor. "My idea," he wrote in his autobiography (one of his twenty-four books), "was that we should set ourselves to pick up the threads of the broken tradition and stand strongly for Gothic as a style for church building that was not dead but only moribund, and perfectly susceptible of an awakening to life again."[6]

In 1892, Cram went into partnership with Bertram Grosvenor Goodhue (1869–1924), an alumnus of James Renwick's office who was particularly gifted in the design of ornamental details, and together they produced some of the most powerful Gothic buildings in America. Like Cram, Goodhue remained firmly opposed to Beaux-Arts classicism, which he considered excessively academic, rigid, and stale. One of the best examples of the impact of the partnership (which also included

---

[6] Ralph Adams Cram, *My Life in Architecture* (Boston: Little, Brown, 1936), p. 72.

RALPH ADAMS CRAM

Frank Ferguson, who was responsible primarily for engineering), and the trend toward a greater simplicity of form, was the commission Cram and Goodhue won for the United States Military Academy at West Point (1903–10). Their ambitious undertaking showed a thorough understanding of Gothic tradition, but also a willingness to adapt and clarify it for contemporary purposes. Confronted with a selection of existing Gothic buildings put up during the previous century, the architects took full advantage of the dramatic site overlooking the Hudson River and skillfully integrated the older structures into a complex that included several new buildings in a simpler but even more authoritative version of the original style. In this case, certainly, the concept of a Gothic fortress for a military academy rising in stepped fashion from the heights commanding a great river seemed both programmatically and symbolically correct. Even today, a worship service in the Cadet Chapel is an almost literal exercise in "muscular Christianity." One need penetrate no farther than the chapel's main portal to be impressed by the building's mission: centered above the entrance is a relief sculpture of a cross in the form of a sword hilt.

Cram and Goodhue's design for Saint Thomas Episcopal Church in New York City is an example of how skillfully the firm could handle a religious commission for a more pacific congregation. Here, a narrow site is exploited to accommodate an asymmetrical composition that contains a truly solemn space, its details rendered with a historicist attention to detail that has been enlived with contemporary energy. While not strictly imitative of European precedent, the building captures the meditative essence of the religious experience, providing an intimate side aisle and chapel for reflection and a grand nave that welcomes the most flamboyant of ceremonies.

United States Military Academy Library

THE UNITED STATES MILITARY ACADEMY CADET CHAPEL, *Cram, Goodhue & Ferguson, West Point, New York, 1910.* Muscular Christianity in the service of war.

SAINT THOMAS
EPISCOPAL CHURCH,
Cram, Goodhue &
Ferguson, New
York City, 1913.
The choice of
Gothic had as much
to do with faith
as with style.

Saint Thomas Church

At least one critic perceived the seed of a new architectural growth beneath the Gothic tracery of Saint Thomas's. Upon its completion, the prolific Montgomery Schuyler wrote, "In the block, without a single tool-mark of ornament, the new Saint Thomas's would already be a noble building. The highest praise the decoration of such a building can deserve is that it heightens and develops the inherent expression of

the structure."[7] In retrospect, one can see that Cram and Goodhue's Gothic imagery, however correct in its historicism, was beginning to yield to increasingly formal and structural demands, and the ornament, however skillful, was becoming steadily less essential to the whole. Indeed, if one were, with Schuyler, to squint at the facade of Saint Thomas's and in the mind's eye strip away the decoration, one would even today be left with a thoroughly satisfying formal composition, one that could survive perfectly well on its own terms as an exercise in pure mass.

Powerful and appropriate as Cram and Goodhue's "hardened" Gothic may have been for a military academy, or their softer version for church buildings, their preferred style faced strong competition from the classical for many public edifices. There is no better example than New York's Pennsylvania Station, designed by Charles Follen McKim of McKim, Mead & White. Here was a building dedicated to modern methods of transportation, and one that made full use of modern technology to serve it. The enormous train shed was a no-nonsense essay in steel and glass, and the complex interpenetration of levels and access ramps acknowledged as no other building of its size had yet done the emerging role of the autombile. Yet few would would have argued with

PENNSYLVANIA STATION, *McKim, Mead & White, New York City, 1910.* The architects brought ancient models to bear on modern transportation.

---

7 Montgomery Schuyler, "The New St. Thomas' Church," in *American Architecture and Other Writings* (Cambridge, MA: Belknap Press, 1961), p. 604.

McKim's decision to use Imperial Rome as the source for the building's public spaces. The main waiting room measured 300 feet in length and was nearly 150 feet high, its vaulted and coffered ceiling springing from massive Corinthian columns to create a space deliberately evocative of the Baths of Caracalla. Visitors arriving in New York through this grand structure could have no doubt that they were entering the epicenter of America's commercial energy; New Yorkers leaving from Penn Station might well feel that they were cultural emissaries bearing enlightenment to the provinces. The demolition of this building in 1963 sent such a shock through even the architecturally uninitiated that New Yorkers swiftly passed the nation's first landmarks preservation law (see chapter Six).

If an updated version of the classical seemed most appropriate for such modern facilities as railway stations in most major American cities, it also appealed to those responsible for honoring the nation's past. The severely Doric Lincoln Memorial by Henry Bacon (1866–1924) in Washington, D.C., is one of the country's most powerful such buildings. It does not directly imitate its classical forebears, but in its stripped interpretation of their forms delivers a comparable serenity that seems perfectly suited to its place, subject, and time. (The Jefferson Memorial, begun more than a generation later in 1939 by John Russell Pope, is an example of how the style, even when it has been bled of much of its artistic vitality, does not lose its power to communicate a dignified message.)

The Lincoln Memorial represents perhaps the highest achievement of the classical in Washington, and the style proved as compelling to the practitioners of government as to those who memorialized its heroes. During the early part of the century, the original plan for the city, drawn up by Major Pierre Charles L'Enfant in 1791, was undergoing significant renewal and expansion (with the assistance of Chicago's Daniel Burnham), and the geometrical forms of the classical repertory proved highly effective at defining the grand boulevards and establishing a stylistic consistency for the expression of a dynamic democratic government.

Foremost among the architects who contributed to the aesthetic improvement of the nation's expanding capital during this period was Paul Philippe Cret (1876–1945). Born in France and trained at the Beaux-Arts, Cret settled in Philadelphia in 1903 and embarked on a career marked by a steady simplification of the classical tradition. His first major work in Washington, designed with Albert Kelsey, was the Pan-American Union (1910), now known as the Organization of American States Building. A slightly florid but nonetheless disciplined palace of stone, it invoked European and even Mayan motifs but was in its lightness and clarity distinctly American. Cret's buildings were unfailingly urbane and mannerly, and made solid contributions to their surroundings by creating a sense of timelessness. After World War I (in which he fought with the French forces), Cret turned to increasingly spare forms, which finally invited the less-than-approving description "stripped classicism" from a number of historians. In this his work showed a close affinity to what was happening in Europe, particularly in Italy and Germany, where authoritarian regimes were finding the orderly formal message of classicism—purged of its democratic associations—an appropriate one for their own repressive purposes. In an unintentionally ironic memorial tribute to his colleague and clubmate, the architect

THE LINCOLN MEMORIAL, *Henry Bacon, Washington, D.C., 1922.* A classic of neoclassicism.

Underwood & Underwood/Corbis-Bettmann

PAUL PHILIPPE CRET

William Adams Delano wrote: "There are many who feel that Paul Cret's influence has been a most healthy one, for he captured the spirit of his time and harnessed it to the chariot of architectural tradition."[8]

During the years immediately following World War I, while the cities of America were booming, the suburbs emerged as a major lure for a new generation of Americans eager to escape the oppressions of urban life. The instinct is familiar from the days of Downing and Davis, but this latest cycle was fueled by a new phenomenon: the proliferation of the automobile. In 1907, Henry Ford had begun to produce what be-

[8] William Adams Delano, "Memoirs of Centurian Architects," in *The Century, 1847–1946.* (New York: The Century Association, 1947), p. 211.

came the legendary Model T, bringing a formerly luxurious product into the reach of many more Americans. Within a few years travelers were no longer confined in their leisure wanderings to the network of railway lines.

Philadelphia was a prime example of a city whose most prosperous residents began to establish themselves in surrounding communities that were within easy reach by train or car, yet far enough away to justify an impression of country gentility. Wilson Eyre was an early practitioner of the pastoral domestic architecture that became identified with the Philadelphia area, and he ultimately emerged as one of the best-known architects in the country. In contrast to the grand resort architecture of the Newport "cottages," or even the Gothicizing fantasies of Andrew Jackson Downing, the buildings done by Eyre and his colleagues expressed a slightly whimsical humility—however disingenuous that quality might seem among clients with the resources to sign checks for entire estates. Often constructed of local stone, they adhered to no single style, but used European vernacular elements to evoke an image of life on the fringes of picturesque English and French provin-

THE PAN-AMERICAN UNION (ORGANIZATION OF AMERICAN STATES), *Paul Cret, Washington, D.C., 1910.* Beaux-Arts at heart, but "stripped."

cial villages of centuries past. The architectural firm of Mellor, Meigs & Howe also flourished by designing such residences, which drew from a wide variety of romantic sources to accommodate the comfortable lifestyle of the suburban squire. Perhaps the ultimate expression of their "architecture of mood," as Robert A. M. Stern has described it, was the sprawling, multibuilding estate of Arthur E. Newbold, Jr., in Laverock, Pennsylvania, built between 1921 and 1928.[9] Based on a Norman farmhouse that Howe had seen during his wartime service in France, it depended for much of its effect on studied irregularities, including an artificially sagging roofline, and strong contrasts of textures and materials to create an overall effect of aged familiarity. The architects went so far as to sprinkle the property with live sheep, ducks, doves, and cows, which were used without apology as promotional elements in photographs of the finished composition.

Colleges and universities provided opportunities not unlike those of the more ambitious suburban estates to create complexes of buildings, but with an overlay of monastic scholarship and all the associations appropriate to it. These were communities intended to be as nearly as possible sufficient unto themselves, and were often isolated physically as well as spiritually from the perceived evils of urban life. Here—at

[9] Robert A. M. Stern, *George Howe: Toward a Modern American Architecture* (New Haven, CT: Yale University Press, 1975), p. 31.

Princeton, the University of Michigan, or Stanford—was America as it wished to be in its moments of highest aspiration. Indeed, *campus*, meaning simply "field" in Latin, was a term first applied at Princeton to describe the country site of the college, but eventually came to represent—even in urban settings like those of Harvard, Yale, Columbia, and the University of Chicago—the American ideal of a scholarly world apart, the fulfillment of the "academical village" of Jefferson's fantasy. Not for American scholars the hubbub of the Sorbonne, or the hard-edged confines of Bologna and Berlin!

More than an idyllic setting was required for an institution of higher learning to satisfy its leaders' yearning for separation, however; the implied passage of time was also a factor. In the 1880s, Harvard's Abbott Lawrence Lowell, who would become the university's president from 1909 to 1933, lamented that "Not one of our older buildings is venerable, or will ever become so. Time refuses to console them. They look as if they meant business and nothing more."[10]

Creating the required venerability meant selecting a suitably antique architectural style. Was it to be Gothic, in deference to the monastic origins of education in France and England? Or classical, to honor the philosophical and artistic legacy of Greece and Rome? Or Colonial, to embrace the idea of a nation that had severed its ties with Europe and was starting anew? Whatever the case, campus architecture had more than the usual mission: It was to educate as well as to house. As the *Yale Alumni Weekly* put it rhetorically as late as 1935: "For a university, is there anything more appropriate than to adapt to new conditions forms, used before, which have become the accepted investiture of the spirit that lies within?"[11] Demonstrating the power of the Gothic to transcend even the most intense institutional rivalries, the dean of the architecture faculty at Harvard in 1928 pronounced the new Harkness Memorial complex by James Gamble Rogers at Yale to be "one of the gems of modern American architecture."[12]

[10] See Paul Venable Turner, *Campus, An American Planning Tradition* (New York: Architectural History Foundation; Cambridge MA: The MIT Press, 1984), p. 117.

[11] *Yale Alumni Weekly*, October 25, 1935, p. 5.

[12] G. H. Edgell, *The American Architecture of To-day* (New York and London: Charles Scribner's Sons, 1928), p. 171.

Not surprisingly, the architects who were selected for these academic commissions employed a variety of styles, for each of which a special appropriateness was claimed. Cram insisted that his Gothic buildings at Princeton were a tribute to the origins of Western scholarship in the medieval monasteries of Europe. A similar argument was advanced by the Philadelphia firm of Day & Klauder, which also did work at Princeton, as well as at Wellesley and Yale. The University of Pennsylvania favored the work of Cope & Stewardson, which tended toward the Tudor and Jacobean in a further evolution of the abiding affection for English academic precedent. Another Philadelphian, Horace Trumbauer, was equally at ease in classical and neo-Georgian, and combined them in

JAMES GAMBLE ROGERS

Yale University Department of Manuscripts and Archives

Carter Wiseman

the Widener Library (1913) at Harvard. (Such architectural ambidex-
terity was common to the profession at the time; before designing his
neo-Gothic and neo-Georgian colleges at Yale, James Gamble Rogers
had provided a sturdy homage to the Greek temple for the New Haven
Post Office on the city's central green.)

The rationale for such dependence on European models in this generation of buildings was, of course, that time-honored forms would
guarantee authenticity and high quality. For Cram, the use of Gothic
for academic buildings also ensured their *spiritual* legitimacy. For university presidents, the attraction was less liturgical, but no less associational. In adding several neo-Georgian buildings to the periphery of
Harvard Yard in the early 1920s, the goal, according to a chronicler of
the period, "was to give Harvard Yard that sense of scholarly seclusion
which the sponsors so much admired in the gardens and quadrangles of

**HARKNESS
MEMORIAL
QUADRANGLE**,
*Yale University,
James Gamble
Rogers, New Haven,
Connecticut, 1921.*
The evocative use
of the Gothic over-
shadowed a skilled
manipulation of
form.

THE UNIVERSITY OF PENNSYLVANIA, *Cope & Stewardson, Philadelphia, 1901. A lingering longing for an academic past.*

Cambridge and Oxford."[13] Writing of the appeal of the neo-Gothic architecture of the residential colleges built at Yale some years later by Rogers, a university historian said: "In Gothic windows, the lights begin to gleam here and there, and one is prone to forget Edison and his white magic, and to think of the candlelight that streamed down into the courts of Cambridge when young Francis Bacon was a student at Trinity."[14]

Occasionally, the exercise could get out of hand. At Yale, Rogers designed one residential college with a Gothic facade facing the street—which was dominated by other Gothic buildings of his design—and a less expensive Georgian one facing the inner courtyard. (He also hired craftsmen to grind down the steps to create the impression that generations of students had already trod them, and to break and re-lead selected windows to suggest that the ages had taken their toll on the stained glass.) The height—literally—of Gothic excess was erected by Charles Z. Klauder for the University of Pittsburgh. His forty-story

[13] Bainbridge Bunting, *Harvard, An Architectural History* (Cambridge, MA: Belknap Press, 1985), p. 158.

[14] Robert Dudley French, *The Memorial Quadrangle: A Book About Yale* (New Haven, CT: Yale University Press, 1929), p. 83.

"Cathedral of Learning" was a grossly overscaled steel building in Gothic costume, but was nonetheless judged a success by at least one tastemaker of the time. Said the dean of Harvard's architecture school: "As a skyscraper, none will deny its effectiveness and beauty."[15] As an academic building, however, it was a catastrophe, as the university discovered as soon as the first class in it ended and every student in the building tried to fit into the elevator.

However beautiful Klauder's tower may have seemed to some, the discontinuity between historical style and contemporary construction was growing steadily less tenable. The forms clearly had to evolve to accommodate the new realities. One senses already in much of the work of the 1920s a certain lassitude, a thinning of the creative blood, an impatience with the predictability of both the architectural problems and their solutions. The celebratory verve of Cram, Rogers, and their colleagues had begun to fade. While the architectural journals still ran regular portfolios of medieval French farmhouses and Venetian palazzi sketched by American designers taking the Grand Tour, they also made room for articles on the work of, for example, Austria's Josef Maria Olbrich and Otto Wagner, who were probing the limits of traditional European architecture.

Betram Goodhue's career provides perhaps the best example of the way in which the more thoughtful American architects confronted design issues in the 1920s as the influence of the Europeans began to grow. Having been cast as a pro-Gothic "church architect" for much of his career, he was eager to experiment with a new style, and embarked on a series of buildings in the so-called Churrigueresque style, a free adaptation of Spanish mission architecture, which culminated in his designs for the Panama-California Exposition in San Diego of 1911–15. But, as with the Gothic, the Spanish for Goodhue was more than a mere cloak, it was a genuinely sympathetic gesture toward tradition. Goodhue sincerely believed that a style based on the Mexican traditions of the region was a way to create a lasting regional identity through architecture. His work for the Panama-California Exposition did much to launch a brief local vogue for the Spanish Colonial, but this too failed to satisfy Goodhue.

In 1913, Goodhue and Cram, who had for years been operating vir-

15 Edgell, op. cit., p. 179.

San Diego Historical Society

tually separate offices in New York and Boston, formally ended their
partnership. The more austere Cram remained wedded to the Gothic.
But the more energetic and romantic Goodhue, having worked in the
Hispanic style in California, gradually began to move in an entirely different direction.

In the Nebraska State Capitol, begun in 1920 but not finished until
1932, and the Los Angeles Public Library (1926), Goodhue began to
slip the bonds of his stylistic heritage. Having been forced to accommodate the classical to satisfy the terms of the competition for the
National Academy of Sciences in Washington (1924), Goodhue dis-

Photo by Sid Spelts, Courtesy Nebraska Capitol Archives

covered that the style need not be limited to the stale version against which he had for so long held such animosity. Thus freed to embrace the simplifying principles represented by the classical, he took on the capitol and the library with an even more fully eclectic sensibility. These buildings were almost entirely about form rather than style or history. Departing from the standard American formula of a Roman dome atop a colonnaded temple box, Goodhue in his capitol design sent a lean shaft soaring out of an essentially astylar base, emphasizing the vertical thrust with thin, uninterrupted piers set forward of the tower windows. While there was ample ornament on the capitol's exterior,

THE NEBRASKA STATE CAPITOL, *Bertram Grosvenor Goodhue, Lincoln, Nebraska, 1932.* A tantalizing vision of a future that might have been—without Modernism.

Goodhue subsumed it into the abstraction of the overall scheme. Heroic figures (by the sculptor Lee Lawrie) surfaced almost organically out of the stonework rather than standing alone, as they had at St. Thomas's, or, indeed, at Chartres. The scheme for the Los Angeles Public Library carried the simplification expressed in the Nebraska State Capitol a substantial step further. The design included a squat tower centered on a spare, symmetrical base, and relegated the major exterior ornamental touches to the main entrances and the pyramidal cap of the tower.

One can sense in these buildings the virtual inevitability of the next phase in the design evolution: the total disappearance of ornament as it had been used for centuries. But Goodhue did not move fast enough for at least one leading critic of the day, Fiske Kimball, who described Goodhue's efforts as "disinfected classicism." Kimball declared that "Goodhue's achievement is more of a negative than a positive character. He has tried to expurgate without bringing much that is deeply creative."[16] There is merit to Kimball's claim, but the real value of Goodhue's achievement has become clear in hindsight. He was exploring new paths, but was reluctant to abandon those that he had already traveled and that linked him to an architectural continuum. Because the American architectural establishment was later to reject so violently its historical sources in return for the temporary excitement of Modernism, Goodhue, who—like Irving Gill—might well have reached a similar destination on his own, appeared by contrast with the Europeans, who had started their journey earlier, to be hopelessly timid, and was soon cast aside.

Goodhue was not the only American innovator to suffer that fate. On June 10, 1922, the *Chicago Tribune* announced an architectural competition to mark the newspaper's seventy-fifth anniversary. The goal was the design of a new headquarters that, according to the organizers, was to "secure for Chicago the most beautiful office building in the world." The first prize was the princely sum of $50,000. The announcement drew 263 submissions from 23 countries. (Goodhue was among them, submitting a blocky, stepped tower resembling an attenuated version of his Los Angeles Library, but he won only an honorable mention.)

16 Fiske Kimball, *American Architecture* (Indianapolis and New York: Bobbs-Merrill, 1928), p. 209.

One of the most memorable submissions was by Adolf Loos, the proto-Modernist Austrian whose name has become most closely associated with a single essay he wrote in 1908 entitled "Ornament and Crime." To the bafflement—and, ultimately, derision—of the judges, Loos submitted a design in the form of a giant Doric column. It struck most of them as paradoxical that an opponent of ornament would suggest a building that appeared to be nothing more than a grossly overscaled piece of ornament itself. But Loos was on to something. He had lived and traveled in the United States as a young man and had been an early admirer of the factories and grain silos that would so influence his European colleagues in their search for fresh formal inspiration. He realized that the United States was still in need of cultural anchoring. And what better anchor than a skyscraper—the most American of building types—in the form of what was, in a wonderfully literal sense, the original tall building, one that carried the most powerful associations with classical antiquity?

Predictably enough, Loos's design was rejected. The winning entry was by Raymond M. Hood (1881–1934), a Beaux-Arts–trained architect who had once worked for Cram and Goodhue, and his partner, John Mead Howells. Their design provided for a massive square shaft rising to a crown that was frosted with all manner of Gothic ornament, including a grove of mini-flying buttresses. It was a sturdy building, but stylistically timid, and the avant-garde critics were merciless. They much preferred the design by Eliel Saarinen of Finland, who took second place with an elegant composition that was also frankly Gothic, but simpler in its ornamentation and much more graceful. Louis Sullivan, who had virtually invented the skyscraper as an art form, said of Saarinen's: "In its single solidarity of concentrated intention, there is revealed a logic of a new order, the logic of living things; and this inexorable logic of life is most graciously accepted and set forth in fluency of form." (Saarinen was so affected by the positive reception of his second-place scheme that he moved permanently to the United States and, with his son, went on to make a major contribution to the development of American Modernism.)

In the *Tribune* competition one could detect in a unique concentration the unresolved state of American architecture in the first quarter of the twentieth century. There were wildly Gothic spires, sober classical blocks (one had a Greek temple perched at the summit), and virtually

RAYMOND HOOD

every possible combination of those two traditions. All of the architects were straining mightily to deal with the structural truths Sullivan and many of his Chicago colleagues had already confronted, but which no other Americans were quite ready to embrace. To a Modernist eye, the entry that asserts itself as the obvious leader is the austere design by the Germans Walter Gropius and Adolf Meyer. But most of the other European entries were as retrograde as those submitted by the Americans. Indeed, they ranged from classical kitsch to a shaft topped with the image of an American Indian complete with war bonnet and raised tomahawk.

THE CHICAGO TRIBUNE BUILDING, *Hood & Howells, Chicago, 1923.* The winner of the competition went on to better things.

Hood understood that his successful design was backward-looking; he had done it deliberately to win, rather than to make an artistic statement. But his motives should not be dismissed as entirely cynical. As Ely Jacques Kahn, a colleague and friend, observed of Hood: "The fact that his detail was Gothic amused him some years later, for, as he put it quite tersely himself, the building was erected when embroidery was in vogue, and he was more concerned with the actual structure than its shell."[17]

---

[17] Quoted in Walter Kilham, Jr., *Raymond Hood, Architect* (New York: Architectural Book Publishing Co., 1973), p. 60.

Soon enough, Hood began to shed that Gothic shell, although his American Radiator Building (1924) in New York, a black brick spire he designed in a more stripped version of the style, was a fine work by any standard. He moved on to design the even leaner News Building (1930), also in New York, and, finally, was the major designer of Rockefeller Center, the unrivaled example of American architectural urbanity in the twentieth century (see page 171).

The wry, plain-spoken Hood was above all a pragmatic man. (When told by an associate during the work on Rockefeller Center that he couldn't hire another draftsman because there wasn't enough room in the office, Hood declared, "Hire another man anyway; there's always one guy on the can.") His gradual abandonment of ornament had less to do with ideology than with the cost, which struck many of his commercial clients as the determining factor. However, many of Hood's colleagues, especially in New York, were drawn less to the structural possibilities offered by tall buildings than to their potential for pure visual effect. Intrigued by the flamboyant use of metal and glass demonstrated with such power at the 1925 *Exposition des Arts Décoratifs* in Paris, architects like Hood's friend Albert Kahn (1869–1942) began to drape their buildings in colored terra cotta and gleaming metal. For the moment, at least, the style that became known as Art Deco seemed to provide a way to shed the historicist baggage of the Gothic in skyscraper design, while maintaining a commitment to the ornament most architects and clients still wanted.

There is no more triumphant example of the skyscraper as entertainment than the Chrysler Building (1930), by William Van Alen (1882–1954). Responding to the New York zoning resolution of 1916, which required tall buildings to be set back gradually as they rose to allow more light to reach the street, the Chrysler is a slender shaft springing from a broader, square box at the base. The vertical thrust of the main body of the shaft is expressed by unbroken piers that culminate in rounded arches on all four sides. But then the fun begins. The first tier of arches is echoed seven times in gleaming stainless-steel plates pierced by triangular windows, and topped by a wonderfully thin spike (assembled in secret and raised through the roof at the last possible minute to beat out a rival for the title of world's tallest building). During the day, Chrysler makes a boldly theatrical gesture evocative of Flash Gordon television shows, but at night it soars into full fantasy, its

© Ezra Stoller/Esto

ROCKEFELLER CENTER, *Raymond Hood and others, New York City, 1933.* Attacked at the time, it became one of the world's most successful urban compositions.

THE CHRYSLER BUILDING, *William Van Alen, New York City, 1930.* A reminder that architecture can be entertaining as well as powerful.

Landmarks Preservation Commission, New York City

triangular windows outlined in zigzag lines of white lights worthy of a super-scale carnival.

The theatrical effects earned Van Alen the title of the "Ziegfeld of his profession," but his building should not be regarded as mere show. Especially in contrast to its near contemporary, the Empire State Building, by Shreve, Lamb & Harmon (1931), it succeeds by most of the standard architectural measures of function, grace, good proportion, and the integration of materials. And although it was roundly ridiculed by the Modernists as gaudy, it has survived to remind us that architecture, in its ancient role of delighting the eye, need not be stripped of entertainment, or even humor.

But humor, and even delight, were qualities for which American architects had steadily less tolerance. Their profession was no longer one dominated by gentlemen amateurs who could swap tales of their days at the Ecole and discuss their commissions at social clubs. American society was opening up, and the architectural schools were changing accordingly, producing more and more graduates eager for a piece of what in the mid-1920s was a building boom. At the annual convention of the American Institute of Architects in 1900, the members had voted to require that, beginning in 1902, candidates for membership would have to be graduates of an approved architectural school or pass a special examination. Those graduates were now entering their maturity, and showing a predictable generational impatience with doing things the way their immediate predecessors had done them. Meanwhile, the wealth that had sustained so many grand domestic commissions was shrinking under pressure from the new tax laws, and American industry was expanding rapidly, creating an ever greater demand for larger and more efficient factory and office space.

At the same time, a new and powerful architectural wind was blowing from the Continent. It had already swept romantic eclecticism from its own precincts, and was about to do the same in America. Indeed, even the most dedicated eclectic could see that modern life and modern materials were calling out for their own expressions in architectural form. Inviting and evocative as the architectural fantasies on American college campuses may have been, they could no longer be justified in the face of what was happening outside their walls. The Gothic buildings at Yale, in particular, came in for a drubbing by one precocious undergraduate, who declared in *Architectural Forum* that "Built to appear matchless in their glory and timeless in their splendor, they actually display the tawdriness of the age and the timidity of its intellectual leaders. Although millons have been sunk into them, they have few treasures to give the young. They are copies, imitations, veritable thefts."[18] (To drive the point home — and provide an example of what was possible — the editors juxtaposed Yale's Gothic Sterling Law buildings with a photograph of the contemporaneous Bauhaus Building by Walter Gropius in Germany.)

Some architects, like Cass Gilbert and Albert Kahn, operated in both realms, doing classical or Gothic when called upon, but turning out industrial and commercial buildings unembellished by any but minimal historical reference. Gilbert's severe U.S. Army Supply Base in Brooklyn (1918) is a marked contrast to his super-Gothic Woolworth Building, and Kahn's manufacturing plants were worlds away from his neoclassical library on the campus of the University of Michigan. These architects differed from the zealots, though, in embracing industrial form as yet another option, rather than as the "true faith" to which so many would soon be called. Nevertheless, it was in these commercial buildings that the guidelines for the future were found, for they responded with simple utilitarian vigor to the new requirements of the day with the materials and techniques that could best satisfy them: steel beams, poured concrete, and large expanses of glass.

The implications of those fundamental elements of a new architecture had been recognized for some years in Europe, where forward-looking architects, as Galen Howard had pointed out in his 1913 *Architectural Record* article, were ready for revolutionary change. *Vers une Architecture*, the seminal book by Le Corbusier, was published in 1923 and appeared in an English translation in 1927 as *Towards a New Architecture*. Its brief but powerful argument about the need for architecture to embrace the message of the machine age instantly became required reading for the American architectural avant-garde.

Increasingly, American architectural journals saw a resurgence of the moralistic tone that had characterized the American architectural debate at regular intervals since Jefferson's day. The eclectics were increasingly condemned as aesthetic weaklings, incapable of a coherent

---

[18] William Harlan Hale, "Old Castles for New Colleges," *Architectural Forum* (June 1931) p. 729.

theory or even originality. Gradually, the early clarity and simplicity of American domestic architecture began to look like the road not taken, while the knowing selectivity of the eclectics seemed more and more irrelevant. The pronouncements of Wright about "organic" architecture, pronouncements that had for years seemed willfully eccentric, took on a compelling new meaning. (Indeed, Wright began publishing again in *Architectural Record*, declaiming on the corruption of the entire contemporary architectural profession, himself excepted.) The comfortable dream into which American architecture had settled following the 1893 World's Columbian Exposition was coming to an abrupt awakening.

The trend did not go unopposed. Referring to the early work of Le Corbusier and his colleagues in Europe, Cram declared in his autobiography: "These things seem to me to be a betrayal of trust, a vicious though unintentional assault on the basic principles of a sane and wholesome society."[19] A few pages later, he expanded on his point and urged his colleagues to stand by the eclectic faith:

> "What we confront to-day is the chaos of change when one era comes to its end and another rises to take its place. This being so, the architect or other artist can only work, so to speak, from hand to mouth. He is and must be an eclectic—an opportunist, if you like. The new must be expressed through new, but perfectly well-chosen works; the old, which still providentially survives, through its old language, adaptable and made intelligible to the modern consciousness; the future—if, by the grace of God, some may be granted an adumbration of its nature—in that idiom that preserves and indicates eternal values supplemented and enriched by that which is good (and that alone) which develops from the peculiar processes of the present time."[20]

One's heart goes out to Cram. He had embraced a particular form of architecture—the Gothic—because he thought it was the best that had ever been, and because he thought its artistic and spiritual traditions would imbue a young nation with the physical and moral examples on which to build a great future. As he looked around him he saw the first signs of collapse. He was determined that they be contained. "It is unnecessary further to emphasize what I mean by the limitations set for

---

[19] Cram, op. cit., p. 272.
[20] Ibid., p. 280.

the operation of the modernist idea in the field of art. It has its own place and it may and should go to it. Its boundaries are definite and fixed, and beyond them it cannot go, for the Angel of Decency, Propriety, and Reason stands there with a flaming sword."[21]

It was a noble sentiment, by a sincere artist, and it should not be read as merely a fearful reaction to a threatening future. The best representatives of American architecture between 1900 and 1933 had shown every sign of eventually shedding their dependence on European precedent for a mature evolution of those precedents in response to American conditions. What shame was there, after all, in acknowledging the source of those examples? To suggest—as so many did—that because the United States was a new political phenomenon it therefore required an entirely new architecture misreads history and the very nature of artistic continuity and influence. American architecture could separate itself from Europe no more than American politics could separate itself from Greece or the *Magna Carta*.

Who was qualified to say that American architecture should settle on a single style, rejecting all others? An enduring article of American faith—artistically as well as politically—was that every citizen was entitled to freedom of expression. How better to serve such a populace than through an eclecticism that drew on the best of the European past while adjusting it to the present?

But the wielders of Cram's flaming sword had little chance against the forces already loosed upon America's architecture. Those forces would sweep away much that was wasteful and absurd, but also much that was durable and humane. However much their successors mocked them, the eclectics knew that cornices and moldings, multipaned windows and classical columns, not to mention color and texture, appealed to those who prefer to live or work in a building rather than to think about it.

As a chronicler of the time put it, "If the detail is reminiscent of Paris or Rome, let us not worry over-much. Style is not the life-blood of architecture; more often it is the jester's cap and bells, the motley for the crowd."[22] The underlying *architecture*, he might have added, was often as sound as ever.

---

[21] Ibid., p. 283.

[22] See Thomas E. Tallmadge, *The Story of Architecture in America* (New York: W. W. Norton, 1927), p. 267.

Modernism and the Abstract Ascendancy

Reminiscing in a Denver hotel room in the late 1980s, Chester Nagel, a retired local architect, cast back nearly fifty years to his days as a student at Harvard University's Graduate School of Design. "We were going to change the world," he said. "Architecture was no longer going to be merely decorative. We were trying to separate ourselves from the bombast of the old. We were looking for the essence, and we found it."[1]

---

[1] Interview with the author, July 10, 1987.

WALTER GROPIUS

Nagel was one of the hundreds of young architects who came to Harvard in the 1930s and 40s to study with a stellar group of European emigrés. They were led by Walter Gropius (1883–1969), founder of the Bauhaus—the revolutionary German design school that had combined architecture, crafts, and the plastic arts in a unique curriculum—and his Hungarian-born Bauhaus colleague Marcel Breuer (1902–1981). Scores of the graduates from that heady period went on to highly successful and influential architectural careers. Indeed, a list of the better-known Harvard alumni of those days reads rather like a directory of the leading American architects from the 1950s to the 1990s: Edward

Larrabee Barnes, Henry N. Cobb, Ulrich Franzen, Philip Johnson, I. M. Pei, and Paul Rudolph, among the most prominent. Until that time, no school of architecture except the Beaux-Arts itself could claim to have produced so many architects who would have such a pervasive impact upon their society. So powerful was the educational experience in that place and time that even those graduates, like Nagel, who did not go on to fame contributed with zeal to the propagation of the faith they absorbed under their Harvard mentors.

These men had been drawn to Harvard from various sources, but in most cases they came because they were dissatisfied with the teaching that was available elsewhere. They were young, enthusiastic, and energetic, and they sensed that a fundamental change was imminent for their profession. I. M. Pei—who would go on to design the East Building of the National Gallery in Washington, D.C. (1978), and the glass pyramid for the Louvre Museum in Paris (1989)—was rather typical in his sentiments if not in his origins. Born in China in 1917, Pei had come to the United States to study at MIT, which was then still dominated by the Beaux-Arts system, and graduated in 1940. "There was something lacking at MIT," he recalled nearly fifty years later. "We were all aware that something was happening at Harvard, but we couldn't even talk about it in the presence of our dean. When I arrived at Harvard, it was a breath of fresh air. It was closer to what I understood architecture to be."[2]

That air was almost entirely European—and overwhelmingly German. Gropius had established the Bauhaus in 1919, and had created a highly influential school before the Nazis forced its closing in 1933. He later emigrated, first to England, and then to the United States. In 1937, Gropius accepted an invitation from the dean of Harvard's Graduate School of Design, known familiarly as the GSD, to take on the chairmanship of the department of architecture.

What Gropius—an earnest and idealistic man who had won the Iron Cross as a cavalry officer with the Kaiser's army in World War I— brought with him was a coherent philosophy of architecture. It was something still lacking in the United States, as the *Chicago Tribune* competition had so dramatically demonstrated.

In brief, the new creed called for a recombination of the arts into a new synthesis. Gropius had written in 1919, in his "Manifesto of the

_____

2 Interview with the author, January 26, 1988.

Bauhaus": "Let us together desire, conceive and create the new building of the future, which will combine everything—architecture *and* sculpture *and* painting—in a *single form* which will one day rise toward the heavens from the hands of a million workers as the crystalline symbol of a new and coming faith." In 1936, in his *The New Architecture and the Bauhaus*, Gropius went on to write that the goal of the new architecture as he saw it was the "composite but inseparable work of art, in which the old dividing line between monumental and decorative elements will have disappeared forever."

In making that proclamation, Gropius owed a substantial debt to Adolf Loos, whose polemical writings proved far more influential than his *Tribune* competition entry. Before he became known for his buildings, Loos had made a name for himself writing for Viennese publications on the need for a new architecture in Europe. He made his greatest impact with his 1908 essay "Ornament and Crime," in which he declared: "As ornament is no longer organically linked with our culture, it is also no longer an expression of our culture." Lack of ornament, he argued, "is a sign of spiritual strength. Modern man uses the ornaments of earlier and foreign cultures as he thinks fit. He uses his own powers of invention on other things."

The essay was widely translated and circulated abroad; Le Corbusier referred to it as "an Homeric cleansing" of architecture. And although Loos himself later argued that he had never intended his message to be taken as a blanket prohibition of ornament (his own architecture made overtly ornamental use of natural materials such as richly colored marble), it became a cornerstone in the orthodox European Modernist structure.

However doctrinaire Loos and the members of the Bauhaus may have seemed in their aesthetic beliefs to those who oversimplified their pronouncements, the Europeans were also committed to what they perceived as the needs of their changing society. The devastation of World War I had been compounded by economic uncertainty and widespread political unrest. As Peter Blake, a former editor of *Architectural Forum*, described the sentiments of the avant-garde European architects of the day, many of whom he came to know personally, "art came second to the basic concerns that dealt with problems of the real world: economic and social justice, overpopulation, poverty, disease." Radical modern architects, Blake went on, "hoped to improve the human condition in an egalitarian society."[3]

Nearly sixty years after Gropius arrived in America, such sentiments seem almost impossibly naive. For all the various powers of architecture, it has never been employed with much success in solving social ills. But the radicals had not yet been disillusioned. They were setting a new agenda for their art, and housing the growing workforce in an affordable and aesthetically innovative setting was very much a part of it. Nowhere in Europe was that made more clear than in the design of the so-called *Weissenhofsiedlung,* a housing complex built in 1927 outside Stuttgart. The competition for the Weissenhof Exposition drew submissions from most of the leading Modernists of the day, including Le Corbusier from France, Gropius from Germany, and J. J. P. Oud from Holland, and was supervised by Germany's Ludwig Mies van der Rohe (1886–1969). The twenty-one separate buildings provided a showcase not just of the latest architectural technology and aesthetic thinking, but of a determination among the participants to bring architecture to bear on the solution of social problems on a large scale. The buildings were intended to be efficient, affordable, attractive, and easy to build, using available industrial materials. While they fell short of satisfying all these criteria, they were without question a testament to the shared goals—social as well as artistic—of the best architectural talents in Europe at the time.

Shortly after Gropius arrived in the United States, he published an article in *Architectural Record* in which he confirmed for his American audience the social aims that had been set out by the organizers of the Stuttgart project: "I want a young architect to be able to find his way in whatever circumstances; I want him independently to create true, genuine forms out of the technical, economic and social conditions in which he finds himself instead of imposing a learned formula onto surroundings which may call for an entirely different solution."[4]

Such sentiments were not unknown in America even before Gropius arrived. The prolific Albert Kahn can certainly be seen as an architect who turned his considerable talents to the industrial realities of the day.

---

3 Peter Blake, *No Place Like Utopia* (New York: Alfred A. Knopf, 1993), p. 5.
4 "Architecture at Harvard University," *Architectural Record* (May 1937) p. 10.

ALBERT KAHN

He designed more than two thousand factories for clients, including
Henry Ford (who introduced the assembly line in one of Kahn's buildings), Walter Chrysler, and Joseph Stalin (who commissioned Kahn's
firm to help speed the Soviet Union's industrialization). In 1938 alone,
Kahn was responsible for roughly 19 percent of the architect-designed
industrial buildings in the United States. But although his work embodied the machine age principles on which European theorists like
Gropius were building their movement (using photographs of Kahn's
factories in their teaching), it carried with it no larger vision of industrial architecture's role in society. An artist Kahn may have been, but he

didn't make an issue of it. "Architecture is 90 percent business and 10 percent art," he insisted. Such pronouncements did not prevent him from designing some exquisite private houses in a variety of historically correct styles, but the apparent architectural schizophrenia caused him no pause at all. In contrast with the Europeans, Kahn felt that art and industry should not overlap.

Another American whose instincts coincided to some degree with those Europeans who were caught up in the potential of industrial architecture was Ralph Thomas Walker (1889–1973), whose Barclay-Vesey Telephone Building in New York, finished in 1926, was selected by Le Corbusier himself as the frontispiece for his *Towards a New Architecture*. Walker's massive and rather grim structure, which he said had actually been conceived of "as a machine," became popular as an American expression of Modernist concerns. But Walker, like Kahn, was careful to set himself apart from what he saw as the doctrinal excesses of the movement.

The ambiguity over Modernism expressed in the works and words of

CHRYSLER TRUCK PLANT, *Albert Kahn, Warren, Michigan, 1938.* For Kahn, architecture was "90 percent business and 10 percent art."

such architects as Kahn and Walker was highlighted with striking effect in March 1932, when *Pencil Points* magazine, the forerunner of *Progressive Architecture*, initiated a debate in its pages over the merits and demerits of the new philosophy of design. The second piece in the series—which included such prominent architects of the time as Ralph Adams Cram, Willliam Adams Delano, Charles Z. Klauder, and John W. Root, as well as Kahn—was by George Howe, who had spent much

GEORGE HOWE

of his career designing *faux châteaux* for the wealthy of Philadelphia, but had now become a convert to Modernism. No more dramatic statement of a doctrinal *volte-face* exists than Howe's declaration in his contribution to the *Pencil Points* series, "Functional Aesthetics and the Social Ideal," in which he declared: "The broker who motors to town every day from an imitation thatched cottage is in fact playing at doll's house. The architect who builds it for him is doomed to produce a work without mature significance. There is more real beauty in one straight line of a well-designed country house, standing in bold relief against the irregularities of nature, than in all the soft contours recreated by the romantic in painful imitation of the peasant's handiwork."[5] And this from the man who only eight years previously had spared no effort or expense in the creation of an imitation French farmhouse—complete with pre-sagged roof—for his client Arthur Newbold!

Whatever his earlier inclinations, Howe in 1932 was writing with special authority about the new developments in architecture. Only a

[5] *Pencil Points* (April 1932) p. 217.

year before, he and his partner William Lescaze (1896–1969) had completed the most dramatic example of high-rise Modernism yet achieved in the United States, the Philadelphia Saving Fund Society Building (PSFS). Since dubbed the world's first truly Modernist skyscraper, the thirty-two-story building is a sleek shaft of glass, steel, and stone divided into discrete zones for a public banking hall, offices, and building services. The ground floor originally housed a series of shops. Above them was the soaring banking room fitted out in polished stone and metal. These elements form a base from which the office tower springs. To the rear, differentiated from the horizontally striped glass-and-steel tower by

PHILADELPHIA SAVING FUND SOCIETY, *George Howe and William Lescaze, Philadelphia, 1931.* The moment of Howe's conversion to Modernist ways.

The Warder Collection

a cladding of stone, is the service tower, which contains elevators, stairs, toilets, and a fire tower.

The entire structure was—and remains—a composition that satisfied both aesthetic and functional demands, dispensing in the process with all vestiges of traditional high-rise architecture, from classical columns to ornamented cornices. Every aspect of the design adhered to the new principles of clarity of function and expression of structure. Howe and Lescaze even designed the starkly simple clocks that provided the only furnishings in the gleaming elevator lobbies. No moldings, no niches or other embellishment of any kind marred the smooth surfaces of the building's public spaces. Nothing could have been further from the cozy fantasies of Howe's earlier estates for his well-heeled suburban barons, or closer to the avant-garde entries in the *Tribune* competition.

Accounts differ about which partner was most responsible for the more radical aspects of PSFS, but it is fair to infer that its unmistakable European look owed much to Lescaze, who had been born and educated in Switzerland, coming to the United States in 1923. Although at the time not yet a convinced Modernist himself, Lescaze had been exposed to the movement during his formative professional years in Geneva and Zurich, and was ready to embrace it when the opportunity presented itself. And while Howe had secured the commission for the PSFS project and developed its basic design before going into partnership with Lescaze, the final version of the building is clearly indebted to Lescaze's sensibilities as well as those of Howe.

The other major Modernists at work in the United States at the time were also European by birth. Rudolph Schindler (1887–1953) was a native of Vienna, but was, like so many of his European colleagues, much taken by the publication in 1911 of Wright's portfolio of buildings and drawings, and in 1914 moved to Chicago. Four years later, Wright hired him, and in 1919 sent Schindler to Los Angeles to supervise work on a house for Aline Barnsdall, a wealthy patron of the local art scene (see page 189). When the house was finished, Wright decided to close his California office (he was fully occupied with the design of the Imperial Hotel in Tokyo and was spending much of his time in Japan), but Schindler chose to stay on, setting up a practice of his own. It succeeded, largely on the strength of a single building, the Lovell Beach House at Newport Beach, California. Completed in 1926, the house

THE LOVELL BEACH HOUSE, *Rudolph Schindler, Newport Beach, 1926. A West Coast vision of the European avant-garde.*

showed scant trace of Wrightian influence, relying on spare, unembellished forms supported by massive poured-in-place concrete frames.

Richard Neutra (1892–1970) had also been born in Vienna, and, like Schindler, had met the radical Adolf Loos, whom he described as "my master and fountain of ideas in architecture."[6] Neutra said that Loos's stories of his own brief stay in the United States, along with the publication of Wright's portfolio, persuaded him to emigrate, which he did in 1923. He came briefly to know Louis Sullivan, and at Sullivan's funeral the following year met Wright in person. Neutra went on to spend several months working for Wright—as well as for Holabird and Roche—before moving on to Los Angeles. There, he formed a loose partnership with Schindler. Neutra's own house for the Lovell family— the Health House (1929)—built on the slope of a canyon in the Holly-

6 Esther McCoy, *Richard Neutra* (New York: George Braziller, 1960), p. 8.

wood Hills, was a crisply modern building distinguished mostly for the use of a prefabricated steel skeleton in its structure, and it made a name for the architect even in Europe. (He was invited to become a visiting critic at the Bauhaus.)

The work done by Schindler and Neutra showed that there was an appetite, however small, for overtly Modernist architecture in America, particularly in California. But like their predecessors Irving Gill, Greene & Greene, and Bernard Maybeck, Schindler and Neutra remained on the edges of the country's architectural mainstream, which still flowed from the East Coast. Moreover, neither was of sufficient stature to consolidate a movement, as Wright had done.

More important, the conditions were not yet right. European painters and sculptors as well as architects may have been eager to cleanse their artistic landscape of an academicism run rampant, giving birth to such movements as *De Stijl*, Cubism, and Constructivism. But

THE LOVELL HEALTH HOUSE, *Richard Neutra, Hollywood, California, 1929.* An interest in Modernist structural expression survived work with Wright.

while the most progressive Americans had also grown increasingly frustrated with neoclassicism and other forms of eclecticism, most were dogged by the fact that historical styles still served the purposes of those Americans most likely to provide patronage to architects: the wealthy, in contrast to the government, which was still the primary client in Europe. Despite the stale state of architectural innovation, Americans with money and interest enough to commission architects were still eager to display it through established forms; their greatest ambition, after all, was to become members of an *establishment*. That impulse had long ago exhausted itself in Europe, where traditional forms represented a social structure that had manifestly failed. But in the United States, a new elite was not yet ready to abandon the trappings of a social prominence so recently gained. And in any case, because the leading architecture schools in the country were still dominated by the Beaux-Arts philosophy, there were few alternative sources of training for architects who might have wished to stray from the established path.

By the early 1930s several forces were combining to change that state of affairs. The Depression had virtually halted construction in America; by the beginning of 1933, fully 85 percent of the practicing architects in New York City were out of work.[7] In the absence of jobs, many sought solace in theory, and Modernism had a tremendous amount of it to offer.

The architectural message itself—whether formal, social, or both—was appealing enough. But the bearers of that message had a special allure. Most of the European architects who came to the United States in the 1930s and 1940s could describe themselves as refugees from oppression. Their work had come under increasing suspicion as the forces of fascism and Nazism gained momentum. After months of escalating pressure from the Nazi government, which found the school's work "un-German," the faculty of the Bauhaus closed it. Gropius had already turned over the leadership to Mies van der Rohe, who tried to find an accommodation with the Nazis, but finally could not. Mies, having visited the United States in 1937, arrived for good in 1938. Had such men come to the United States merely as talented bearers of new architectural tidings, they would surely have been embraced by the avant-garde. But perceived as they were as exiles from oppression, they fulfilled one of America's most cherished criteria for citizenship.

---

[7] *Architectural Record* (July 1991) p. 162.

Beyond that, Modernism as presented by Gropius, Breuer, and Mies appealed to the persistent American Puritanism that had surfaced so often in informed architectural debate since Colonial times. Architecturally speaking, Modernism was an even "purer" version of the creed. "Less," Mies van der Rohe declared in one of his most famous aphorisms, "is more."

Not to be overlooked as a reason for the warm welcome extended to the new arrivals was that, with the onset of the Depression, what limited building there was had to be done in the most economical fashion. The emphasis placed by the Modernists on rational design, the expression of structure, and the use of industrial materials—not to mention the virtual elimination of ornament—gave their message a very practical appeal.

Although the conditions may have been ripe for the development of a new way of making architecture in America, the so-called Modern movement was still known only to a relative few. It was given its public certification in February 1932 with a remarkable show at New York's Museum of Modern Art—then only three years old. Organized by Alfred Barr, the museum's director, the art historian Henry-Russell Hitchcock, and Philip Johnson, then a young curator, MoMA's first architectural exhibition attempted to summarize the most progressive developments in contemporary European and American architecture. Those developments, the organizers believed, had produced a style expressing several design principles: a concern with volume as opposed to mass and solidity, regularity as opposed to axial symmetry, and the proscription of "arbitrary applied decoration." The show, entitled "Modern Architecture: International Exhibition," drew relatively little attention at the time except among the avant-garde, but the museum took the bold step of sending it on a national tour, giving the show, and the book based upon it—*The International Style: Architecture Since 1922*—a much larger audience.

The combination of the show and the book served as the introduction to European Modernism for most Americans concerned with the subject, and in retrospect can be seen as a seminal event that affected American design well into the 1960s. But the impact had much to do with the fact that the organizers had edited the original "product"—European Modernism—in one highly significant respect. The refinement was symbolized by the addition of the word "*Style*" to the title of the book.

From the start, the Europeans had considered housing a fundamental element of the overall architectural mission. Unlike Americans, who had traditionally conceived of ideal residential architecture as isolated buildings—whether Jefferson's Monticello, or Davis's Lyndhurst—these architects focused their attention as well on the needs of large numbers of people living in close proximity. In this, they went well beyond the contemporary American efforts, such as those of Clarence Stein and Henry Wright in their garden suburbs, which, for all their charm and innovative planning, embodied few really fresh ideas about an architecture that had to accommodate the pressures of social and industrial change in a country fast becoming centered on its cities. In *Towards a New Architecture*, Le Corbusier had called for an architecture that would consider a house as a "machine for living in." By that, he meant a dwelling that exploited all the advances in materials and convenience that were becoming available. He carried the concept over into mass housing with his concept of a "Ville Radieuse," an urban setting made up of enormous apartment towers set among parks, but within easy reach of a system of superhighways.

Megalomaniacal as the Le Corbusian vision seems in the wake of so much disastrous urban renewal that was inspired by it, the concept was at its heart deeply humane. The goal was to create a city free of the congestion and squalor that had defined so much European city life for centuries, and at the same time take advantage of the technology that allowed architects to build into the sky and create transportation systems of unprecedented speed and efficiency. (The architect's drawings for the scheme included biplanes soaring perilously between the towers.) Le Corbusier's city and the *Weissenhofsiedlung* were, from the perspective of their time, based as much on concepts of high social responsibility as they were on principles of architectural art.

Hitchcock and Johnson, however, embraced the movement represented by Le Corbusier and Mies more for its novelty as a style than for its potential as social theory. For these museum curators, who were both well-born and thoroughly insulated from the harsher social realities with which the radical Europeans were grappling, Modernism meant something almost entirely aesthetic. Indeed, Johnson was to insist for the rest of his architectural career on the futility of addressing social issues through architecture. In the introduction to their book, Alfred Barr declared that "It should be made clear that the aesthetic qualities of the

Style are the principal concerns of the authors," noting that they had made "little attempt to present here the technical or sociological aspects of the style except in so far as they are related to problems of design."

Not surprisingly, the framers of the MoMA show had trouble dealing with Frank Lloyd Wright. Here was a homegrown architect of unmatched power and originality who had, through the publication of his work in Europe, contributed substantially to the underlying principles of Modernism itself (especially in his use of free-flowing interior spaces). And yet, his own architecture bore little resemblance to the works that had so captivated Hitchcock and Johnson. Wright's "organic" forms, his overt use of ornament, and his enduring enthusiasm for natural materials simply did not conform to the "machine" aesthetic that had seduced the MoMA curators. Unable to tailor Wright's nonconforming architecture to their purposes, the organizers assigned him the role of senior statesman. "One very great architect," Alfred Barr wrote of Wright in their catalogue, "is included who is not intimately related to the Style, although his early work is one of the Style's most important sources." Wright was hardly pleased by his relegation to the status of godfather, and although he eventually made a sort of peace with the museum, he never quite forgave it for the slight.

Apart from Wright, the most important of the few Americans who were included in the show were Neutra, for his Lovell House, and Howe and Lescaze, for their PSFS Building, which Hitchcock and Johnson found interesting largely because of its dramatic cantilevering of the main facade. The other prominent Americans were Raymond M. Hood and J. André Fouilhoux. Their McGraw-Hill Building, designed for a publishing company and finished in 1931, was praised by the organizers of the museum show for its "lightness, simplicity, and lack of applied verticalism," apparently a reference to the Gothicizing impulse of other New York skyscraper architects, such as Cass Gilbert in his 1913 Woolworth Building. But Hitchcock and Johnson criticized Hood and Fouilhoux for their "heavy ornamental crown," which they considered an "unhappy and illogical break in the general system of regularity." In fact, Hood was oblivious to such abstract concerns, preferring to concentrate on the practical requirements of the program—in this case publishing and book production—rather than the aesthetic theories to which he might bend them. At a symposium at the Museum of Modern Art following the show, Hood responded with characteristic clarity to the criti-

McGraw-Hill Company

cisms from the curators: "I wish we could all work with our own sense of discipline and be free as the devil. . . . We should keep away from 'style' and for once we will make of this style a freedom of the spirit."[8]

The language of the judgments passed by Johnson and Hitchcock is evidence enough of their primarily aesthetic concerns. Much of what

---

[8] See Robert A. M. Stern, Gregory Gilmartin, and Thomas Mellins, *New York 1930* (New York: Rizzoli, 1987), p. 580.

made Howe and Lescaze's Philadelphia skyscraper such a powerful building was not just its cantilevers but its sensible organization of services: shops on the street floor, banking room above, offices above that, with a separate service tower at the rear. In fact, Howe's tower has been interpreted as owing at least as much to the Beaux-Arts tradition of clear planning as it did to the new stylistic trends. The shape of McGraw-Hill was, as Hitchcock and Johnson acknowledged, determined largely by zoning restrictions, but one of the aspects that distinguished it most was the one that most displeased the critics: the "ornamental crown," which displayed the company name in enormous letters visible to millions of New Yorkers, making a powerful advertisement of the entire building. In this, it was like PSFS, which also displayed its name across its crown, if in a more elegant fashion. In both cases, the aspects that had most to do with the buildings' success were held against them because of aesthetic criteria.

A comparable attitude informed the analysis of the MoMA show's European housing entries, which were found praiseworthy largely because they were so handsome, not because they brought architectural intelligence to bear on the problem of accommodating large numbers of residents in efficient, economical ways.

The formalist attitude espoused by Hitchcock and Johnson should not have come as a surprise. Without a long history of architecture of its own, and as a society in a constant state of social and technological change, America had long ago acquired the habit of taking its inspiration from disembodied sources rather than from original monuments within an established context. While Hitchcock and Johnson had actually seen most of the buildings they included in their show, they had what might be called only a touristic appreciation of the historical and social processes that had produced the forms that so attracted their aesthetes' eyes. The fact that their analysis could not make room for the most creative American architect—Wright—is a telling indictment of their essentially doctrinaire priorities.

But Hitchcock and Johnson were not alone in ignoring the origins of the work they espoused. Although Gropius had been one of the founders of the Modern movement, and continued to insist on the social obligations of his art, he, too, became a vigorous participant in the aestheticism that came to dominate the American version of the phenomenon. Shortly after his appointment at Harvard, Gropius took the remarkable step of dropping architectural history from the curriculum of the Graduate School of Design. Thereafter students took the subject as an elective rather than a requirement, and had to seek it out in the lecture halls of Harvard College rather than those of their own school. So hungry were Gropius's supporters for a change from the old ways of doing things that this excision of architectural memory performed on their education met virtually no resistance. Gropius's followers eagerly agreed with his position that creativity would be stifled by exposure to the influences of architectural history. "When the innocent beginner is introduced to the great achievements of the past," he declared, "he may be too easily discouraged from trying to create for himself."[9] With some bitterness, the Harvard-trained critic and historian Bruno Zevi complained in 1994 that "When I was at Harvard, from 1940 to 1942, we did not learn that there could be a modern use of old architecture, that modern interpretation of past monuments was possible and vital. Gropius, Breuer . . . and the other design professors did not care."[10]

But such judgments lay either deep in the minority or far in the future during the early days of the Modernist revolution at Harvard. When Gropius was introduced at the May 1937 meeting of the American Institute of Architects in Boston, he was given a standing ovation, and another after he finished his speech.[11] The symbolic rejection of what had gone before was further emphasized by the fact that in taking up his Harvard post Gropius was replacing a Frenchman—Jean-Jacques Haffner—who was an alumnus of the Ecole des Beaux-Arts.

Even in the early days, however, the high price of the revolution was evident to those with an open mind. One of the most regrettable aspects of the embrace of the new thinking and its attendant devotion to abstraction was that it did away with much of the traditional Beaux-Arts training in draftsmanship. In the traditional schools of architecture, students were still required to draw with painstaking care from plaster casts of classical architectural details, a practice that forced them to investigate with eye and hand the most intimate details of architectural form.

---

[9] See Wayne Andrews, *Architecture, Ambition and Americans* (New York: The Free Press, 1964), p. 259.

[10] Bruno Zevi, quoted in the *GSD News* (Fall 1994) p. 41.

[11] Reginald Isaacs, *Gropius, an Illustrated Biography of the Creator of the Bauhaus* (Boston: Little, Brown, 1991), p. 228.

However, because the practice was associated with ornament, and because the new emphasis was on the grand scale of cities as well as on individual buildings, draftsmanship in the traditional sense gave way increasingly to an increased enthusiasm for scale models. These were often beautiful in both concept and execution, but they encouraged an approach to architecture from above, rather than at eye level. One need only compare the delicate effects of a pre-Gropian Harvard thesis rendering with the Olympian manipulation of rectilinear forms of a typical GSD studio model of the 1940s to appreciate the shift in sensibility from the specific to the general. Even Gropius eventually conceded the loss.[12]

But at the time, the price certainly seemed worth the gain. Indeed, the shift in perception from the intimate to the abstract was encouraged by the fact that society's demands on architecture itself were changing. Modern technology made it possible to raze depressed sections of cities and rebuild them with relative ease. The terms "slum clearance" and "urban renewal" entered the American planning vocabulary, symbolizing simultaneously the optimism and the callousness of the impulse to change. The result was all too often a scheme that did not consider the issues of how buildings relate to each other or to their users.

A striking example of the effect of such thinking is provided by the early career of one of Gropius's best students, I. M. Pei. After graduation from Harvard, Pei briefly joined the GSD faculty, but soon went to work for William Zeckendorf, one of the country's leading real estate developers. Zeckendorf was a man of extraordinary ambition and considerable architectural sophistication. He approached his business on the grand scale. Working closely with Pei and several of Pei's fellow Harvard alumni whom he had brought into the office, Zeckendorf would research development opportunities for cities around the country, and then phone the local officials to make a proposal. If they expressed interest, Zeckendorf and his team would fly to the designated city in the company plane, study the "target" a few times while circling, and, once on the ground, present their scheme for the city's future. The technique was a marvel of enterprise, but frequently produced a rather harsh result. The geometrical abstraction of the planning done by Pei and his colleagues for downtown Denver, for example, remains compelling at the level of geometry, but was uninviting from the sidewalk.

---

[12] Ibid., p. 237.

United Nations

UNITED NATIONS
HEADQUARTERS,
Wallace K. Harrison
and Max Abramovitz,
New York City, 1950.
A world apart for the
world body.

A grander but similar case is represented by the headquarters for the United Nations in New York, designed by Wallace K. Harrison (1895–1981) and Max Abramovitz (1908–) and finished in 1950. The three main elements of the complex (which were derived from an original scheme by Le Corbusier) are distributed in a sculptural arrangement that has considerable appeal when seen in isolation; the enormous slab of the Secretariat is balanced happily by the lower buildings housing the General Assembly and other official functions. But the ensemble has virtually nothing to do with the existing street patterns of the city, let alone the rest of New York architecture, and can be oppressively chilly as a pedestrian experience.

The effect can be sensed even more clearly in Gropius's own 1949 design for the Harvard University Graduate Center in Cambridge. As an abstract composition, it has unquestionable power; as a setting for daily student life, it pales before the no less carefully planned, but much more humane, neo-Gothic intricacies of James Gamble Rogers's Memorial Quadrangle at Yale.

The damage done to the urban fabric by the triumph of such abstract compositions can be sensed immediately by comparing them to the plan for New York's Rockefeller Center, the first stage of which was built between 1932 and 1940 by a group of architects whose primary design member was Raymond Hood. Here, the Beaux-Arts emphasis on symmetrical arrangement of forms endured, and the overall composition— comprising fourteen buildings on nearly twelve acres—also responded with great sensitivity to the scale of the adjoining streets and avenues, creating an urban oasis that was nonetheless gracefully integrated into the existing fabric. The slightly retrograde "Moderne" aspects of the design were roundly criticized by the avant-garde, but the Center's urbanistic gestures—whether in the relationships in mass and scale among the separate buildings, the eventual inclusion of a public skating rink, or the temporary addition of rooftop gardens—more than outweighed its supposed transgressions.

The most powerful example of the impact the new abstract way of thinking was to have on American architecture, particularly that of American cities, is the work of Mies van der Rohe. The son of a master mason in the ancient German city of Aachen, Mies, like Wright, had no formal architectural training. He worked off and on for three years with the Modernist pioneer Peter Behrens, who had striven to integrate traditional forms with the demands of modern industrial society. But for

HARVARD UNIVERSITY GRADUATE CENTER, *Walter Gropius and the Architects Collaborative,* Cambridge, Massachusetts, 1949. Intellectually appealing, but not a comfortable place to be.

UPI/Corbis-Bettmann

all his own dedication to the materials and mechanics of building, Mies grew increasingly concerned with form as an element in his work. Between 1921 and 1922, he produced two radically visionary designs for skyscrapers. Pierced by service cores, with floor slabs extending outward from them, the buildings were designed to be clad entirely in glass. They were never built, but the pristine image Mies created of an ideal, crystalline edifice (whose precise function was not specified) had a lasting impact on the sensibilities of his Modernist colleagues and was eventually to emerge in altered form as the definitive architectural icon of the era.

Apart from the glass skyscraper projects (and his work for the *Weissenhofsiedlung* in Stuttgart), the building by Mies that was to have the greatest influence on his art and that of his followers was the German Pavilion at the 1929 World's Fair in Barcelona. A building of almost sublime intellectual content, it was made of crisp planes of travertine, polished marble, onyx, and glass that intersected with a lightness and geometric rigor comparable to paintings by the most radical abstract painters of the day. The free-flowing spaces of the interior evoked something of the feeling of Frank Lloyd Wright's work, which Mies had encountered through the Wasmuth Portfolio, but the floor plan could stand alone as a work of abstract graphic art. Here was an early but definitive statement of Mies's lifelong search for ways to reduce architecture to its fundamentals. In a telling remark made in the 1950s, Mies said: "I remember the first time I went to Italy. The sun and the blue skies were so bright, I thought I'd go crazy! I couldn't wait to go back to the north, where everything was gray and subtle."[13]

Mies's reputation had risen rapidly in Germany, and in 1930 Gropius, who had resigned as director of the Bauhaus two years earlier in hopes of calming internal artistic and political problems, suggested Mies for the post. Mies's tour lasted a mere three years, until pressure from the Nazis forced him and the remaining faculty members to close the institution for good. Not long afterward, Mies was invited to design a vacation house in Wyoming for a wealthy American family. (The invitation arose out of a recommendation by Alfred Barr at the Museum of Modern Art.) The house was never built, but the trip to America to

---

[13] Ibid., p. 207.

MIES VAN DER ROHE

work on its design had furthered contacts between Mies and some of the leading architectural schools about a teaching position.

The first contact came from Harvard, but Mies balked when he learned that Gropius would also be a candidate, and in 1938 he went instead to Chicago to become director of architecture at the Armour Institute, which was renamed the Illinois Institute of Technology (IIT) two years later following a merger with a local college.

The appointment was a wonderful coincidence, since Chicago was far more celebrated for skyscrapers than Cambridge. And Mies, on the strength of his all-glass projects alone, had established himself as the most innovative theorist in that medium. Although he later insisted that Chicago had no real influence on his work, a man who liked to characterize his own goal as an architecture of *beinahe nichts*, or "almost nothing," could not have avoided absorbing at least some of the no-nonsense practicality of the local architectural tradition. And although he may have been a surpassing artist, Mies seldom dwelt openly on the aesthetics of his work, preferring to emphasize such themes as "standardization of construction" and "economic considerations."

The firsthand experience of construction was something that had begun to disappear from American architectural training at about the time the architecture schools emerged as powerful institutions after the Civil War. That lack compounded the longstanding American proclivity to create high-style architecture based largely on graphic sources, as opposed to the European tradition, which relied on precedent and the experience of "master builders" skilled in construction as well as design. Mies was determined to restore that tradition, and totally revised the IIT curriculum to require a thorough knowledge of construction in all its phases.

But the curriculum was not the only area in which the new director made sweeping changes. Shortly after his appointment, Mies was asked to create a new campus for the school. The result became the first entirely modern academic complex in the country, and remains perhaps the most complete combination of Modernist architectural and planning ideals ever built, making even Gropius's graduate student housing complex at Harvard look slightly romantic. Over a period of fifteen years, Mies designed virtually all of the important structures for the eight city blocks of the new IIT campus, arranging them in an asymmetrical composition that created distinct exterior spaces without actually walling any of them off. What ultimately emerged was a three-dimensional expression of Mies's search for an architecture that was so thoroughly reduced in both form and function to its essence that it could be turned to almost any use and, he hoped, repeated with relative ease. Aware that the modern age would make constantly changing demands on the uses to which a building was put, Mies strove mightily for an architectural *Urtyp*, an essential form that would be infinitely flexible.

As a result, many of the buildings at IIT have an almost industrial look, and none of the forms clearly identifies its use. The insistence on this interchangeability of parts reached a slightly bizarre level with the design of the campus chapel, which was almost indistinguishable from the classroom and research buildings that surrounded it. The highest expression of Mies's reductivist impulse at IIT, however, was Crown Hall, finished in 1956. Intended to house IIT's school of architecture as well as its institute of design, the building is an enormous box, its roof suspended from four great girders spanning the width of the building, and thus eliminating any need for interior supports. In Crown Hall, Mies succeeded in creating what was in his mind the ideal work of architecture—one that was fundamentally simple, but also totally adaptable. In so doing, he showed his admiration for Albert Kahn's enormous factory spaces, but elevated them to the highest aesthetic plane through the knowing manipulation of proportion and a perfectionist's devotion to detail.

But it was the Miesian skyscraper that became the icon of urban America in the 1950s, fulfilling the promise of the glass towers Mies had conceived in the early 1920s. The Depression and World War II had slowed or halted expansion in virtually every area of American life except the military. Now, with peace and a new prosperity fueled by a growing corporate community, the country had an urgent need for new buildings of all sorts. And Mies was perfectly positioned to serve that need. Having consolidated his academic base of operations at IIT, Mies in 1947 was granted—largely through the intercession of Philip Johnson—a retrospective exhibition at the Museum of Modern Art in New York. With that stamp of approval, and the attendant publicity, Mies became an obvious candidate for the major commercial commissions of the day. (He had also come to look the part, expanding considerably at the waist, wearing elegantly tailored double-breasted suits, and indulging in fine cigars and many martinis.)

Mies had already come to the attention of a Chicago real estate developer who asked the architect to design a pair of twenty-six-story apartment towers at 860–880 Lake Shore Drive. In these speculative towers, finished in 1951, Mies succeeded in reducing the high-rise concept to its simplest terms, departing from the "traditional" Modernist system of wrapping a thin skin around an internal structure, and creating instead a steel frame rather like a cage of prefabricated steel members. In so doing, he created an opportunity for visual interest that sheer surfaces of glass, stone, or metal could not. With great skill and subtlety, Mies had narrow steel I-beams, the basic "stud" of modern construction, welded to the exterior of each of the structural columns of the buildings. His purported aim was the stiffening of the frame of each bay, but more important was the creation of a surface texture that relieved the potential monotony of a smooth facade, while emphasizing the verticality of the overall form. The architect later explained that he had used

Carter Wiseman

CROWN HALL,

ILLINOIS INSTITUTE

OF TECHNOLOGY,
Mies van der Rohe,
Chicago, 1956.
A jewel of a building
that could be used
for almost anything.

the device primarily because, without it, the building simply "did not look right."[14]

Predictably enough, Mies was criticized for such behavior by doctrinaire followers of Hitchcock and Johnson, who felt that he had indulged in a concealed form of ornament in violation of their stylistic canon. Indeed he had, but in such a way as to celebrate—albeit symbolically—the structural underpinnings of the building, much as Louis Sullivan had in adding vertical elements to the Wainwright and Guaranty buildings where no structural columns were required.

Mies's major monument remains the Seagram Building (1958) on New York's Park Avenue, where the architect took his technique to heights that were nothing less than sublime. Blessed with an enormous budget made possible by the owner's distillery business, the architect was able to indulge his taste for fine materials, using bronze for his ap-

---

[14] See Franz Schulze, *Mies van der Rohe, a Critical Biography* (Chicago: University of Chicago Press, 1985), p. 243.

plied I-beams, and expensive tinted glass. Seagram's cost per square foot came to nearly twice that of comparable buildings going up at the time. But as in his Chicago apartment towers, Mies infused what might have been a mere box with art through his sure sense of mass, proportion, and scale. As with all masterpieces, documenting the details never explains the result. The only proper way to appreciate Mies's accomplishment is

© Ezra Stoller/Esto

THE SEAGRAM BUILDING, *Mies van der Rohe, New York City, 1958.* The most famous Modernist skyscraper was covertly ornamental.

to compare it with the imitations that it spawned in cities across the land, where the absence of his eye for the relationship among parts—height to width, spandrels to columns, and such details as the slightly rounded form of the applied I-beams—produced buildings of similar size and shape, but without Seagram's serene self-assurance.

Apart from the lushness and elegance of the building itself, the distinguishing aspect of Seagram is its position on its site. Rather than fill the entire allowable space, which would have required the sort of regular setbacks used by Hood at McGraw-Hill, Mies set the tower ninety feet back from the front of the lot line and thirty feet in on either side, creating a far more dramatic effect. With the grand forecourt, which is broken only by symmetrical reflecting pools and invokes the interplay of water and mass Mies had explored with such virtuosity at the Barcelona Pavilion, the tower soars 516 feet with overwhelming effect, while allowing its admirers to appreciate its subtle beauty from an appropriate distance.

If imitations of the Seagram Building help demonstrate its quality as an object, an immediate precursor, the twenty-four-story Lever House (1952), is a reminder of how much Mies had improved on the competition. Designed by Gordon Bunshaft (1909–1990) of the firm of Skidmore, Owings & Merrill for a site across Park Avenue from the one Seagram was to occupy, Lever owes a considerable debt to Mies's own earlier imagery of high-rise design, but is fundamentally different in its composition. It is essentially a pair of opposed slabs, a vertical one rising at the edge of its horizontal counterpart. Although convincing enough as pure geometry (which alone created a critical sensation at the time of its completion), the scheme suffers upon close examination. Its main failing is that the open space created by lifting the lower slab on columns—unlike the plaza at the front of Seagram—does little to enhance the tower above, and is actually a rather bleak area for pedestrians. At the same time, the sleekness of the tower's surface, despite its blue-green glazing, contributes to an instant reading of its entire message, ultimately rendering the form predictable. Mies's tower, by contrast, changes constantly, if subtly, as a result of the crisp manipulation of color and surface shadows, making the even simpler form steadily more complex the longer it is pondered. The closest competitor in this regard is the Equitable Savings and Loan Association Building in Portland, finished in 1948, by Pietro Belluschi, who managed a similarly sensitive effect on an almost entirely flush surface by varying his materials—glass and aluminum—with comparable skill, if at humbler scale.

Ironically, it was in the speedy proliferation of the skyscraper form that its greatest potential for harm finally lay. Whether scaling the heights of elegance, as Seagram and the Equitable did, or trolling the aesthetic depths, as did so many lesser versions, they were ultimately perceived as repetitive, impersonal, and authoritarian. Not coincidentally, those very qualities attracted the attention of the country's expanding corporate community, which saw in these large new forms an opportunity to affirm the power of financial success. In this, the commercial patrons of the 1950s differed not at all from the great Renaissance merchants of Florence and Rome, who had embraced the *palazzo* form for much the same reason, or indeed the Woolworths and the Singers. Unfortunately, what appeared at the beginning of the corporate high-rise era to be easily replicated was in fact not at all. For all Mies's insistence on the wide applicability of his architecture, the best examples of it—Crown Hall; the house he designed for Edith Farnsworth (1951) outside Chicago; 860–880 Lake Shore Drive; and Seagram—were virtually custom-made. When imitators tried their hand at his example, the results inevitably fell short, as any number of "Miesian" buildings of the 1960s bear witness.

And for all the insistence by the Modernists that they were originally inspired by social goals, the architecture to which they gave birth had less to do with the lessons of the machine in service to society than with an underlying urge for mechanistic order. There was little concern for context, and a clear aversion to the old architectural fabric. In a memorable scene from the film version of Ayn Rand's 1943 paean to individualism, *The Fountainhead*, the architect Howard Roark, played by Gary Cooper, declares: "My ideas are mine! Those who accept them must do so on my terms!"

More the pity for the United States, whose fledgling urban identity had shown considerable strength along with its many weaknesses, but was in desperate need of nurture and was ill-equipped to resist a European-bred movement that appeared so alluringly self-confident.

The greatest irony was that a country whose most eloquent architectural spokesmen—Jefferson, Sullivan, Wright—had for so long com-

LEVER HOUSE,
Gordon Bunshaft,
New York City, 1952.
The dominance of
the geometry
compromised the
impact on the street.

Rotch Visual Collections

**THE EQUITABLE
BUILDING**, *Pietro Belluschi,
Portland, Oregon,
1948.* A triumph
of skin.

THE FARNSWORTH HOUSE, *Mies van der Rohe, Plano, Illinois, 1951.* Skyscraper abstraction at domestic scale.

plained about its own dependence on Europe was so ready to embrace yet another European import. What made the capitulation acceptable to many was that the movement had been promoted as an *international* style. But beneath that camouflage was the fact that the nation still did not yet have enough confidence in its own—the Goodhues, the Gills, the Wrights—to stay an independent course.

One can only wonder where the best American architects of the 1920s and 1930s might have emerged had they not been overwhelmed by the European influence. Certainly one clue is provided by the insistent individuality of Frank Lloyd Wright, who had receded from the public eye following his marital upheavals, but was now ready to reappear on a wave of interest in a new romanticism that was soon joined by a growing group of architects with little patience for the chilly rationalism of the Modernist pioneers.

The Romantic Resistance

E ven stripped of its original social mission, the Modern movement's abstract aesthetic proved compelling well past the demise of its founders. By the late 1980s, there was even talk of a Modernist revival. But even in its heyday, the philosophy as expressed in architecture left some practitioners—as well as clients and users— unsatisfied. All but overwhelmed by the industrial and corporate imperatives embodied by the rationality of orthodox Modernism was a lingering appetite for something warmer, more humane—more romantic. For all their excesses, the eclectics had provided buildings with which people could connect at a personal and associational level. The classical pillars on a courthouse evoked images of Athenian democracy and Roman law, no less than the Gothic gargoyles on a college library evoked images of medieval scholars bent over their parchments. If such imagery was used indiscriminately from time to time, it was at least interesting to the eye. Finials and ornamental vergeboards were things that could be measured by the eye and related instantly to buildings one had seen before. However overblown some eclectic facades might seem, passers-by knew that the buildings had been touched by human hands, while a Modernist curtain wall proudly proclaimed its machined origins and extended no invitation. Abstraction and utility, for all their allure to the mind, left much to be desired by the heart. Frank Lloyd Wright had known that from the outset, and a generation of others would learn it soon enough.

Of all the buildings Wright designed, one of those he most cherished was among his earliest. It was the sixty-foot-high windmill he built on his family's farm in Spring Green, Wisconsin, in 1896. It was—and is—a wonderfully simple object in the landscape, contrasting with the attenuated erector-set form of the standard metal version so common across the American prairies. In plan, the tower is an octagon pierced by a diamond-shaped form, and in elevation these two rise to a lookout monitor, which is topped by the fourteen-foot wheel, giving the whole a vague resemblance to a modern airport control tower with a radar rig on top.

For Wright, the most important aspect of the tower was its unusual structural bracing, which he predicted accurately would outlast the factory-made models on the surrounding farms. In recognition of the way the two basic forms embraced each other, the architect christened this piece of unorthodox engineering "Romeo and Juliet." The gesture can fairly be interpreted as a characteristic case of Wright tweaking the Midwestern morality of the day, but he could have done that with any number of titles. It would not be stretching the interpretation to say that Wright saw in this structure, with its deep foundation and elemental function, a symbol of the drawing together of natural and mechanical forces that so informed his entire career.

By the time Wright left for Europe in 1909, the Prairie houses alone would have constituted a full and brilliant career for most architects. But his durable genius was to be given new energy by what he saw dur-

Pedro E. Guerrero

"ROMEO AND JULIET," *Frank Lloyd Wright, Spring Green, Wisconsin, 1896.* An early design that combined fantasy with durability.

ing his excursion abroad, especially in Germany and Austria. In Berlin, the pioneering architect Peter Behrens had among his employees at various times Walter Gropius, Mies van der Rohe, and Le Corbusier. In Vienna, Adolf Loos was stripping his buildings of applied ornament, while others, like Otto Wagner, Joseph Maria Olbrich, and Josef Hoffmann, were seeking to integrate new forms of ornament into their designs by turning to exotic sources beyond the European tradition. Sinuous plant forms swirled across the facades of major urban monuments, whose entrances were often announced with heroic sculptures of abstracted human figures, and gilt inlay and ceramic tiles added even further to the visual mix.

Although Wright came into direct contact with much of what was happening on the European architectural frontiers, it is fair to assume that he also absorbed considerable history as well. After all, he was a mature man of forty-two, an internationally known architect, and had never before been to Europe. No doubt to avoid further scandal over the abandonment of his family for a married woman, Wright left scant documentation of his sojourn abroad. But despite his repeated insistence throughout his life that he was never influenced by any other architect except Louis Sullivan, this proudly provincial midwesterner with such an insatiable aesthetic appetite was surely absorbing everything he could use from what he saw on his travels, which took him and Mamah Cheney to London, Paris, Berlin, and Vienna, as well as to Bavaria, the castles of the Rhine Valley, and Tuscany.[1]

Having concluded work on the portfolio the Wasmuth firm was about to publish in Berlin, Wright in 1910 returned to the United States and embarked on the construction of his retreat at Taliesin. In addition to a refuge, Taliesin eventually became a community, providing work space and accommodations for "apprentices" who paid to do chores while studying architecture at the feet of the master. One of the earliest projects to be developed at Taliesin was Midway Gardens, a recreational complex for the South Side of Chicago. Completed in May 1914, the project was especially noteworthy for its ornamentation, which included freestanding sculptural figures. While Wright would not admit it, the inspiration appears to have been the strikingly similar figures by the Viennese Secessionist architect Josef Hoffmann. (Successful as the Gardens proved for a short period, they were put out of business by Prohibition, and were demolished in 1929.) If Wright's work until his departure for Europe had been characterized by a steady simplification and refinement of forms, it now took on a new and intricately decorative dimension that can probably be attributed to his experience in Europe. Characteristically for Wright, however, the ornament he developed and the ways in which he used it were unique, showing once again his extraordinary ability to draw inspiration from disparate sources and integrate them in his own fashion.

---

[1] Anthony Alofsin, *Frank Lloyd Wright, the Lost Years, 1910–1922* (Chicago and London: University of Chicago Press, 1993). Alofsin describes in detail what little is known about Wright's European trip, and speculates with authority on what the architect may have absorbed from the experience.

Pedro E. Guerrero

Midway Gardens marked the return of Wright's creative vigor following the European exile, and the atmosphere of Taliesin was, according to apprentices of the period, nothing short of electric. Wright's own description of the enterprise conjures up images of a medieval court, with modern equivalents of knights, ladies, and vassals paying homage to their lord. But the storybook aspects of Taliesin assumed tragic dimensions on August 15, 1914. While Wright was away, one of his employees went berserk, murdering seven people, including Mamah Cheney and two of her children (by her earlier marriage), and burning much of the compound to the ground.

The ghastliness of the event would have destroyed most men. Yet after an extended period of grief Wright seemed almost to take strength from the tragedy, embarking on a series of buildings that constituted an entirely new phase in his artistic development. Having rebuilt the destroyed portions of Taliesin, Wright was offered an extraordinary commission. Even before his 1905 trip to Japan, he had been an admirer of

TALIESIN,
Frank Lloyd Wright,
Spring Green,
Wisconsin, 1911.
A personal statement
of refuge and retreat.

Japanese prints, and he soon became an authoritative collector. Apparently through his contacts in collecting circles, Wright's name was proposed to a Japanese group looking for an architect to replace Tokyo's old Imperial Hotel, which had been built in 1890 to accommodate Westerners visiting the city, and was by now too small. Wright was asked to take on the project, and spent much of the following five years dedicated to it. The commission provided him not only a spectacular architectural opportunity, but also a welcome second exile in which to recover from the personal horrors that had overtaken Taliesin.

The new Imperial Hotel displayed an innovative combination of influences. Its symmetrical H-shaped plan was almost Beaux-Arts in spirit, and unlike anything Wright had undertaken up to that time. Although he had always expressed contempt for the French academic tradition (to the point of turning down Daniel Burnham's offer of the all-expenses-paid course in Paris), Wright had to have seen some of its most impressive buildings during his visit to France. And since the Beaux-Arts system was uniquely suited to large monumental commissions—and the Imperial client was not likely to favor radical organizational schemes—Wright could be forgiven for turning to that system in taking on a building of a scale he had never attempted. One need only contrast the organization of the hotel with his free-flowing plan for the McCormick House to realize that Wright in Japan was working with a new set of organizational tools.

Beyond the hotel's plan, its most striking element was its ornamentation. Here again, Wright seems to have absorbed the impact of applied ornament from his European trip, and used it with a richness that, at times, approached vulgarity. It is as if he were trying out every conceivable variation on the primary geometric forms—circle, square, triangle—without waiting to discipline them. And although the ornamental scheme had a certain internal consistency, it bore no direct relationship to anything specifically Japanese. Indeed, it seemed more closely related to contemporary Viennese ornament, much of which Wright may have seen on his Continental tour. Wright here seems once more to be creating a world unto itself, in formal terms, at least, rather like that at Taliesin.

Apart from the unprecedented scope of the design, the most compelling aspect of the Imperial Hotel was its engineering. The architect took special pains to protect the building against the earthquakes that

were common to the area, and set it on a forest of concrete piers driven into the ground. The floors were cantilevered off the piers in a way Wright likened to trays balanced on a waiter's fingertips. The exterior walls were self-supporting shells. Wright's precautions were amply justified when an earthquake struck in 1923, destroying much of the surrounding city, but leaving the hotel intact. (It fell to wreckers in 1968.)

Wright's increasing interest in ornamental systems found further expression in a series of houses begun in California during the final phases of the Imperial Hotel project. The first and most powerful of these was for a wealthy Los Angeles patron of the arts, Aline Barnsdall. Built in the hills overlooking the city, the Barnsdall House (1921) was constructed primarily of poured concrete in crisp, geometrical forms that strongly recalled those of Mayan architecture. Wright had never been to the great Mayan sites, but numerous books on them were available to him, and models of the major monuments had been exhibited at various times in the United States, giving Wright all he needed for yet another excursion into the integration of exotic forms into his own evolving ornamental schemes. In this case, he transmuted the client's favorite flower, the hollyhock, into the theme for all of the building's ornament.

More than ever before, Wright began to integrate ornament and structure in the Millard House, completed in 1923 in Pasadena and

BARNSDALL HOUSE, *Frank Lloyd Wright, Los Angeles, 1921.* The ornament demonstrated Wright's continuing explorations of new forms.

known as "La Miniatura." Here, he developed what he called a "textile block" system of concrete blocks, so named because of the way the blocks were "woven" together by metal rods to create an integrated structural fabric. The system, which Wright hoped would lead to a standardized method of building quickly and at low cost, in fact proved highly impractical—some thirty individual molds were required to produce the various shapes required by the Millard design. But it was yet another expression of Wright's search for ways to combine technology with nature. While he abandoned the strip windows of the Prairie houses, he still welcomed the natural world, in this case through openings pierced in the concrete blocks themselves.

California proved only a temporary diversion for Wright, but it marked the completion of a transitional phase in his career. He had left for Europe in 1909 as a brilliant but essentially regional talent. As a result of his exposure to the great monuments and latest architectural movements of Europe, and then to contemporary Japan, Wright stood virtually alone among his contemporaries in the scope of his firsthand knowledge of architecture outside America. Although Taliesin would be struck by fire twice more, personal tragedy was now largely behind him. Wright's second marriage, to Miriam Noel, in 1923, ended in divorce four years later, but in 1928, he married his third and last wife, Olgivanna Lazovich, an immigrant from Yugoslavia who was as devoted to mysticism as she was to Wright. With the formidable Olgivanna at his side, Wright began to emerge as a force above and beyond his sources in the American heartland.

Yet commissions eluded him. Apart from the California houses, he had little to do—a situation that was soon compounded by the onset of the Depression. Wright responded by concentrating on the Taliesin Fellowship, a formalization of the apprentice system that he developed shortly after construction of his Wisconsin retreat. And he began to explore visionary schemes that revealed more than ever the romantic instincts that were so deeply embedded in his being. They ranged from a cathedral to a planetarium to high-rise towers for New York City. But what unified them all was the persistent vision of an ideal community in which the residents could indulge their separateness from what Wright would come to call the "mobocracy."

In 1935, Wright gave physical form to an idea that had been gestating for years, and which he christened "Broadacre City." Even while designing mansions for such wealthy clients as Robie and Barnsdall, Wright had been concerned about housing for the middle classes. With the onset of the Depression, these concerns became urgent and widespread. As originally conceived, Broadacre City would have occupied four square miles of land, on which each of fourteen hundred families was to have its own acre. The community was to be sustained by farming and small factories, the traffic patterns organized for maximum efficiency and safety, and the housing constructed of largely prefabricated units. Impractical in any number of ways, Broadacre City nonetheless attempted to address the problem of how to integrate housing with the automobile, an issue shunned by many planners of an even more romantic stripe who continued to look for ways to minimize the presence of cars. Although Wright characteristically denied any links to the utopian communities proposed over the years by American religious leaders, his community had unmistakable links to his views about the proper way to live in an independent land. In that sense, Wright's plan differed substantially from the rationalist schemes of his European contemporaries, who tended toward more socialistic ideals.

Ironically, the essentially isolationist—and anti-urban—quality of Wright's populist thinking expressed in Broadacre City and his related designs for economical "Usonian" houses saw its most forceful expression over the next two decades in three designs for the very rich. (To be sure, wealthy clients were almost the only ones available at the time.) The first of these buildings was a weekend retreat for the Pittsburgh department store magnate Edgar Kaufmann. The site was a remote one, on a cascading stream roughly two hours' drive from the city. Wright embraced the setting, producing a work of architecture so compelling in its sensitivity to both form and nature that it has become one of the classics of modern architecture. Begun in 1934 and finished three years later, Fallingwater—as the building was named—was a series of overlapping concrete trays set into a wooded slope and anchored to the underlying rock. The most dramatic aspect of the building was the way two of the trays extended out over the stream at a point where it cascaded over a low waterfall.

While the crisp geometry of the trays bears a superficial similarity to the spare planes then in use by the European avant-garde, it was used in ways unthinkable to Gropius or Mies, whose goal most often was to emphasize the distinction between the man-made and the natural. The

FALLINGWATER (THE KAUFMANN HOUSE), *Frank Lloyd Wright, Bear Run, Pennsylvania, 1937.* Wright's supreme achievement in blending the natural and the man-made.

IIT campus could have been located almost anywhere, and that was part of its power: It stood deliberately apart from its surroundings. By contrast, Fallingwater could not have been anywhere but where it was. Wright accomplished this site-specificity by exploiting the topography as he had in no previous building, sliding the horizontal forms over and under each other, but then stabilizing them by allowing the bedrock to emerge inside the house as the base for one of his signature stone chimneys. Although the horizontality is familiar from Wright's Prairie houses, here it takes on added energy as it is integrated into the sloping site. If the dominant horizontality of the Robie House created a sense of movement across its narrow site, Fallingwater seems to be simultaneously emerging from and receding into its elemental sources in the surrounding earth; from certain angles, the house actually seems to be in the grip of stony fingers reaching up out of the ground. As in no other building he designed, Wright embodied in Fallingwater his convictions about the bonding of the man-made and the natural in a unified whole.

The second major project of this period in Wright's career was the S. C. Johnson & Son Administration Building, in Racine, Wisconsin, begun in 1936 and completed in 1939. Like the Larkin Building in Buffalo, the Johnson Building was to be a place that celebrated the virtues of work (the company manufactured wax and other household products), but also made it an uplifting experience. And even more than in the Larkin Building, Wright in Racine pushed his technological inventiveness to the limit. The focus of the building was an enormous room for administrative workers. Above it was space for executive offices, as well as a theater, the form of which provided a bridge to an adjacent structure for parking cars.

Like the Larkin Building, the Johnson complex was entirely inward-looking, a self-contained ideal environment. Wright provided no windows in the main workroom, but suffused it with light by creating a roof skylight and a clerestory of glass tubes bonded together with caulk. Supporting the roof was a cluster of concrete columns that swelled gently upward to circular plates, creating the impression of attentuated mushrooms, or lily pads. The plates were joined where they met, creating a rigid structure for the entire building.

The saga of the "lily pad" columns has assumed legendary proportions in the history of American architectural engineering. When Wright proposed them, the local building inspectors balked, insisting that the spindly columns were too weak to support their intended loads. In a deft publicity gesture, Wright had a test column piled high with sandbags and invited local press photographers to attend. The column eventually collapsed, but only after demonstrating that it could hold forty-eight tons more than the twelve required by the inspectors. Far more problematical were the Pyrex glass tubes Wright used to light the

JOHNSON & SON ADMINISTRATION BUILDING, *Frank Lloyd Wright, Racine, Wisconsin, 1939.* The main space was supposed to suggest a church.

interior. Over the years, the caulking failed, producing leaks, a problem solved only years later with flexible silicone sealants.

For all the debate over Wright's innovations in structure and materials, the greatest achievement of the Johnson Building was its magical interior experience. The room created by the sixty closely-spaced twenty-one-foot-high columns is reminiscent of a dense but sheltering forest, while the atmosphere created by the translucent tubing is almost submarine, and even otherworldly. The overall gentleness of the space is amplified by the alternating curves of the balconies overlooking the entrance, which, in Wright's characteristic fashion, is compressed by the addition of a bridge linking the mezzanine balconies, making the arrival in the main space all the more dramatic. Even with the clatter and bustle of a normal workday, the main room still has an almost religious quality—appropriate enough for a company whose founder expected devotional loyalty from his employees. The addition of a research tower, completed in 1950, only added to the quasi-religious impression of the overall complex by creating the equivalent of a church spire.

By now, Wright had established a second headquarters for his operations, at what became known as Taliesin West (1938), in the desert outside Scottsdale, Arizona. Used primarily in the winter, when the Wisconsin Taliesin was lashed by winds and snow, the Arizona outpost was a successor to the Ocatilla camp near Phoenix that Wright and his entourage had built of wood and canvas while working on the design for a resort in the area some years before. Taliesin West was a more elaborate complex, integrating living quarters with a large drafting room, service buildings, and even a small auditorium where weekly black-tie recitals were conducted to instruct the apprentices in the social as well as the architectural graces.

Although Taliesin West shares many of the familiar Wright touches from the Prairie days—a long, low profile, a dynamically irregular plan, and compressed entries—it is absolutely appropriate to its arid site. Just as the Wisconsin Taliesin seemed to belong to its hill, suggesting a medieval keep, Taliesin West seemed to bond with the desert, the spare and almost primitive shapes evoking the spirit of prehistoric encampments. The masonry walls are made of local stone of varied colors pressed into a concrete matrix, making the connection between the desert floor and the building almost seamless, while exploiting the materials for their naturally decorative potential. The walkways intersect with the buildings at unexpected (but carefully planned) angles, presenting a succession of arresting visual compositions. For all that, nothing about the imagery is imitative or literal. As at Fallingwater, but in a totally different setting, the forms seem to have evolved—to use Wright's favorite word—"organically," from the site.

Taliesin West is as much or more about landscape design as it is about architecture in the conventional sense. And it is proof that Wright's proclamations about searching for the roots of architecture in nature were more than theoretical. Although the Robie House was located in Chicago, Wright wished to see it as an abstraction and evocation of the surrounding prairies. Taliesin West confirmed even more clearly his belief in the possibility of linking the natural and the man-made. Again, it does so in a regionally appropriate way; this was not a transplant of a foreign idea to an inhospitable setting. In the desert, Wright demonstrated

TALIESIN WEST, *Frank Lloyd Wright, Scottsdale, Arizona, 1938.* Even in the desert, Wright showed an uncanny understanding of the land.

that he was not a prisoner of any natural setting, but was able to embrace a site with an uncanny understanding of its essence. What unified the projects was their self-containment.

There is no greater expression of that persistently inward-looking aesthetic than the Solomon R. Guggenheim Museum in New York City, begun in 1943 but not completed until 1959. Here, Wright took abstract form and modern technology to their contemporary limits, using reinforced concrete to create a soaring spiral that swelled as it rose, creating a building that was as much sculpture as it was architecture.

With ample justification, critics of the building have attacked the Guggenheim for ignoring both its urban context and its role in exhibiting art. Indeed, there was and would be nothing like it on the staid Fifth Avenue streetscape, and the continuous slanted ramp Wright used instead of horizontal floors made the display of conventionally framed paintings especially difficult. Nonetheless, the elemental power of the formal concept was enough to overwhelm the building's shortcomings.

While the Guggenheim confirmed the fundamentally introverted nature of Wright's architecture, it also marked the culmination of a trend that had been evident for many years. If Wright's early buildings seemed to cling to the earth, embedding themselves in their sites, the Guggenheim seemed ready to spiral off its own foundations. And his conceptual drawings of the period show other, even more levitational impulses at work. If Wright's romanticism had begun with Romeo and Juliet in the farmscape of Wisconsin, it seemed at the end of his life to have evolved into a fascination with the celestial.

Meanwhile, however, the influence of European rationalism had proven far easier than Wright's for American architects to follow, and the spiritual offspring of Gropius and Mies were transforming the American cityscape in the image of their mentors. But even before Wright died, in 1959, his relentless attacks on Modernism were finding sympathetic listeners among younger architects who had begun to tire of the inaccessibility of much that they had been taught.

FRANK LLOYD WRIGHT, 1953

One alternative was to embrace the plastic potential of the new materials for which many orthodox Modernists had such affection, partic-

Pedro E. Guerrero

ularly concrete. Once Wright's Guggenheim had set an example of architecture as abstract sculpture, a few younger architects began to pursue what might be called a more literally symbolic version. The Finnish-born Eero Saarinen (1910–1961) had actually wanted to become a sculptor, but followed the path of his famous father Eliel, and embarked on architecture instead.

Although the elder Saarinen did not win the *Chicago Tribune* competiton, the attention his runner-up design attracted prompted him to visit the United States for the first time, in 1923, and he decided to stay, becoming head of what developed into the influential Cranbrook Academy of Art in Bloomfield Hills, Michigan. There he concentrated on the design of the campus, and on a curriculum that embraced arts, crafts, and furniture, as well as architecture. Meanwhile, Saarinen's son was emerging as more than a mere assistant to his father, and in 1948,

THE SOLOMON R. GUGGENHEIM MUSEUM, *Frank Lloyd Wright, New York City, 1959.* Hard on paintings, but a sublime work of architecture.

G. E. Kidder Smith/Corbis-Bettmann

when both competed for the Jefferson National Expansion Memorial in St. Louis, Eero prevailed.

Eero Saarinen's design, which was not executed until 1964, was a 590-foot-high catenary arch in stainless steel. Although the form was elegantly simple, and the technology was contemporary, the image was fundamentally romantic: a gateway to the West symbolizing in almost literal terms the opening of the vast American landscape to the pioneers of the past century.

This combination of Modernist method with romantic imagery was only partially apparent in Saarinen's other major design of his early years, the General Motors Technical Center in Warren, Michigan (1946–57). This multibuilding complex showed a strong debt to the geometrical compositions of the campuses at IIT by Mies. But Saarinen departed from that precedent in his treatment of an enormous water tower, which the architect rendered as a monumetal work of sculpture in gleaming stainless steel.

A more forceful expression of Saarinen's willingness to tailor his architecture to both the practical and the thematic needs of his clients was the pair of residential colleges he designed for Yale University (1962). Responding to the prevailing Gothic style of the nearby buildings that had been designed by James Gamble Rogers some thirty years before, Saarinen created a complex of irregular low forms punctuated by towers, and clad the entire composition in a layer of randomly shaped stone set in a matrix of poured concrete not unlike the combination Wright had used at Taliesin West. In sympathy with the historic references of the earlier buildings, the Saarinen colleges evoke a scholastic European past, but they do so in a vernacular that has shed any direct borrowings from specific periods—including European Modernism. Much more than Rogers, Saarinen was willing to inhabit the spirit of the place, and to seek out forms appropriate to it, rather than to impose forms based on tradition or aesthetic ideology.

Saarinen's impulse to honor the spirit of the commission in symbolic terms took a dramatically different shape at the headquarters for the John Deere Company, in Moline, Illinois (1963). Deere was a leading manufacturer of farm machinery, and Saarinen selected as one of his primary materials for the building a type of steel that weathered to a handsome brown color. He used the steel to enclose the main building

EERO SAARINEN in an enormous cage, communicating simultaneously a practicality of structure and an affection for the innumerable rusting plow blades and tractor frames that document the passage of generations of farmers across the American landscape. "Farm machinery is not slick, shiny metal but forged iron and steel in big, forceful, functional shapes," the architect explained.[2]

Saarinen's legacy as a romantic was made most secure by a trio of buildings he undertook beginning in the late 1950s. The Ingalls Hockey Rink (1959), also at Yale, became an instant landmark because of the sweeping form of its roof, which was suspended from a narrow concrete spine. This was not a literal interpretation of the movement of skaters, but its curved profile seemed highly appropriate for the commission, and the dramatic interior succeeded admirably at communicating the special combination of grace and violence represented by the sport the architecture was intended to accommodate.

---

[2] Aline B. Saarinen, ed., *Eero Saarinen on His Work* (New Haven, CT, and London: Yale University Press, 1968), p. 82.

At Idlewild (now Kennedy) Airport in New York City, Saarinen turned concrete to even more ambitious purposes, creating in his terminal for Trans World Airlines a shape that was unapologetically symbolic of flight. To most visitors the building looks very much like a bird about to take wing, although Saarinen protested that his goal, as at the hockey rink, was merely to express an abstraction. The TWA Building, which was begun in 1956 and completed in 1962, was criticized for appearing to be made entirely of sculptural concrete, when in fact the structure was braced by an internal web of reinforcing steel. But the fundamental message of the material as an expression of the architectural purpose emerged with unmistakable clarity despite the dissembling.

A more refined example of a similar program was Saarinen's terminal building for Dulles Airport, outside Washington (1962). There, he seemed less seduced by the attraction of doing something just because the materials made it possible. The imagery at Dulles is less literal than at either Ingalls or TWA, and the structural system more easily understood: an enormous sheet of concrete slung from a set of concrete hooks. Or, as Saarinen described it, "like a huge, continuous hammock suspended between concrete trees."[3] At Dulles, Saarinen caught the essence of the building's function without succumbing to a more simplistic—and therefore more perishable—effect. But while Dulles remains a modern monument to the confluence of use and imagery (and has since been expanded according to Saarinen's original designs), it is also handicapped by its uniqueness. No lessons flowed from this building because, apart from copying it, there was no way to expand its application. In the end, Saarinen's was, like Wright's, an architecture of emotion applied to specific requirements and sites.

In the 1950s and 1960s, an increasing number of architects began, like Saarinen, to find ways to return to architecture the human presence of which it had been so thoroughly stripped during the machine age. Among these were such figures as Edward Durell Stone, Minoru Yamasaki, and Philip Johnson (who, despite his original loyalty to Mies, had, as an independent architect, become increasingly impatient with Modernism). But most of their work of the period was dogged by superficial attempts to embellish, rather than rethink, the forms that had emerged under Mies and Gropius. Stone made a career of draping oth-

---

[3] Ibid., p.104.

TWA TERMINAL, *Eero Saarinen, New York City, 1962.* Architectural sculpture that verged on the literal.

erwise unexceptional boxes with ornamental screens of concrete, while Yamasaki turned to attenuated, rather effete columns to pretty up his work, producing such insubstantial designs as the Woodrow Wilson School of Public and International Affairs at Princeton (1965), and, in 1977, the overbearing 110-story World Trade Center towers in New York City. Johnson, meanwhile, immersed himself in a series of buildings whose combination of predictability and superficiality moved one critic to describe them as "ballet-classicism."

An architect who confronted the burdens of the Modernist legacy with considerably more courage was Paul Rudolph (1918–1997), who had studied under Gropius at Harvard, but had rapidly grown disillusioned and had set off on his own course. Rudolph was no less a romantic than Saarinen, but while Saarinen searched for an appropriate form for each of his commissions, Rudolph seemed eager to find a language that would apply to everything he did. The vocabulary on which

he eventually settled was a coarse one. His favorite material was concrete poured with a corduroy texture made even more rugged by hammering the raised ridges to expose the underlying aggregate of stone. The technique created a powerful visual effect, assuming an almost ornamental quality in some cases. But it was a hostile surface and contributed to Rudolph's reputation as a major figure in the "brutalist" phase of modern architecture.

In at least one of Rudolph's buildings, however, the abrasive treatment of the concrete came together with a lyrical sense of sculptural form and interior spatial gymnastics to create a classic of its period. The building was the Art and Architecture Building at Yale University, completed in 1963. Although plagued from its dedication by failures ranging from inadequate heating and ventilating to the stingy studio spaces accorded the students of painting and sculpture, the building had an undeniable authority. Purely as sculpture, it presented a dynamic as-

DULLES AIRPORT, *Eero Saarinen, Chantilly, Virginia, 1962.* A building about the feeling of flight.

semblage of horizontal and vertical forms that came together with a rare sense of equipoise. The effect was especially welcome on its urban site, where the building provided a strong statement at a location where the street grid changed direction, and completed a formal and historical progression that included a neo-Gothic classroom building, and a neo-Renaissance art gallery with a 1953 Modernist addition. Rudolph's interior, if it proved confusing to get around in, was an unmatched excercise in spatial interpenetration. Ceiling heights ranged from seven to twenty-eight feet; and although officially described as as a nine-story building, it had thirty-six changes in level expressed in landings and mezzanines that fed into each other both horizontally and vertically with spectacular theatrical effect.

The Art and Architecture Building confirmed Rudolph's boldness in abandoning the faith to which many of his Harvard classmates continued to cling in favor of a more autonomous course. But in breaking away, Rudolph ultimately succumbed to excess. The very idea of using hammered concrete as an interior surface—as he did at Yale and at the University of Illinois, among other places—seemed symbolic of Rudolph's willingness to subject his buildings' users to a certain amount of physical pain should they brush up against the walls. His architecture, not to mention his plans for redeveloping New York City's waterfront, eventually verged on the bombastic, leaving him rather isolated in his profession—heroic, to be sure, but trying too hard. In Rudolph's defense, the need to break away from the powerful legacy of Gropius and Mies almost guaranteed a measure of excess, just as the need to sever the ties with neoclassicism had created an offputting absolutism among the early Modernists.

The one leading architect who seemed to have no need to do open battle with his predecessors was Louis I. Kahn (1901–1974), who produced in a remarkably short time a magisterial body of work that fundamentally redirected the way architectural questions were posed and answered.

Kahn loved elemental forms modulated by exquisite details. He had a unique sense of materials and of the ways in which they can be joined together. He had a confident way with grand spaces, but also understood the importance of nooks and crannies. He had a sublime sensitivity to light, and he had an unashamed reverence for architectural history, from which he drew enough sustenance to reinvigorate and

Michael Marsland

steady an art that had, in the aftermath of Modernism, all but lost its
way. Although Kahn was not prolific, he built enough buildings of such
high quality to gain him the undisputed status of heir—spiritually if not
stylistically—to Wright, Le Corbusier, and Mies.

Born on an island off Estonia in 1901, Kahn came to the United
States in 1906 with his mother and siblings to join his father, who had
settled in Philadelphia. Kahn abandoned plans to study painting, and
instead enrolled as an architecture student at the University of Pennsylvania under Paul Cret. Adept at music, too, Kahn helped to pay his way
through Penn by playing the organ in Philadelphia movie houses.[4] At
the time, Penn was one of the most powerful schools of architecture in
the country, and Kahn would never lose his affection for Cret or for the
Beaux-Arts classicism promulgated by his teacher. In 1941, Kahn joined
forces with George Howe, who gave Kahn a firsthand taste of Modernism in its most refined American form. Kahn went on to become a
visiting critic and faculty member at the Yale School of Architecture,

**ART AND
ARCHITECTURE
BUILDING**,
*Paul Rudolph,
New Haven,
Connecticut, 1963.*
The brutalist
execution was
mitigated by the
spatial dynamics
of the interior.

[4] Remarks by Rodney Armstrong, former librarian at the Phillips Exeter Academy, on the occasion of the library's twentieth anniversary, November 7, 1991.

and in 1950 won a fellowship to the American Academy in Rome. The experience lasted only three months, but allowed Kahn to wander not just among the monuments of Roman antiquity but as far afield as Greece, Palestine, and Egypt.

Kahn was a famously passionate man whose followers came to treat him as something of a guru and quoted his aphorisms—such as, "What does the building want to be?" and "What does the brick say?"—as close to holy writ. His early career spanned both the Depression and World War II, a period when architectural work was scarce, and he spent many years working on socially redeeming but aesthetically undernourished housing designs for factory workers and veterans. His first major building—not finished until he was fifty-two—was the addition to the Yale University Art Gallery, a commission he won in 1951 in part through the efforts of his former associate George Howe, who had become chairman of Yale's department of architecture. A spare building that turns one blank wall to the street, while greeting the courtyard behind with a delicately composed glass facade, the gallery betrayed a debt to the geometric order of the reigning architectural philosophy. But inside, it showed a bold interest in changing the accepted rules. The rectangular form is pierced by an exposed concrete cylinder housing the main staircase, and a similarly exposed rectangle, which contains the elevator and other mechanical necessities. In isolating these functions and leaving their raw forms exposed with such sculptural vigor, Kahn was showing an early commitment to what became his philosophy of "served" and "servant" spaces. He took the concept further by spanning the exhibition areas with ceilings of reinforced concrete molded into tetrahedrons. The form—which was derived from the space frames developed by Buckminster Fuller—was left exposed so that the visitor to the gallery was made instantly aware not just of the way the building was constructed, but also of the decorative dimension of the structure itself. (The visual intrigue was increased by assorted pipes and wires, which normally would have been concealed, but which Kahn threaded through holes in the ceiling concrete.)

After the Yale Art Gallery, Kahn went on to design the Richards Medical Research Building at the University of Pennsylvania (1965). There, he took the ideas formed at Yale to another, but vertical dimension, evoking in many who saw it the romantic imagery of the towers of Italian hill towns—which the architect had admired during his first trip to

Europe, in 1928—while honoring the system of served and servant spaces by housing the utilities in the towers and suspending the laboratory spaces between them. Among the many virtues of the Richards Building is the way Kahn assembled the parts. The compositions of materials and colors remain pleasing in themselves (and particularly sensitive to the palette used by Cope and Stewardson for their neo-Tudor quadrangles nearby); and they are strengthened by the forthright fashion in which the architect put the structural elements together. The joinery of the building makes immediate visual sense, even to the uninitiated; there is no doubt about what is held up by what. By blending his architectural parts with such skill, Kahn created a building that remains convincing to one's understanding of structure, but beautiful to look at as well. Unfortunately, Kahn's attention to the aesthetics of the building overwhelmed his concern for its function, which proved woefully inadequate to the scientists who had to work in the laboratories.

If the Richards towers seemed to invoke the hill towns of Tuscany, the Salk Institute for Biological Studies in La Jolla, California (1965) showed Kahn's abiding affection for the ruins of ancient Rome. It also showed Kahn's enduring debt to Paul Cret and the Beaux-Arts, which has traditionally been criticized for its emphasis on symmetry and axiality, but under Cret was interpreted as a search for subtle variations on the underlying order to create designs that were, if orderly, also fresh. At Salk, Kahn created two parallel rows of four-story towers. The towers served as private studies for Salk researchers, who conducted their work in the laboratories that were distributed along the outside of the complex and linked to the towers by bridges and exposed staircases.

Down the center of the composition Kahn placed a masonry court

YALE ART GALLERY, *Louis I. Kahn, New Haven, Connecticut, 1953.* Contemporary function with a whiff of Roman ruins.

sliced by a narrow canal that conveys a thin stream of water to a sculptural falls facing the Pacific Ocean. The crisp solemnity of this open-ended complex rightly forces a comparison with Jefferson's campus for the University of Virginia (UVA). Like UVA, Salk is an "academical village," one devoted to the life of the mind in no less a fashion than a monastery. And like UVA, Salk is organized according to a plan that distributes isolated zones for study along both sides of a shared space intended for casual meetings among the residents. What Jefferson's Lawn did by pointing its students westward to a future across the continent, the central space at Salk did in symbolizing a quest for knowledge as infinite as the sea to which it opens. Indeed, Salk can be seen as a spiritual and physical continuation of its Virginia predecessor. (In 1996, another research building was added at the eastern end of Kahn's original complex. Although designed by architects who worked with Kahn on the original building, the addition created a sad echo of the building by McKim, Mead & White that had closed the open arms of Jefferson's Charlottesville pavilions.)

RICHARDS MEDICAL RESEARCH BUILDING, *Louis I. Kahn, University of Pennsylvania, Philadelphia, 1965.* A successful evocation of Tuscan hill towns, it failed science.

Kahn's fascination with Roman ruins (which, because of their elemental nature, he found more interesting than better-preserved monuments) found a comparatively delicate expression in his library for the Phillips Exeter Academy in Exeter, New Hampshire (1972). On the surface, the Exeter Library is a remarkably simple building, a box within a box. The outer one is made of brick, a concession to the most common material on the campus and an evocation of New England mill architecture. But its four-square mass and unblinking, deepset windows give it a brooding, atavistic presence. The library might be merely blocky had the architect not designed the outer box so that its corners do not meet. This is a device that Kahn used elsewhere in the building (having refined it since he introduced it at the Richards laboratories) to create the impression that the forms are in suspension, and lighter than they might seem to be if clearly connected.

The interior of the Exeter building is dominated by an enormous atrium. Each of its four walls—which constitute the inner box—is cut away in a four-story circle of concrete. Surrounding the atrium are the bookstacks. At the perimeter of the building are lounge areas and study carrels. No zone is isolated from the others, and daylight is filtered throughout by means of a skylight monitor above the atrium, as well as through the peripheral windows. The building is a fulfillment of the vision Kahn articulated when he declared, in his runic way, "A man with a book goes to the light. A library begins that way."[5]

The beauty of the Exeter concept—like the concepts for so many Kahn buildings—is that it is at once geometrically tough and thoroughly humane. And unlike the Richards laboratories, it also satisfies the needs of the users, while creating an atmosphere that ennobles their scholarly activities. The balconies around the central space present a constantly changing scene of students moving among the shelves, while the space itself commands a sense of awe at its formal abstraction. This is a masterly combination of the timeless and the daily.

One of the most powerful elements of the Exeter design was the use of natural light. Nowhere was Kahn more successful in his use of that basic architectural ingredient than at the Kimbell Art Museum in Fort Worth, Texas (1972). The idea for the building was, like Exeter's, a sim-

---

[5] See David Brownlee and David De Long, *Louis I. Kahn: In the Realm of Architecture* (New York: Rizzoli, 1991), p. 129.

ple one: a succession of one-story barrel-vaulted spaces. But they are set aglow by Kahn's lighting system. A slot along the tops of the vaults admits a steady stream of daylight, which is met by metal reflectors that bounce it back upward to wash the polished concrete of the gallery ceilings, making them seem to hover above the darker zones of the galleries below. The otherworldly effect is amplified at the ends of the vaults, where Kahn left a thin arc of glass separating the wall from the roof.

At the Yale Center for British Art (1974), which was Kahn's last major work, he brought together many of the most successful elements of his earlier buildings. In doing so, however, he confronted a special set of demands created by the urban site. Although the building was a part of Yale University, and diagonally across the street from Kahn's 1953 art gallery (as well as Rudolph's Art and Architecture Building), that street was considered an unofficial boundary by the city of New Haven, and the site for the center was viewed as part of the city rather than of the campus. Among the resulting conditions was that retail shops be included to provide tax revenue. Kahn, who had grown up in the center of Philadelphia, had always been devoted to the life of the city and its meaning for culture. Indeed, one of his most repeated aphorisms was: "The city, the gathering of persons, each a singularity, their ways of living and their ways to express, is a place where a boy beginning his life can sense what he would become."[6] Accordingly, Kahn came up with a scheme that embraced the required shops by aligning them along both street facades at the ground-floor level and inserting the entrance to the Center at the corner.

Because of its location in the middle of a city, the British Art Center can be seen as an even more difficult challenge than some of those Kahn buildings that had no need to adjust to an existing architectural context, such as the Salk Institute. The commitment to structural expression remained, however: the facade is a crisp composition of rectangular forms separated by concrete piers and beams that make their load-bearing function abundantly clear. (They grow thinner as they rise, reflecting in both fact and symbol the reduced weight they must carry.) The concrete members create a regular grid, but the "filling," while deftly asymmetrical, expresses the interior function: glass is used where

6 Quoted in Paul Heyer, *Architects on Architecture* (New York: Walker and Company, 1966), p. 389.

SALK INSTITUTE,
*Louis I. Kahn,
La Jolla, California,
1965.* Comparable
to Jefferson's UVA
Lawn as a sacred
place in American
architecture.

offices and galleries require windows, while blank metal panels are used where they do not.

One of the qualities that make this and virtually all of the rest of Kahn's work at once timeless and accessible is his craftsman's sense of how materials are used and how they are assembled. In this, he shared something with Mies, who, at his best, remained dedicated to explaining visually how architecture is made. One need only look at the way the arches and rain gutters are fitted to the columns at the Kimbell Art Museum, or the delicate intersections between the concrete and the wood paneling at the Yale Center for British Art to understand how tactile was Kahn's grasp of his art. It was also the medium through which he communicated most directly with his buildings' users.

If one of the reasons for the discarding of Modernism was implicit in its beginnings—the abandonment of ornament—then Kahn found a way to satisfy the longing for the affective properties of ornament even if he did not resort to it in the traditional sense. By revealing a joint with such explicitness, Kahn created shadow lines that gave his architecture texture, but he also made a connection with the viewer, who instinctively relates to the process of construction. In this sense, too, Kahn showed a kinship with Mies, and even Sullivan, both of whom had expanded their definitions of functionalism to include the appetite of the viewer for visual pleasure. Indeed, Kahn's celebration of joinery is not unlike Mies's addition of the customized I-beams to the Seagram Building's facade. But Mies was so chaste about the gesture that it remained all but imperceptible to the layman. The rough clarity of the way the concrete columns meet the arches of the Kimbell is apparent to anyone who has ever placed one child's toy block atop another. Not surprisingly, Kahn often said that he preferred the relative bluntness of the Temple of Hera at Paestum to the elegance of the Parthenon.

Kahn used materials in a way that anticipated the effects of weather and age, and in this he departed radically from the Modernists. The stains that rapidly appeared on the stucco of Gropius's Graduate Center at Harvard made it look shabby and cheap. By contrast, the streaks on the concrete and the bleaching of the teakwood panels at Salk made

THE EXETER LIBRARY, *Louis I. Kahn, Exeter, New Hampshire, 1972. Sublime spaces that worked well.*

Cervin Robinson

the building appear durable and strong, recording years of salt spray and bright sunlight. Kahn's are clearly buildings with a past—and a future. Over the protests of his client, Kahn used panels of treated stainless steel on the facade of the British Art Center. The effect, he predicted, would be that "On a gray day, it will look like a moth; on a sunny day, like a butterfly."[7] He may have overstated the case, but the effects of New England winters on the metal have given it an alluring patina that enriches, rather than spoils, the visual impact.

By using such elemental techniques, Kahn did much to return architecture to the understanding of the user. He reclaimed it from the realm of the abstract, and, without succumbing to literal romanticism, delivered it back to the senses. Indeed, what most distinguishes all of Kahn's works is a quality of being at once monumental and intimate, a combination that had eluded most of the Modernists. That is largely because Kahn took extraordinary pains not just with his overall forms, but with his materials and the ways in which they were treated at the scale of the user. Just as the concrete at Salk is about to become oppressive, there is a welcome stretch of teak to warm the eye. Just as the abstraction of the main space at Exeter is about to overwhelm, a fireplace provides a touch of domesticity. Just as the planar geometry is about to become relentless at the British Art Center, there is an expanse of linen wall covering to soften the impact.

But surely Kahn's greatest achievement was his ability to transcend period and style. His fascination with the Roman ruins he saw during his stay at the American Academy is clear in the starkly massive forms he employed at Exeter and Salk. Yet these forms do not actually resemble the examples on which they are based, and can be understood at an instant even by those who have never seen the Baths of Caracalla. Kahn seemed able to distill from some of the most powerful relics of architectural history their underlying, primordial message about what buildings mean in simplest terms as places of shelter, of work, of worship.

Yet in so doing, Kahn did not remain tied to history. While the Richards labs became notorious for their failure as settings for scientific

---

[7] Kahn to Jules Prown, the first director of the Center, quoted in Jules David Prown, *The Architecture of the Yale Center for British Art* (New Haven, CT: Yale University Press, 1977), p. 43.

research, the concept of served and servant spaces that informed the design had as much to do with larger contemporary needs as it did with the romantic images of medieval towers in the Tuscan landscape. The scientific requirements were better accommodated at Salk, which, if it seemed almost primitive in its tribute to the sea and the sun, was also based on a determination to serve scientists interacting at the highest levels of modern research.

Kahn differed fundamentally from his more romantic late Modernist colleagues. Wright was never able to free himself from himself; in every one of his major buildings a sense lingers that the architect was eager to remind users and visitors alike that the architecture had been made by him, and him alone. Kahn's buildings project no such feeling of authorship, and seem instead to have evolved. In that sense, they are surprisingly anonymous, allowing the experience of the architecture to take precedence over the identity of its creator. Unlike Saarinen, Kahn never fell prey to the allure of symbolic sculptural form. Thrilling as the Ingalls Rink and the TWA Terminal may be as virtuoso performances, they are limited by their literalness. Once the initial impact has receded, the buildings have little to offer. Unlike Rudolph, Kahn never seemed angry at what had gone before. Where the Art and Architecture Building at Yale stakes out its ground in opposition to what Rudolph perceived as the aridity of the Bauhaus tradition and its reflection in Kahn's art gallery across the street, the Kimbell Art Museum, for example, simply transcends the issue of precedence, combining the most modern of lighting devices with the most ageless of forms to create spaces that seem both immediate and timeless.

But the overall impact of Kahn's work—and the most fundamental way in which it differed from that of his romantic contemporaries—was due to the underlying sense of order that pervaded it. There was nothing gratuitous about his architecture. If a Saarinen building was powerful for the specificity of its imagery—TWA, Ingalls—it was weakened as a part of his overall *oeuvre* by its lack of a relationship with his other works. Although Rudolph's best buildings show a greater consistency, they also express a limited vision, one that the architect attempted to apply in one form or another to most of his major commissions. The Kahn buildings, while richly varied in form, are unified by a commitment to rational order, and in this Kahn again showed his debt to the

THE KIMBELL
ART MUSEUM,
*Louis I. Kahn, Fort
Worth, Texas, 1972.*
Kahn's masterwork
in the manipulation
of light.

Beaux-Arts training he had received at Penn under Cret. One can only speculate about what would have happened had Kahn attended Harvard under Gropius, where the concept of order was inseparable from the idea of the machine. Kahn's order reflected far more the time-tested ways in which architecture was used. In simplest terms, the distinction was between the mechanistic and the humanistic.

In a related way, Kahn's sense of order also differed from Wright's, for Wright insisted that the ultimate model for architectural form and organization lay in nature, hence the concept of "organic" architecture. Again, Kahn turned to human experience, but that of the heart in concert with the mind. "Architecture," he told a group of Yale students in 1963, "is what nature can not make."[8] "Science finds what is already

---

[8] Brownlee and De Long, op. cit., p. 100.

THE YALE CENTER FOR BRITISH ART, *Louis I. Kahn, New Haven, Connecticut, 1974.* A craftsman's sense of materials.

there," he said in a 1967 lecture, "but the artist makes that which is not there."[9] "Nature," he said on another occasion, "makes its designs through the tenets of order."[10]

Such poetic aphorisms were typical of Kahn, and occasionally reached levels of obscurity that puzzled and even embarrassed his most devoted supporters. In his fondness for such pronouncements Kahn

---

[9] Ibid., p. 95.
[10] Quoted in *What Will Be Has Always Been, the Words of Louis I. Kahn*, compiled by Richard Saul Wurman (New York: Access Press and Rizzoli, 1986), p. 260.

shared much with Sullivan and Wright, among other architects who felt compelled to tell their clients and critics what their architecture meant by associating it with cosmic forces. It is a practice indulged in by many lesser architects, and the better writers among them can be entertaining if not inspirational. But when all the verbiage is stripped away, the architecture must speak for itself—and is all too often disappointing. In Kahn's case, his buildings were more eloquent, and certainly more comprehensible, than his pronouncements. His was a unique synthesis, and it remains unequaled.

The Power of Preservation

t was perhaps predictable that, as Louis Kahn was probing ancient architectural history in search of inspiration for his buildings, other American architects would begin to reassess the value of the shrinking supply of their country's own, more recent historic structures.

To be sure, the process was a gradual one, having begun as far back as the founding of the earliest historical societies—in Massachusetts, in 1791, and in New York, in 1804. And it had continued fitfully into the twentieth century. But the growing appreciation of America's architectural past had been violently interrupted in the 1930s with the arrival of

European Modernism and its dedication to starting the history of architecture anew. By the 1960s, however, the shortcomings of this revolution were becoming increasingly clear, and efforts to reestablish links to the past had taken on increasing momentum. Spurred by the demolition of several nationally known monuments—and negative public reaction—many architects turned with unprecedented enthusiasm to saving the best of the nation's built legacy. The eventual result would be a fundamental rethinking of the role of architecture in America.

By 1960, Modernism had existed for some forty years, if one marks its beginnings in the work of the European pioneers of the 1920s. The compelling intellectual appeal of its rationalism and abstraction was no longer either new or exotic. Moreover, Americans had had several decades to assess that movement from a user's point of view. Many of the individual buildings designed by Mies, Gropius, and their American disciples had unquestionable architectural merit, but many lesser works by their imitators had contributed to an all-too-frequent sameness, particularly in the nation's major cities, where uninflected glass towers proliferated to face each other with emotionally mute results.

This sameness helped concentrate the attention of both the public and the professional architectural community on the physical variety that had been lost in the name of progress. Americans were coming to see that the "Victorian atrocities" and "Romanesque piles" so despised by many Modernists had much to recommend them after all, especially in the way they interacted with their architectural neighbors. Even some of the nation's slums that had been cleared with such zeal in pursuit of urban renewal were now recognized in hindsight to have been preferable in their scale and detail (not to mention their role in fostering a sense of community) to the faceless structures that often replaced them. Whatever their individual stylistic identities—neoclassical, Queen Anne, pseudo-Gothic—they had historical roots with which one could associate. And for that reason alone, those that survived began to strike a newly responsive chord among people who had grown weary of the "clean slate" promised by the proponents of architectural revolution.

Time had not been kind to the products of that revolution. Without constant and often costly care, their pristine surfaces had suffered. Weather streaked the concrete and the stucco, and urban grime dulled the shiny curtain walls of glass and steel. As similar buildings went up around the early monuments like Lever House and the Seagram Building, the "new" buildings actually began to look rather old, or at least worn out, while many of their older neighbors, such as McKim, Mead & White's 1918 Racquet and Tennis Club, began to look stately and mature. For all of its intellectual appeal, the Modernist vocabulary fell demonstrably short in dealing with the process of aging.

Much of the public had never embraced Modernism with the enthusiasm of the academy and, later, the corporations. As the passage of time steadily exposed the failings of Modernism, a collective sigh of relief could be heard across the land: "At last, it's over. We always liked the old stuff better anyway!" Aesthetes as well as lay people joined in the chorus. At first gradually, and then quite suddenly, preserving the best of the architectural past became nothing short of a cause.

At heart, the very concept of preservation posed a challenge to what America was all about. It was, after all, a society founded upon newness. The old—whether political, social, or architectural—was almost by definition bad, and should therefore be cast aside. It was an article of American faith that new was better than old. Had not the nation itself been established on the principles of revolution and the abandonment of the old ways of Europe?

Moreover, much of the most prominent architecture of the eighteenth and nineteenth centuries—the mansions of Massachusetts, the plantations of Virginia, the resorts of the Hudson Valley—had been built by the rich and socially prominent, and the early preservationists tended to be members of the same stratum of society. There was at first little popular sympathy for preserving monuments to—and for—the elite. Every artistic generation tends to rebel against those immediately preceding it, while "rediscovering" the virtues of those further back in time. Consistent with this pattern, the United States even in the nineteenth century quite naturally looked for its aesthetic examples to the great cities of Europe, which had long had an appreciation and tradition of preservation that Americans were, as a people, too young to have developed.

Certainly, much of what had been built in this country in the early years had been done in haste and had little architectural merit on the great scale. But as the country grew older and more appreciative of its history, increasing numbers of people began to realize that holding on to some of their past was essential—and that the monuments to that past were at risk.

At first, however, attention focused less on architectural merit than on association with the outstanding figures of American history. One of the first achievements of the early preservationist efforts was the purchase by the State of New York in 1850 of the building in Newburgh used by George Washington as his headquarters during the last two years of the Revolutionary War. In arguing the case for the building's preservation, New York's governor at the time, Hamilton Fish, declared that "there are associations connected with this venerable edifice which rise above the consideration of dollars and cents."

But the major push for preservation in the United States began with an organization called the Mount Vernon Ladies' Association, which was founded in 1853. Spearheaded by Ann Pamela Cunningham of South Carolina, the group struggled for years with Washington's heirs to preserve the home of the nation's first president, mounting the first nationwide publicity campaign for such purposes. With much badgering, cajoling, threatening, and dealing, the campaign eventually succeeded, setting an example for future preservationists of prevailing against strong odds. (The campaign also established the role of women—at the time a virtually powerless group in the world of architecture itself—in the continuing efforts to preserve the nation's built heritage.)

A related aspect of the early preservation movement was that, at least in the beginning, it had virtually nothing to do with the academy. It was a grass-roots phenomenon, and it drew its energy as much from local pride as it did from issues of historical significance. Even the earliest architectural schools in the country, it should be remembered, were direct offshoots of the French Ecole des Beaux-Arts, and were no more likely to embrace authentic American buildings than were their Modernist successors.

With the success of efforts like those of the Mount Vernon Ladies' Association, however, preservation organizations spread steadily westward to embrace Spanish and Native American structures. (In California, a vigorous effort was led by an organization with the colorful name of the Native Sons of the Golden West, who in 1892 succeeded in preserving Sutter's Fort in Sacramento.) But the strongest and most forward-looking support for preservation remained along the East Coast. The attempts to preserve the Massachusetts village of Deerfield, the site of notorious massacres by Indians and French troops in 1675 and 1704,

were launched in 1847, and became the first major example of an organized preservation movement in New England. What distinguished
the Deerfield effort from its predecessors was its concentration on saving and restoring an entire community, rather than isolated buildings of
importance, thus recreating an overall architectural context that would
amplify the historical experience of the visitor. The Philadelphia Centennial of 1876 did much to call further attention to the nation's Colonial heritage, including its buildings, by exhibiting "a colonial
homestead of a generation ago," and a "New England Farmer's Home"
attended by hostesses in period costumes.

Monticello, the hilltop home of Thomas Jefferson, was among the
first cases in which association with a historical figure intersected with
architecture of superior quality. The building had been bought in 1836
by Uriah Levy, a lieutenant in the United States Navy who had come
into a fortune and developed a personal passion for saving Jefferson's
homestead. Levy's will indicates that Jefferson's stature as a framer of the
United States was his prime motivation, but Monticello was also a monument to American architecture even more than Mount Vernon was,
and in his wish to leave Monticello to the "People of the United States,"
Levy made a lasting contribution. (Because of disputes within the Levy

**MOUNT
VERNON LADIES'
ASSOCIATION**

MOUNT VERNON, *Arlington, Virginia, anonymous, 1770. A shrine more to its owner than its architecture.*

family over the will, the building was brought to the brink of ruin, but in 1924 was finally sold to a private foundation dedicated to its preservation as a public shrine.)

The turn of the century saw an expansion of the preservationist concern to the governmental level. The Antiquities Act of 1906 gave the president the power to designate buildings and landmarks on federal land as national monuments. The act was not strictly speaking about architecture, but when William Sumner Appleton established his Society for the Preservation of New England Antiquities, in 1910, the role of design was firmly fixed on the private preservation agenda. The goal of the organization was, according to its founder, to save and perpetuate buildings that were "architecturally beautiful or unique."

The trend could be detected in the commercial world as well. In 1915, the White Pine Bureau, an organization of lumber producers, launched a bimonthly architectural publication intended to promote the use of pine as a building material. Although it was at heart an advertising vehicle, "The White Pine Series" included serious essays on traditional American architecture and its lasting value for the present and the future. The series was illustrated with photographs, plans, and drawings of "wood construction, critically described by representative American architects, of the most beautiful and suggestive examples of architecture, old and new, which this country has produced." The frontispiece for the first issue was a photograph of the Parson Capen House.

Not surprisingly, the move toward architectural preservation took place in step with comparable attempts to save the nation's most distinguished natural sites. In 1916, the National Park Service was established, and while its primary goal was to protect the natural environment, with the passage of time the service found itself caring for important structures on its lands as well.

A mixed blessing for the fledgling cause of preservation was the emergence at about this time of what became known as "house museums"— buildings assembled from, or containing fragments of, historic structures that were not themselves preserved. The Metropolitan Museum of Art opened its American Wing in 1924, displaying intact pe-

MONTICELLO, *Charlottesville, Virginia, Thomas Jefferson, 1785.* Its rescue marked a turning point in the preservation movement.

Rotch Visual Collections

riod interiors that had been removed from several significant historic buildings. However, while the practice provided a glimpse of period design to greater numbers of people than ever before, it posed a serious threat to many endangered buildings, which might have been better served by being preserved as built rather than stripped of their beams and paneling for displays in a contrived setting These museums were nonetheless a positive development in that they made the architecture of the past accessible to many who might not otherwise have encountered it.

Increasingly, Americans found themselves on the move, thanks largely to the proliferation of the automobile. In 1914, the United States recorded 1,664,000 passenger vehicle registrations. By 1926, that number had leaped to 19,267,000. The impact on historic sites grew accordingly. The National Park Service registered 240,000 visitors in 1914; by 1926, the total was 2,315,000, turning the thoughts of preservationists to the idea that even relatively out-of-the-way sites might be saved by attracting larger numbers of visitors.

The most influential of these activists was William A. R. Goodwin, the rector of the eighteenth-century Bruton Parish Church in Williamsburg, Virginia. In 1924, he had approached John D. Rockefeller, Jr., for help in financing a new building at the College of William and Mary, where Goodwin was teaching. (An earlier overture to Henry Ford had failed.) Goodwin had spent much of his career restoring his own historic church, and he now felt that such efforts should be expanded to include the historic community around it.

The motivation behind the preservation of Williamsburg was not merely associative. Although many of the Williamsburg buildings had provided a stage for historic events and the actions of great Americans, Goodwin's project was about architectural quality and correctness, at least as far as it could be determined. Later critics would attack Williamsburg for recreating the image but not the reality of the Colonial period. They pointed to the fact that roughly half of the buildings were reconstructions modeled on a combination of surviving fragments and informed speculation. (The Capitol building was rebuilt on its original foundations, but in the absence of the original plans was modeled on a print found in an Oxford University library.) And the patrons had no interest in reflecting the less pleasant aspects of the Colonial past. Indeed, slavery was virtually banished from the history promulgated by the

restorers, as it was at Monticello until the 1980s. As one critic put it, "What Williamsburg presents is upper-class WASP history. The streets are clean; the slave cabins and outhouses have been suppressed. It is history without depth and without continuity. The clock has stopped and the past has been enshrined behind glass. And having put history in its niche, one can admire it and forget it."[1]

WILLIAM A. R. GOODWIN, ON LEFT, WITH JOHN D. ROCKEFELLER, JR., AT COLONIAL WILLIAMSBURG

Nonetheless, Williamsburg and many comparable, if less ambitious, preservation efforts (such as Old Sturbridge Village in Massachusetts, and Henry Ford's outdoor museum of Greenfield Village in Dearborn, Michigan) helped to create a new level of awareness of the nation's architectural past, however flawed or incomplete the social and physical context. In the process, they gave birth to what amounted to a new area

[1] Constance M. Greiff, *Lost America, from the Atlantic to the Mississippi* (Princeton, NJ: Pyne Press, 1971), p. 7.

COLONIAL WILLIAMSBURG, *Williamsburg, Virginia, anonymous, 1700s.* While a "sanitized" monument, a monument nonetheless.

of architectural practice. To execute a restoration properly required craftsmen familiar with the tools, materials, and techniques of the past, as well as researchers able to determine from surviving fragments of stone, mortar, paint, and wallpaper where the materials had come from and how they had been used by the original builders.

Although sensitivity was spreading about the value of preservation, it was not yet sufficient to prevent the loss of some of the nation's finest monuments. The year 1930 became a black one in preservation history when H. H. Richardson's masterful Marshall Field Wholesale Store in Chicago was destroyed, a loss made even more tragic in light of the city's reputation as the birthplace of modern American architecture.

Spurred in part by such vandalism—as well as a desire to employ architects put out of work by the Depression—the Historical American Buildings Survey (HABS) was established in 1933 under the auspices of the National Park Service to document the history of the nation's building arts through measured drawings, photographs, and other historical data. (HABS became the nation's primary training program for preservation professionals.) Shortly thereafter, HABS struck an agreement with the American Institute of Architects to help administer the program through local AIA chapters, and with the Library of Congress to maintain HABS documentation on a permanent basis.

Just as the increase in automobile traffic in the 1920s had introduced ever greater numbers of Americans to their widely scattered architectural heritage, the expansion of air travel after World War II gave many architects and preservationists their first exposure to the monuments of Europe and the organizations—such as the French *Commission des Monuments Historiques*—that preserved them. One indirect result was the chartering by Congress in 1949 of the National Trust for Historic Preservation, a private organization devoted to encouraging the preservation of historically significant buildings and places by acting as a clearinghouse for information and coordinating the efforts of preservation groups.

But the saga of destruction continued, taking with it, in 1950, McKim, Mead & White's Low House in Bristol, Rhode Island. The Low House was accompanied into oblivion in the same year by Frank Lloyd Wright's majestic Larkin Building, which had been one of Buffalo's most prominent landmarks. In a painfully ironic case, the National Park Service itself was responsible for demolishing Frank Furness's 1879 Provident Life and Trust Company in Philadelphia, in 1957.

In the face of such setbacks, the preservation movement received an enormous, if unexpected, boost in 1961 with the publication of a book entitled *The Death and Life of Great American Cities*. The author, Jane Jacobs, was a magazine writer with no professional experience in either architecture or planning; in fact, she didn't even have a university degree. But she brought to the questions of modern American urban life an unprecedented passion and a skilled eye that had been lacking among the credentialed experts. In her book, Jacobs struck at the core of Modernist abstraction as expressed in urban architecture and planning by studying "how cities work in real life."[2] In a chapter entitled

---

[2] Jane Jacobs, *The Death and Life of Great American Cities* (New York: Vintage Books, 1961), p. 4.

Buffalo and Erie County Historical Society

"The Need for Aged Buildings," she made clear that architectural quality was not her main concern: "By old buildings I mean not museum-piece old buildings, not old buildings in an excellent and expensive state of rehabilitation—although these make fine ingredients—but also a good lot of plain, ordinary, low-value old buildings, including some rundown old buildings."[3] But if Jacobs was moved less by architecture than by people—whom she saw as victims of the urban renewal policies that had been spawned by Modernism—her criteria nonetheless posed a fundamental question to contemporary architects: Was their own work serving its purpose? And what, precisely, was that purpose?

In Jacobs's view, the purpose was the nurturing of an intensely tex-tured, richly chaotic experience of cities developed through the partic-ipation of the users. With unsparing logic and masses of examples,

[3] Ibid., p. 187.

Jacobs demonstrated that the tidy abstractions of Modernist architects and urban planners had little to do with what really made a city work, but a great deal to do with the designers' concern for order and authorship. Although architectural preservation as such did not play a major role in her polemic, it benefited enormously from it, because implicit in Jacobs's opposition to the sort of reductive approach demonstrated by a Mies van der Rohe on the IIT campus was an endorsement of the organic architectural fabric—whether humble or grand—that such schemes so often swept aside.

Nevertheless, the losses continued. Adler & Sullivan's 1892 Schiller Building, in Chicago, was razed in the same year Jacobs's book came

out. (Over the years, Chicago has confirmed that it is better at innovation than appreciation, compiling a lamentable record of demolishing architectural monuments.) Countless lesser structures were suffering a similar fate as urban renewal—in restrospect a cruelly ironic term—swept the land. By the early 1960s, roughly 25 percent of the buildings that had been listed on the Historical American Buildings Survey since its creation in the 1930s had been destroyed. And the greatest number of those had been built before 1830. More recent architecture, like Chicago's Schiller Building, was being targeted at an alarming rate.

Surely the most painful example was the demolition of New York's Pennsylvania Station, in 1963. The condition of McKim, Mead & White's spectacular combination of Roman bath and modern train shed had been declining for years, and its noble spaces had been repeatedly violated with garish signs and ticket counters that obscured the original elegance of the design.

The owners of the station, the Pennsylvania Railroad, had long been eager to replace the building with a more modern facility, on top of which they planned to erect a sports complex and an office tower. In a notorious letter to the *New York Times* in defense of his plans to demolish the station, the president of the railroad asked rhetorically: "Does it make any sense to preserve a building merely as a 'monument' when it no longer serves the utilitarian needs for which it was erected?"

The question had never been posed with such cruel effect before. But the answer quickly emerged: There is more to architecture than utilitarian needs, especially when it takes the form of a major work of art. Despite strident protests by scores of prominent architects and hundreds of aroused New Yorkers, the railroad went ahead with its plans, dumping the ornamental sculpture of the once-gleaming edifice among the swampy flats of New Jersey.

As the full impact of Penn Station's demolition resonated beyond New York, national public sentiment began to build for safeguards against future losses. While no one would ever wish to celebrate the passing of such a fine work of architecture, the sacrifice of Penn Station was redeemed to a large degree by the momentum it gave to the preservation of other buildings. It was no coincidence that the year after the loss of Penn Station, Columbia University established the first American academic program in historic preservation, under the architect and

Museum of the City of New York

historian James Marston Fitch. The successful Columbia program led to the establishment of scores of similar programs in universities across the United States.

But the most significant event in the history of the movement up to that point was the establishment of the New York City Landmarks Preservation Commission, on April 19, 1965. In setting up the new body, the nation's dominant city—which was both celebrated and damned as a place where commerce traditionally took precedence over culture—committed itself to a review of all buildings that were at least thirty years old, and granted itself the power to designate the best of them as official landmarks. Unlike similar legislation elsewhere in the country, this law had teeth, in the form of substantial fines and other penalties for owners who disregarded it.

The decision by New York City to create a landmarks commission with credible enforcement powers did much to stiffen similar efforts around the country. The city of Portland, Oregon, set up a Historical Landmarks Commission in 1968, and embarked on a vigorous campaign to halt the spread of demolition in its downtown area. One of that city's major preservation achievements was saving the 1872 New Market Theater, which had been at the heart of Portland's cultural life in the 1870s and 1880s, in a spirited fight with developers who wanted the site for an office tower. In St. Louis, threats to Louis Sullivan's Wainwright Building were fended off long enough for the state of Missouri to buy the building and expand it for use as government offices, while in Los Angeles a plan to demolish Bertram Goodhue's Central Public Library stalled in the face of citizen protests. In Denver, the history associated with the old Brown Palace Hotel persuaded the owner to renovate it rather than replace it.

Such scattered efforts gained national endorsement in 1966 with the passage by Congress of the National Historic Preservation Act, which stipulated that major historic works of architecture must be preserved. An assortment of inducements—including tax credits and grants-in-aid—was later created to encourage the saving of important buildings, and through the National Trust for Historic Preservation, aid was extended to private preservation organizations across the country. An expansion of the National Register of Historic Places guaranteed that protected buildings could not be demolished without due process.

In San Francisco, arguably one of the most picturesque of American cities, the threat posed by real estate development was especially acute, because the most historically significant areas were so tightly concentrated; a demolition that might be absorbed by a larger, more spread-out urban area could leave gaping holes in San Francisco's fragile fabric. The city's vulnerability became painfully apparent in 1965, when the local redevelopment agency wiped out the old vegetable district for Golden Gateway Center, a complex of towers and town houses.

Encouraged by preservation efforts in New York City and Washington, D.C., San Francisco in 1967 set up a Landmarks Preservation Advisory Board. Although the board had no power to prevent demolitions—

McGraw-Hill Company

JAMES
MARSTON
FITCH

it could only demand a delay—the manifest value of such a body was clear to most San Franciscans, and virtually all of the board's officially designated buildings were saved. By 1985, San Francisco had issued its Downtown Plan, which built upon the work of the advisory board by protecting in perpetuity 249 architecturally or historically significant buildings; it provided partial protection for 200 more.

Although the momentum for preservation was building, and was being accompanied by legislation, opponents continued to attack the laws and designations, which inevitably presented restrictions on use and maintenance. The debate came to a head in the fight over Penn Station's surviving New York sibling, Grand Central Terminal, the 1913

Beaux-Arts monument to train travel designed by the firms of Reed & Stem and Warren & Wetmore. The building's setting had already suffered grievous damage when, in 1963, a fifty-nine-story office building designed by Walter Gropius and Pietro Belluschi had been erected on a site just to the north. The possibility that Grand Central might be further defaced—or even follow Penn Station into architectural oblivion—prompted the city's landmarks commission within months of its creation to consider designating Grand Central's elegant exterior, which it did on September 21, 1967.

The designation took place over the protests of the owner, the Penn Central Transportation Company, which decided in 1972 to challenge the landmarks law on the basis of "economic hardship," arguing that designation deprived the company of the income it could reap by building a fifty-five-story office tower (designed by Marcel Breuer) atop the terminal. The New York State Supreme Court ruled in the owner's favor, declaring that the law in this case constituted a "taking of property" without just compensation. The decision was overturned on appeal, but Penn Central decided to carry the case to the United States Supreme Court.

The final phase of the campaign to save Grand Central took on national proportions not seen since the days of the Mount Vernon Ladies' Association. The high point was a highly publicized train ride from New York to Washington that included a host of the nation's most prominent architects, as well as Jacqueline Kennedy Onassis, the widow of President John F. Kennedy. In the end, the landmarks law was upheld by a six-to-three vote of the U.S. Supreme Court, on June 26, 1978. The ruling gave the practice of designating landmarks a federal seal of approval. While frequently challenged on procedural grounds, the legislation was now stronger than it had ever been. By 1997, the New York City Landmarks Preservation Commission had designated 964 buildings, 98 interiors, 9 parks or other scenic landmarks, as well as 69 historic districts.

Judicial endorsement of the historic designation concept raised some troublesome questions, however. For one, it provided official public support for what was necessarily a subjective—in the view of some, elitist—process. For another, because it did not provide for financial compensation, the law raised the potential of a very real burden on owners who could not afford to maintain their properties or might wish to demolish or alter them. Just as preservation had originally challenged the

traditional American faith in the sanctity of the new, it was now challenging the no less sacred American reverence for private property.

Any number of strategies were subsequently devised to compensate owners of designated landmarks for possible financial loss. The most creative—and effective—was the transfer of development or "air" rights. According to air-rights legislation, the owner of a designated site could sell the unbuilt space above a protected building to the developer of another, undesignated site. The purchaser would then be able to add the equivalent of the space above the historic property to his own project. The trade-off often meant exceeding height and bulk restrictions in other parts of a city, but that was widely considered preferable to sacrificing a historically important building. The transfer of development rights proved especially useful in San Francisco, where the practice did much to facilitate administration of the preservation ordinances already in place.

GRAND CENTRAL TERMINAL, *New York City, Reed & Stem, Warren & Wetmore, 1913. A failed attempt to destroy the terminal solidified the landmarks legislation.*

Although it was helpful in dealing with commercial properties, the practice of transferring development rights often fell short when the designated buildings were dedicated to not-for-profit and religious institutions. Nowhere was this made more clear than in another New York City battle, this one over St. Bartholomew's Episcopal Church. Designed by Bertram Goodhue and completed in 1919, the Park Avenue church was designated a city landmark in 1967 for its "handsome modern versions of Romanesque and Byzantine architecture," of which it was considered an "outstanding example." Since its founding the church had served a wealthy, socially prominent congregation. But as the city around it changed, becoming less residential and more commercial, the congregation began to shrink, reducing both the reach of the church's ministry and the income from donations. In 1978, a new minister was appointed, and in short order announced plans to take the church's message to the airwaves by creating a television program.

To cover the cost of the new venture, the minister proposed to demolish the parish house adjacent to the church and combine its air rights with those over the church itself to erect an office tower. The local landmarks preservation commission refused the proposal, arguing that the new building would overwhelm the old one, compromising its architectural integrity, while depriving an increasingly congested area of the city of a physical as well as an architectural oasis.

Like the owners of Grand Central Terminal, the leaders of the church turned to the courts, but their appeal was based on significantly different grounds. Lawyers for St. Bartholomew's argued that by restricting the church's use of its assets, the landmarks commission was actually compromising the church's First Amendment guarantee of the free exercise of religion.

Again, the battle went all the way to the U.S. Supreme Court, which this time refused to hear the case. The effect was to endorse a lower court ruling that landmarks designation did not interfere with the church's mission. The case was clouded, however, by the wealth of this particular church, which was widely mocked in the press for claiming that foregoing the office tower and maintaining the existing building up to commission standards would impose a financial "hardship," one of the few grounds on which owners of landmarks could be granted exceptions to the law.

For less wealthy churches and other non-profit institutions, the cost

of preserving and maintaining their properties according to governmental rules was often a serious burden, and in some cases threatened to force them to close. Many such cases were brought in the years following the St. Bartholomew's battle, and a few owners were allowed to alter or demolish their buildings when no other solution could be found. But the issue was a persistent one, and served to focus the attention of the community at large on whether and how its architectural heritage might be maintained. Whatever the legal arguments, common sense argued for sharing the burden imposed on owners of architecturally significant buildings who could not sustain them alone.

The net effect was a substantial increase across the country in private community groups dedicated to raising money for preservation. But the debate over the preservation of buildings owned by non-profit organi-

ST. BARTHOLOMEW'S EPISCOPAL CHURCH, *New York City, Bertram Grosvenor Goodhue, 1919.* An attempt to alter the site expanded the preservation debate into religion.

zations also fueled a strategy for commercial properties that came to be known as "adaptive re-use." In brief, the idea was to take a building that had outlived its original purpose and save it from destruction by assigning it a new function. Thus Chattanooga's Terminal Station, which had seen its last train depart in 1970, eight years later became a restaurant. Denver's 1882 Temple Emanuel, which over the years had lost its congregation, became first a warehouse, and then a retailing complex. Among the most intriguing examples of the practice of finding new uses for old buildings were the conversion of the venerable Lone Star Brewery building in San Antonio, Texas, to serve as an art museum (which adopted the slogan, "We're brewing art"), and the incorporation of thirty-six abandoned Quaker Oats grain silos in Akron, Ohio, into a design for a Hilton hotel.

Since the practice could apply equally well to distinguished buildings and to vernacular structures that had some aggregate value as "context," the traditional focus on preserving individual monuments rapidly expanded to include entire districts or neighborhoods. The survival of the distinguished cores of such cities as Charleston, South Carolina, and Savannah, Georgia, had already demonstrated the wisdom of saving historic districts. Indeed, the first local legislation establishing such a district was passed in 1931 in Charleston. That was followed by New Orleans, which in 1937 gave legal protection to the *Vieux Carré*, the city's French Quarter. Not surprisingly, this legislation also faced legal challenges, but the Supreme Court had held in 1954 that "It is within the power of the legislature to determine that the community should be beautiful as well as healthy, spacious as well as clean, well-balanced as well as carefully patrolled."

The historic district concept presented a new preservation opportunity: saving areas that were aesthetically greater than the sum of their individual parts. Alarmed by the widespread demolition of old neighborhoods that did not have the historic credentials of its French Quarter, New Orleans, for instance, in the early 1970s imposed a moratorium on demolition in the entire downtown area until a comprehensive approach to preservation and development could be established. In the early 1960s, Seattle's Pioneer Square district was a largely abandoned area that seemed destined for demolition and replacement with parking lots. But by early 1977, there were 187 retail businesses in the

Carter Wiseman

neighborhood, and the assessed value of local property had gone up 114 percent over the 1969 level, compared to a 79 percent gain in the assessed valuation of property in the city as a whole. Worried by the development pressures on San Francisco's Jackson Square area, which contained numerous commercial buildings that had survived the 1906 earthquake and fire, the local landmarks board began designating so many of them that the city government's hearing process was soon overloaded. The result was an effort to develop a comprehensive plan for the area, which in 1972 became San Francisco's first historic district.

There and in other cities where concentrations of vernacular architecture survived, community activists launched efforts to plug the gaps caused by past demolitions, turning to architects who were willing to come up with "infill" designs that would enhance the overall character of the area. To the surprise of many commercial real estate developers

HISTORIC DISTRICT, *New Orleans, Louisiana, anonymous, 1800s.* Proof that groups of buildings can be as important as individual monuments.

who assumed that new was always better, many of the urban areas that were saved by this strategy became financial successes.

One of the earliest and most notable examples was New York's SoHo district, which had been all but abandoned when the nineteenth-century cast-iron factories and warehouses lost their industries, but was reborn when artists who had been driven out of other neighborhoods by rising rents discovered that the old loft spaces were just right for over-size canvasses and large-scale metal sculptures. Another success was in San Francisco, where an old chocolate factory was converted in 1964 as the centerpiece of a mixed-use retail complex called Ghirardelli Square. Boston's waterfront market, which had fallen into disuse in the 1950s and was to be torn down, was given new life in 1976 as the Faneuil Hall Marketplace, a complex of boutiques, restaurants, and specialty food shops designed by the architect Benjamin Thompson in an innovative collaboration with a real estate developer, the Rouse Corporation. The project was echoed by similar ones in Baltimore and New York, where the harborfront markets created out of down-and-out warehouses became the catalysts for local renewal efforts. Between 1975 and 1976, the National Endowment for the Arts carried out a survey of nine San Francisco neighborhoods to assess the concentrations of the highly ornamented Victorian row houses that had been such a part of the city's architectural tradition since the 1890s. Through community action, many were saved from destruction, and in the following years "the painted ladies," as the restored buildings became known, proved a major boon to the city's tourist industry.

In many cases, recycling older buildings proved considerably less expensive than building from scratch, giving developers an added reason to rethink their traditional fondness for demolition. The trend was reinforced by the Tax Reform Act of 1976, which provided financial benefits to owners who reused older buildings rather than demolish them. Without intending to, this legislation did much to provide an alternative to the normal forms of urban renewal, which called for demolition and new construction. By creating such incentives to maintain old buildings, the act spurred the refurbishing of entire neighborhoods, which in many cases became attractive to a wealthier clientele. Thus the "urban pioneers" who had sought out low-income housing with some architectural allure were frequently replaced by "gentrifiers," contributing to a self-perpetuating demand for better municipal services, and eventually rescuing many urban areas that might otherwise have been razed.

It was this shift from a traditional focus on individual structures that, along with the steady disenchantment with Modernist forms, laid the groundwork for what became in the 1970s and 1980s nothing less than an architectural counterrevolution. In the process, strict attention to architectural quality was often overlooked, as was historical accuracy. Accordingly, the success of the preservation movement was causing it to reexamine its foundations. Should the economic potential of a South Street Seaport—New York City's oldest surviving waterfront area—be allowed to dictate which buildings were saved and how? If context was to be judged desirable as a setting for individual buildings of high quality, where should the historic district lines be drawn? At what age should a building or a district qualify for protection? And what level of excellence—determined by whom—should trigger designation?

There was little public dissent over the designation of Mies's 1958 Seagram Building. But in the late 1990s, preservationists in Denver mounted an (unsuccessful) campaign to save a complex of downtown buildings that had been designed by I. M. Pei and his colleagues between 1954 and 1960. The buildings were hardly the best of the architects' work, but they were important at the time they were built as early examples of integrated, multi-use commercial development. Should preservation include the saving of buildings that perhaps do not meet the highest design standards, but nevertheless constitute documents of a particular movement, or of a particular architect's aesthetic growth?

Beyond those questions emerged the one—harking back to the preservation of George Washington's wartime headquarters—whether underrepresented groups, such as African Americans, could make a preservationist argument based on their own communities' cultural or political history. The New York City Landmarks Preservation Commission, for instance, briefly considered designating Harlem's Audubon Ballroom. The building had scant architectural distinction, but it had become a shrine of sorts after the black activist Malcolm X was assassinated there. In the end, the building was not designated, but the debate sparked by such issues helped alter the way many American architects thought about their work, by elevating their awareness of the past and forcing a closer scrutiny of what constitutes architectural value over time. In the realm of design, it gave them permission—denied by Mod-

Rotch Visual Collections

ernism—to study and use forms that had been validated by trial and error over centuries. No less important, the preservation movement changed the perspective of architects to include the context in which their buildings were located. It was no longer quite as acceptable to think of architecture as an art of designing buildings in isolation—or with the expectation that the surroundings would eventually be adjusted to accommodate them. Moreover, preservation made clear that the context need not be of uniformly high architectural quality to provide a valuable totality. The idea that mediocre buildings might be valuable for the support they provided to better buildings in their midst contributed to a reexamination of the entire fabric of American building.

In the end, the most important long-term effect of the preservation movement was a growing feeling that Americans had an architectural heritage of their own, after all. What took many by surprise, however, was the idea that, for architectural purposes, not all of the past lay in the history books. In the eyes of a few bold theorists, some of that heritage lay just down the street—and out on the commercial strip. All that was needed for such sentiments to be embraced by the high-design community was a manifesto, and it was not long in coming.

The Outbreak of
the Ordinary

In 1966, New York's Museum of Modern Art made the second of its most important publishing contributions to the history of American architecture in the twentieth century. Having brought out *The International Style* in 1932, helping to launch European Modernism in the United States, MoMA produced thirty-four years later a no less influential volume entitled *Complexity and Contradiction in Architecture*. The author was Robert Venturi, then forty-one, a Princeton-trained architect from Philadelphia. Vincent Scully, a Yale professor of architectural history who was one of Venturi's earliest enthusiasts and became his most vigorous academic advocate, declared in his introduction to the book that it was "probably the most important writing on the making of architecture since Le Corbusier's *Vers une Architecture*, of 1923." The decade following the book's publication would bear out Scully's prediction.

As an undergraduate, Venturi had come to know firsthand the vigorous neo-Gothic buildings of Ralph Adams Cram, who had designed McCormick Hall, home to Princeton's school of architecture, although as a Quaker Venturi could be forgiven for minimizing Cram's message of "muscular" Christianity. Venturi earned his bachelor's degree in architecture *summa cum laude* in 1947, and a master's in fine arts in 1950. At the time, Princeton was unique in having an architecture school that had since its founding in 1921 been thoroughly integrated with a program in art history and archeology, and one of Venturi's chief influences while a student was the revered Jean Labatut, the French-born director of Princeton's graduate architecture program. While still emphasizing the Beaux-Arts principles in which he himself had been schooled, Labatut encouraged his students to look closely at the best works of architectural history—regardless of period or style—and to avoid what he called the "creeping architectural sameness promoted by dictatorial educators."[1] Considering that Walter Gropius had since the 1930s made Harvard's Graduate School of Design the place to be for architectural talent at the time, while relegating the study of architectural history to elective status, Labatut's dogged dedication to aesthetic open-mindedness was bold indeed. And as the later renown of his students would demonstrate, Labatut's guerrilla resistance to the hegemony of Modernism was to prove him something of a hero in retrospect.

After graduation from Princeton, Venturi returned to Philadelphia and worked briefly for the ex-partner of Louis I. Kahn, Oskar Stonorov. He then spent two and a half years with Eero Saarinen during the period when the Saarinen firm had just won the commission for the St. Louis arch and was designing the General Motors Technical Center complex in Michigan. These marked the beginning of Saarinen's most vigorously creative years, during which he was developing his ideas about approaching each commission as a distinct formal challenge, and

---

[1] See C. Ray Smith, *Supermannerism: New Attitudes in Post-Modern Architecture* (New York: E. P. Dutton, 1977), p. 79.

the experience must have been an electric one for the young Venturi. Nevertheless, in 1954, having won a Rome Prize, he decided to leave Saarinen for a two-year stay in Italy as a fellow of the American Academy. Venturi's Italian sojourn was to leave him no less changed than it had Louis Kahn, but in substantially different ways.

Kahn's experience in Rome had focused on the great monuments and ruins of the classical period; Venturi was drawn instead to the work of the great Italian Mannerists of the 1500s—especially Michelangelo—as well as to the major architects of the Baroque such as Bernini and Borromini. What attracted him to these architects, he later said, was the way they twisted the rules and traditions that underlay their architecture, layering their buildings with a multiplicity of meanings, and even injecting some humor.

When he returned to the United States, in 1956, Venturi secured a position in Louis Kahn's office, spending nine months as a junior designer and as Kahn's teaching assistant at the University of Pennsylvania. Kahn had recently finished his term at Yale's school of architecture, during which time he had designed the addition to Yale Art Gallery, and was at work on his seminal Trenton Bathhouse. As in the case of so many other American architects who had gone on to prominence (Wright being the outstanding example), Venturi had the combination of luck and savvy to seek out mentors—first Saarinen, then Kahn—who were themselves on the threshold of fame, but before they had been overburdened or corrupted by it. One scholar has argued persuasively that such contact with great talent at an early stage has been part of the training of virtually every major figure in American architectural history. These contacts, she writes, "occurred *early* in the practice of the employers, the senior architects, and just at that point when they were producing not their first designs, but the first designs that would make them famous. . . . Those younger architects, who later became famous themselves, were present at the time of their employers' sudden surges of inventiveness and strong design that led to fame."[2] This certainly seems to have been true in Venturi's case, for both Saarinen and Kahn were approaching the peak of their early creative energies while Venturi was in their offices.

---

[2] Roxanne Kuter Williamson, *American Architects and the Mechanics of Fame* (Austin, TX: University of Texas Press, 1991), p. 7.

With the growth of the preservation movement, many American architects were already beginning to focus on the value of the country's earlier—and frequently despised—architecture. But even as a child, Venturi had developed a fascination with the work of Philadelphia's historic buildings, particularly those of Frank Furness. In the introduction to a 1991 monograph, Venturi described his feeling for his iconoclastic Philadelphia forebear as "absolute unrestrained adoration and respect." Furness's architecture, Venturi wrote, "elates me by its quality, spirit, diversity, wit, tragic dimension."[3]

Having started his own practice in 1957, Venturi, who remained on the Penn faculty, in 1962 transferred his main teaching efforts to Yale at the invitation of Paul Rudolph, who had become chairman of the architecture department. By then, Venturi was at work on his first important building, Guild House, a low-cost Philadelphia housing project for the elderly, begun in 1960 and completed three years later. At first glance, Guild House is a remarkably unassuming building. Venturi selected an especially dark shade of brick to make the six-story structure blend in with what he described as its "smog-smudged" neighbors. The floor plan followed apartment house precedents of the 1920s. The double-hung windows were reminiscent of similar housing projects across the land. But lurking beneath the apparent ordinariness of Guild House was a slyly intellectual agenda. The oversize letters spelling out the building's name over the main entrance invoked the "supergraphics" in vogue at the time and were intended, according to the architect, to "contradict" the expectation that an old folks' home should remain anonymous, if not actually camouflaged. The stripe of white-glazed brick on the facade was—again, according to the architect—intended to suggest "the proportions of a Renaissance palace." The stout column of polished black granite at the main entrance proclaimed a certain level of luxury, while highlighting the contrast with the humble brick of the facade. To top the building off, Venturi selected an oversize, nonfunctioning television antenna in gold-anodized aluminum. It was, he said, to be read simultaneously as sculpture and "a symbol of the aged, who spend so much time looking at T.V."

---

[3] Robert Venturi, Introduction to *Frank Furness, the Complete Works*, edited by George E. Thomas, Jeffrey A. Cohen, and Michael J. Lewis (New York: Princeton Architectural Press, 1991), p. 6.

If the interpretations proposed by the architect do not seem immediately apparent to the average passer-by, that is the point. This was intended to be an architecture of "complexity and contradiction," provoking a second look and inviting analysis as well as surprise. As such, however, it raised the question—which would become increasingly applicable to the works of Venturi's followers—whether a building is important, or good, or even interesting, merely because the architect says it is. And with the growth of Venturi's fame, theoretical pronouncements about architecture would begin to compete aggressively with the buildings themselves for public attention and critical debate.

Soon after starting work on Guild House, Venturi embarked on a smaller but no less influential building, a house for his mother in Chestnut Hill, Pennsylvania, which was completed in 1964. Again, the first impression was of plainness, even banality. But on closer examination, the facade emerged as a carefully calculated composition. The overall form—which recalled for some critics the Low House by McKim, Mead & White—was symmetrical, but the sense of balance was subtly disturbed by the uneven placement of the windows. The arc of molding above the entrance was interrupted by both the lintel (which was so

GUILD HOUSE, *Robert Venturi, Philadelphia, 1963. The explanation was more appealing than the building.*

© *Wayne Andrews/Esto*

insubstantial as to have no apparent structural purpose) and the enormous slot that converted the whole diminutive building into an enormous broken pediment in the Chippendale fashion. Inside, the snug spaces collided in unconventional and unexpected ways.

If it all seemed a bit confusing, this was, again, intentional. In describing the building's main staircase, the architect wrote not long after its completion that "considered as an element alone in its awkward residual space, [it] is bad; in relation to its position in a hierarchy of uses and spaces, however, it is a fragment appropriately accommodating to a complex and contradictory whole and as such it is good."[4] (There was another staircase that went nowhere, dead-ending at the ceiling.) The message seemed to be: Bad is good; good is bad. Where, a reasonable observer might have wondered, were we headed?

Except for Venturi, no one seemed quite sure. But these two build-

VANNA VENTURI HOUSE, *Robert Venturi, Chestnut Hill, Pennsylvania, 1964.* The original "contradictory" dwelling.

---

[4] Robert Venturi, *Complexity and Contradiction in Architecture* (New York: Museum of Modern Art, 1966), p. 119.

Venturi, Scott Brown & Associates, Inc.

ings nonetheless attracted immediate attention among the architectural elite, and while its members were wrangling over what Venturi was up to, he launched himself onto the national architectural stage with the book that attempted to sum it all up. *Complexity and Contradiction,* much of which was written in 1962 in collaboration with Denise Scott Brown, a junior faculty member at the University of Pennsylvania, displayed a wide-ranging knowledge of architectural history (accumulated at the knee of Jean Labatut and his fellow Princeton professor, Donald Drew Egbert). With postage-stamp-size illustrations used rather like slides in a lecture, Venturi documented his view that the best architecture of the past was not as simple or as orderly (or "classical") as it might look. Michelangelo's Laurentian Library, Venturi reminded his readers, was an evolutionary distortion of the Renaissance precedents on which it was based. Borromini's San Carlo alle Quatro Fontane "abounds in ambiguous manifestations of both-and."[5] Jefferson's "combination of column sizes at the University of Virginia contradicts the maxim that every magnitude requires its own structure."[6] And so forth.

Venturi saw the Modern period as the moment when the organic growth of architecture was abruptly and unhappily halted. Beginning with Mies van der Rohe, whom he condemned for allowing "nothing to get in the way of the consistency of his order,"[7] Venturi launched a general assault on his immediate predecessors and their shared creed. In the book's opening section, entitled "Nonstraightforward Achitecture: A Gentle Manifesto," he declared:

Architects can no longer afford to be intimidated by the puritanically moral language of orthodox Modern architecture. I like elements which are hybrid rather than pure, compromising rather than clean, distorted rather than straightforward, ambiguous rather than articulated, perverse as well as impersonal, boring as well as interesting, conventional rather than designed, accommodating rather than excluding, redundant rather than simple, vestigial as well as innovating, inconsistent and equivocal rather than direct and clear. I am for messy vitality over obvious unity.[8]

If Venturi's older colleagues—Saarinen, Rudolph, even Johnson—had grown increasingly restive with the lingering restraints of their Modernist mentors, here, at last, was a *laissez passer* for a younger generation to explore entirely new territory. Again taking direct aim at Mies, whose aphorism "Less is more" had influenced architectural thinking for so long, Venturi declared: "Less is a bore."

In fact, there was not really a great deal new to Venturi's observations; since the discovery of *entasis* (the slight swelling of classical columns to compensate for the illusion that straight-sided columns shrink at the middle), students of architectural history had written innumerable doctoral dissertations on the irregularities and peculiarities that were integral elements of great design over the centuries. But in the clean-sweeping that characterized the Modernist revolt against the excesses of

---

[5] Ibid., p. 34.
[6] Ibid., p. 62.
[7] Ibid., p. 58.
[8] Ibid., p. 22.

eclecticism and neoclassicism, the search for pure solutions had rendered such ornamental refinements irrelevant, and in some eyes almost sinful. Relatively few practicing architects of the day were as knowledgeable about architectural history as was Venturi. His genius as a practicing architect was to *set aside* Modernist doctrine instead of trying to tinker with it (as Saarinen and Rudolph had), and look again at the architectural continuum that had been so abruptly interrupted in the 1920s and 1930s.

In fairness, Venturi did not cast out all the great form-givers. On the contrary, he praised selected works by Wright and Le Corbusier, and even made grudging room for Mies (citing approvingly his covertly ornamental use of the I-beams on the facade of the Seagram Building). Venturi's overarching point was that, whatever their faults, all forms of architecture were admissible as part of a greater whole. The greatest sin—of which Modernism was thoroughly guilty—was to have become exclusive rather than inclusive.

The new lands Venturi chose to explore were not, however, merely some underappreciated zones of architectural history. They were also the built world of everyday America: gas stations, fast-food restaurants, shopping centers. In his most provocative and best-known challenge to the received architectural wisdom, Venturi boldy asked, "Is not Main Street almost all right?"

The reaction to *Complexity and Contradiction* spanned the critical spectrum. Most loyal Modernists were appalled, especially by the idea that the work of mere builders might be considered appropriate sources for study by *architects*. But others saw the book's apostasy as an avenue of escape from the excesses of the recent past. Indeed, it provided permission to rethink the entire architectural proposition—and to be a bit naughty in the process. Considering the stasis of architectural thinking at the time, Venturi's fearless willingness to offend his elders was nothing short of thrilling, especially to his students.

The year after *Complexity and Contradiction* was published, Venturi and Scott Brown married, and both continued teaching at Yale, which they had by then helped to transform into the most vigorous architecture school in the country. One Yale studio course in particular consumed their attentions, and led to another publication that poured fuel on the fire ignited by their first book. In 1972, Venturi and Scott Brown,

Venturi, Scott Brown & Associates, Inc.

**THE LAS VEGAS
STRIP**, *ca. 1960.*
Venturi's insight
was to look again
at ourselves.

with their collaborator Steven Izenour, brought out *Learning from Las Vegas*, a compendium of research they and their students had done during and after a trip along Route 91, the main street of the celebrated Nevada gambling resort, which they described appreciatively as the "archetype of the commercial strip."

Among scores of other pronouncements that shocked the architectural establishment was one that claimed that "Las Vegas is to the strip what Rome is to the Piazza."[9] Here was a rather touching recurrence of the familiar need on the part of so many American architects to associate themselves with the nobility of the classical tradition, even while, in this case, asserting that the classical in the traditional sense was no longer relevant to the existing American condition. But having riveted the attention of the architectural community with their initial heresies, Venturi and his co-authors were quick to declare their respect for the virtues they felt their predecessors had betrayed. "Since we have criticized Modern architecture it is proper here to state our intense admiration of its early period when its founders, sensitive to their own times, proclaimed the right revolution," they wrote. "Our argument lies mainly with the irrelevant and distorted prolongation of that old revolution today. . . . We think the more directions that architecture takes at this point, the better."[10]

In mapping the new directions, the book divided buildings into two superficially simple categories: the "ducks" and the "decorated sheds." Venturi had derived the concept of the duck from a famous piece of vernacular architecture on New York's Long Island, a building in the shape of a duck that marked the location of a poultry farm and served at the same time as its most prominent advertisement. Venturi included the major Modernist monuments in the duck category because the individual buildings served, in his eyes, as sculptural embodiments of their purposes. (The Seagram Building said, "Business," and "Modern Architecture.") At the other end of the spectrum were what Venturi called "decorated sheds," such as Howard Johnson motels with their distinctive orange roofs, and other unpretentious buildings "where systems of space and structure are directly at the service of the program, and ornament is applied independently of them," in brief, "architecture with symbols on it."[11]

For all the talk about the virtues of Las Vegas, Ho-Jos, and the vernacular architecture of commerce, some of Venturi's most polemical thoughts in this book emerged in a comparison of his Guild House with Paul Rudolph's 1966 Crawford Manor, a high-rise residence for the el-

---

[9] Robert Venturi, Denise Scott Brown, and Steven Izenour, *Learning from Las Vegas* (Cambridge, MA: The MIT Press, 1972), p. 14.

[10] Ibid., p. xi.

[11] Ibid., p. 64.

Steve Rosenthal

derly in New Haven, Connecticut. More perhaps than any other archi-
tect of the generation immediately preceding Venturi's, Rudolph rep-
resented the self-assured brutalist. Indeed, his Art and Architecture
Building at Yale remains a landmark of the period, and Crawford
Manor was executed in the same style, and in the same rough concrete.
Although Rudolph had invited Venturi to teach at Yale, Venturi was
merciless—and rather self-serving—in pointing out the "irrelevance" of
Rudolph's concrete castle for the old in contrast to the virtues of Guild
House.

Noting that both buildings were comparable in use, size, and date of
construction, Venturi assaulted Rudolph's tower mainly for trying to be
something it was not, particularly in contrast to its Philadelphia cousin.
"The system of construction and program of Guild House are ordinary
and conventional and look it," Venturi wrote; "the system of construc-

**THE "DUCK"
BUILDING**,
*anonymous, Long
Island, New York,
1940s.* A "joke"
that became a
serious text.

tion and program of Crawford Manor are ordinary and conventional but do not look it."[12] The architect proudly described his own work as "ugly and ordinary." Rudolph's sin, Venturi explained, was in trying to make his solution to the same humble problem look "heroic and original." The examples make for a powerful comparison, but there are few cases in architectural history in which such an Oedipal moment is so articulately played out.

Whatever Freudian dimensions it may have involved, the criticism hit Rudolph, and—by extension—the surviving Modernists, where they were weakest: in their unrepentant self-importance, and their failure to accept life as it was, rather than as they thought it should be. Venturi also targeted their hypocritical if unconscious attitude toward architectural symbolism. Modern architects, he wrote, "have substituted one set of symbols (Cubist-industrial-process) for another (Romantic-historical-eclecticism) but without being aware of it."[13] Indeed, the Modernist claims about the "honest" expression of materials and the irrelevance of applied ornament had long since been discredited by the likes of Saarinen and Rudolph in the search for more visually powerful forms.

The critics were again perplexed. Writing in the *New York Times*, the critic Ada Louise Huxtable called the Yale studies (which included another one entitled "Learning from Levittown") brilliant. But she focused on a troubling issue when she went on to say: "I have a kind of love-hate relationship with Venturi designs, more for their ideological input, their profound comments on our culture, their intense and often angry wit, their consummate one-upmanship, than for their architectural results."[14]

A pair of buildings Venturi was completing at the time illustrated Huxtable's conundrum in textbook fashion. The Trubek and Wislocki houses (1971), on the Massachusetts island of Nantucket, were a witty excursion backward into the New England saltbox vernacular. Characteristically, though, Venturi fiddled with the standard window treatment, upsetting the traditional symmetry just enough to remind the visitor that an architect had been at work, but not so much as to break

---

[12] Ibid., p. 65.

[13] Ibid., p. 94.

[14] Ada Louise Huxtable, "Buildings You Love to Hate," *New York Times*, October 10, 1971.

the associative link to the seafaring past. In the end, however, it was the *idea* of fiddling with the expected, rather than the visual appeal of the buildings themselves, that had the greater impact.

Venturi was not about to suggest that he and his collaborators had come to their conclusions without help. Along with Italian Mannerism they cited a major debt to Pop Art, whose leading figures—Andy Warhol, Robert Rauschenberg, and Roy Lichtenstein, among others—had been elevating such common objects as Campbell soup cans and comic books to the level of museum collectibles. Denise Scott Brown, echoing Venturi's remarks about the relationship of the strip to the piazza, wrote in a 1971 article entitled "Learning from Pop" that the "forms of the Pop landscape are as relevant to us now as the forms of antique Rome were to the Beaux-Arts, as Cubism and the machine were to the Modern movement."

But Venturi's theories were not merely an architectural extension of the other visual arts of the day. They were also influenced by an intense component of social upheaval, and from one point of view might be seen in retrospect as an inevitable product of contemporary America. By the time *Learning from Las Vegas* was published, President John F. Kennedy had been assassinated, and demonstrations for civil rights were consuming many American cities. The war in Vietnam was escalating, and the main focus of the protests against it proved to be the nation's campuses. The universities—and particularly the architecture schools—were in turmoil. In 1968, students at Columbia and Harvard, taking a cue from their counterparts at Berkeley, occupied campus buildings and brought teaching to a halt. All across the land a feeling was growing that the traditional sources of authority were suspect.

Venturi's approach to architecture was well suited to such turbulent times. While student revolutionaries were chanting, "Power to the people," Venturi promised nothing less than to return *architecture* to the people, and joined in the aphoristic spirit of the times by declaring that his colleagues "should use convention unconventionally," that "an artful discord gives vitality to architecture," and that "architecture is evolutionary as well as revolutionary." As a sloganeer, Venturi was already in close competition with Mies and Kahn.

Beneath the apparent populism of the Venturi–Scott Brown platform, though, lingered a persistent inconsistency. However enthusiastic Venturi might be about "low" culture, he could not escape his "high"

EDEN ROC HOTEL, *Morris Lapidus, Miami Beach, Florida, 1954.* No irony, just architecture people liked.

art sources and sympathies. He remained at bottom an elitist, a product of Mainline Philadelphia and Princeton who had flourished in the academic stratosphere of the American Academy in Rome, the University of Pennsylvania, and Yale. This was no Morris Lapidus, the ebullient master of architectural kitsch and designer of Miami Beach's 1954 Eden Roc Hotel, who—despite his Columbia architecture degree—really appeared to enjoy the glitz. There was no starker demonstration of the difference between the academicism of a Venturi and the forthrightness of a Lapidus than an exhibition at the Architectural League of New York in 1970 sparked in part by the interest in Venturi's work. In the course of remarks on his career, Lapidus declared: " . . . whether it's a hospital, a school, or an office building, or an apartment house, people still have the desire for a little color, a little excitement, a little sense of being uplifted, or being titillated, of being given a little injection of joy through visual and tactile senses."[15] No one ever accused Lapidus of condescension, but Venturi could not shake the charge, and some Gropius acolytes and others went so far as to accuse him of "slumming."

As the years passed, not all of Venturi's critics were limited to the older generation. Robert A. M. Stern, who in his twenties had served as midwife to Venturi's theories by publishing an early version of *Complexity and Contradiction* while editor of the Yale architectural journal, *Perspecta,* in 1965, observed years later that "Venturi and his partners look at the past with a twisted smile."[16] Indeed, one senses a bit of a smirk even in the mature architect's presentation of himself to the public. In the formal photograph for the brochure accompanying the 1991 Pritzker Prize, which was promoted as the architectural equivalent of the Nobel and awarded to Venturi for "changing the course of architecture in this century," the architect is seen posing in front of an architectural model wearing a slightly frayed button-down shirt, the collar buttons of which are unbuttoned. This studied insouciance goes to the heart of the problem that had compromised Venturi's double-take architecture from the outset. A committed radical might have turned down such an establishment endorsement as the Pritzker Prize, but such a gesture might have seemed (horrors!) heroic. The better—more "complex and contradictory"—course was apparently to accept the award, but dress badly for the photographer.

Beneath such apparently lighthearted gestures was an implied retreat from architecture's traditional role as a communicator of communal messages and values, however offensive they might seem to some in retrospect (the power of the papacy as expressed by Bernini, the hegemony of corporate America as expressed by Mies). Venturi proclaimed his goal to be a pluralist architecture, but it has always been the role of architects to make lasting choices, stylistic as well as programmatic. Taking one's cues from strip malls has a certain energetic appeal, but is not likely to endure—any more than humor is—without the context of the time in which it was created.

The problem was that one had to "get" Venturi's architecture in

---

[15] Morris Lapidus, *An Architecture of Joy* (Miami: E. A. Seemann, 1979), p. 220.
[16] Robert A. M. Stern, *Pride of Place, the Search for a Usable Past* (Boston and New York: Houghton Mifflin/American Heritage, 1986), p. 35.

order to appreciate it. This had not been the case with Wright or Kahn—although, as is the case with all great art, the more one knew about their work, the better it was. And with the passage of the radical sentiments of the 1970s, Venturi's tweaking of the architectural establishment seemed both less bold and less interesting. What became increasingly apparent about his work and that of his collaborators was that by elevating the breaking of rules to the realm of art, they were ducking judgment by any standards except their own. If a critic found a Venturi building wanting, the architect could simply respond that the critic didn't understand it. The key to the understanding, of course, was in the architect's pocket.

Predictably enough, the intellectual support that had flourished for Venturi's novel theories in the 1960s began to fade with familiarity. But another reason was that those theories fell short—at least in the eyes of many potential clients—in satisfying an enduring human need, validated in architecture over centuries, for aspiration. In his early writings and designs, Venturi seemed to have concluded that aspiration, perhaps because it is so often betrayed by reality, should be abandoned. The argument makes sense, but it hardly inspires. While the TV antenna atop the home for the elderly in Philadelphia may have reflected a fact of life, it hardly reflected the way the residents might be expected to think of themselves.

As a self-proclaimed ironist, Venturi seemed to have missed the fact that his own "gentle manifesto" was in its way no less absolutist than the Modernist manifestos it was intended to refute. If his predecessors had embraced the machine with an enthusiasm that became oppressive, Venturi embraced the ordinary with an enthusiasm that encouraged the suspension of qualitative judgment altogether. By judging Main Street—most often the product of real estate values and traffic patterns—to be almost all right, he implicitly condemned "higher" values, including those of the Princeton education that presumably helped him analyze the ills of American architecture in the first place. In a sense, this amounted to aesthetic suicide. Venturi was trying to have it both ways, to be a prince accepted by the paupers. But invoking high art as a source does not elevate low art in the making.

By trying to make an intellectual's case for anti-intellectualism, Venturi came perilously close to indulging in the sort of "radical chic" that in the 1970s persuaded some celebrities to organize fund-raisers for radicals and revolutionaries. Such cross-over thinking can be entertaining for a while, but it is virtually impossible to sustain. Not the least of the reasons is that it ultimately involves a confrontation with questions of right and wrong. And in this, Venturi flew in the face of American architectural tradition, at least as it was represented by Jefferson, Downing, and Cram, to name only three of the most outspoken American commentators on the subject. From the outset, Venturi had insisted on suspending moral judgment. "Just as an analysis of the structure of a Gothic cathedral need not include a debate on the morality of medieval religion, so Las Vegas's values are not questioned here," he wrote in *Learning from Las Vegas.*[17] Granted, but one might argue that without medieval religion, there would have been no Gothic cathedrals. The conviction that a building is not only beautiful but stands for something the builder believes in has been a component of great architecture since the Pyramids, however much Venturi might have wished to deny it, and the absence of some comparable commitment in his own work contributed to its frequent insubstantiality.

By abstaining from value judgments, Venturi was also opening a wedge between theory and practice that would grow dangerously wide in the coming decades. It is all very well to debate values in the abstract, but rendering them in brick and concrete requires the support of a client. Apart from rare patrons with a taste for risk, the American architectural clientele has always been drawn to designers who promised buildings of lasting value. And Venturi's built architecture often failed to satisfy his theoretical ambitions.

In *Complexity and Contradiction*, Venturi had cited the literary critic Cleanth Brooks, author of the landmark study *The Well Wrought Urn*, in support of his argument that complexity and contradiction are elements in all great art, literature as well as architecture. "It is not enough for the poet," Venturi cites Brooks as writing, "to analyze his experience as the scientist does, breaking it up into parts, distinguishing part from part, classifying the various parts. His task is finally to unify experience." In response, Venturi wrote: "In the validly complex building or cityscape, the eye does not want to be too easily or too quickly satisfied in its search for unity within a whole. . . . And it is perhaps from the everyday landscape, vulgar and disdained, that we can draw the com-

[17] *Learning from Las Vegas*, p. xviii.

Venturi, Scott Brown & Associates, Inc.

WU HALL, *Princeton University, Venturi, Scott Brown & Associates, Princeton, New Jersey, 1983. A quintessentially academic building.*

plex and contradictory order that is valid and vital for our architecture as an urbanistic whole."[18]

Many of Venturi's supporters were enthralled by such a fundamentally literary approach to architecture, but even they remained guarded about the success of Venturi's own designs in unifying the diverse architectural experiences he claimed they represented. Nevertheless, while many of the corporate clients who had found Modernism to their liking avoided Venturi, the academic and institutional worlds remained enthusiastic. By 1995, his alma mater Princeton had commissioned three buildings and numerous landscaping and renovation projects by its famous alumnus. The most successful was Wu Hall, completed in 1983, a mixed-use structure intended as the centerpiece of a new residential complex for the campus.

Wu Hall makes a respectful contribution to the varied architectural

[18] Venturi, op. cit, p. 103.

palette of the surrounding area, and resolves many of the conflicts posed by its difficult site, yet its allusions (primarily to English manor houses) and deliberate discordances (expansion joints bisecting an appliquéd keystone motif) grow no more melodious with repeated visits. As in so many of Venturi's designs, the subtle alterations of the expected seem to be done more to be different than to produce something pleasing to look at. Unlike Kahn's best work, which seems timeless, much of Venturi's seems almost instantly dated, and for such a durable medium, that quality is hard to claim as a virtue.

With time and acceptance, Venturi's architecture began to take on a certain probity, but traces of the original renegade impulse endured, often in rather strained form. In the Seattle Art Museum, completed in 1991, the architect produced a sturdy masonry box that contained a number of remarkably sensitive gallery spaces. But the entrance was dominated by an enormous staircase that seemed intended primarily for cocktail receptions rather than communication among floors. The

SEATTLE ART MUSEUM, *Venturi, Scott Brown & Associates, Seattle, Washington, 1992.* The experience belies the buildup.

exterior displayed the institution's name in oversize (updated Guild House) letters—this time incised into the limestone—and it was embellished with a cacophonous assortment of colored arches and motifs vaguely reminiscent of the Northwest Indians whose relics accounted for much of the museum's collection. There is a sense here that the ideology of contradiction and complexity was struggling to survive against the traditional imperatives of monumentality. Wearing a funny hat to a formal affair is entertaining only until the other guests get used to the practice, at which point they are entitled to ask whether the ensemble is attractive or just an attempt to provoke. It is almost as if Venturi had become a captive of his reputation: In order to sustain his image as a radical theorist, he had to keep designing buildings that illustrated the theory, but in order to sustain his increasingly mainstream career, he could not let the theory get out ahead of his increasingly mainstream clients.

Venturi strove mightily to talk his way out of the conundrum. In a speech delivered in May 1994 at a Harvard University conference entitled "The Architecture of Science," the architect stuck to his—increasingly murky—justification for his work. A portion of the printed version read: "An aesthetic IRONY is that accommodation to Place in this architectural context promotes a rhythmic exception within generic order and creates thereby aesthetic tension." Unlike Kahn, whose rambling prose could be forgiven in light of a superior architectural product, the thinness of Venturi's pronouncements was made more apparent by the transience of his designs.

The Seattle Art Museum pointed up one of the problems faced by Venturi and those of his followers who wished to pursue historical ornament as a means of communication over architectural time: Few had had any hands-on training in traditional design. True, Venturi and others knew their history texts and had visited the great monuments of Europe, but none had undergone the sort of apprenticeship in masonry that had given Mies such a feel for materials, and few had been forced to study the details of historical architecture from any but an academic or literary perspective. Little wonder, then, that many of Venturi's details, while satisfying his theoretical call for historical resonance, seemed so graceless in their proportions and execution. For three-dimensional products of a radical text, they are curiously mute—and increasingly formal. Venturi, of course, would celebrate the fact as an intentional—and positive—example of contradiction.

Whatever the failings of his buildings, and however windy many of his writings in their defense, Venturi and his collaborators had succeeded in restoring some basic common sense to the thinking about American architecture. Instead of a European concept of what ought to be, architects who chose to could concentrate on what America was—and what people liked. Venturi unmasked the pomposity of such free-standing architectural "monuments" as the (prize-winning) 1968 Boston City Hall by Kallmann, McKinnell & Knowles—not to mention Rudolph's Crawford Manor—and acknowledged the central presence of the automobile as a fact of American life. He reminded the functionalists that the purely ornamental shutters on a suburban split-level could have a very real and perfectly acceptable symbolic value—and that lots of people actually liked living in suburbs, depressing as they might be to the design priesthood. To criticisms of both his work and his theories, Venturi had a suitably pluralist response. "Like any artist, I'm sorry when people don't like or understand my work," he said in 1991. "But as in the case of any artist, there's only so much I can do about it."[19]

If Venturi had provided a thinking-man's manifesto for the rejection of Modernism—and the re-embrace of history—the so-called Postmodernists to whom his theories gave birth were about to take his revolution in a very different, if far less thoughtful, direction.

---

[19] Quoted in Leigh Catesby, "Visions of Venturi," *Princeton Alumni Weekly*, November 6, 1991, p. 12.

The "Whites," the "Grays," and Postmodernism

he publication of *Complexity and Contradiction* provoked a flood of other books that took up similar themes of architectural regret and revisionism. The critics Charles Jencks and Nathan Silver in 1972 published *Ad Hocism*, arguing that architecture would be better served by the qualities of surprise and incongruity than by the rationalism of Gropius and Mies. The book's illustrations included images of a Casablanca shantytown and a violin case modified to carry a shotgun. In 1974, Peter Blake, himself a once fervent Modernist architect, sallied forth with a confessional entitled *Form Follows Fiasco: Why Modern Ar-*

chitecture Hasn't Worked, in which he documented the failures of Modernism with the zeal of a convert. A 1977 book by C. Ray Smith entitled *Supermannerism* attempted to place the collapse of Modernism in a historical continuum comparable to that of the closing phases of the Italian Renaissance. Taken together, these publications constituted a sort of collective *mea culpa* for the previous architectural era, a group confession in which each penitent seemed determined to be the most contrite about the sins of the past.

The published message was augmented by an architectural event that, more than any other, came to symbolize the death of Modernism in the public as well as the professional mind. The Pruitt-Igoe housing complex in St. Louis had been designed in 1955 by Minoru Yamasaki as a model public-sector project. To a large degree, Yamasaki's St. Louis buildings embodied what remained of the *Weissenhofsiedlung* ideal, incorporating simple, geometric forms, modern—if humble—materials, and facilities for shared activities. But the ideals were quickly betrayed by the social ills of the time, and the buildings eventually became little more than slums, wracked by the effects of drugs, crime, and poverty. The situation had deteriorated to such an extent that in 1972 the local authorities decided to demolish the central portion of the complex, and did so in spectacular fashion, with dynamite. The explosion took with it not only a blighted set of buildings, but also one of the last hopes of early Modernism to improve the lot of the working class through architecture. In the bargain, the demise of Pruitt-Igoe gave critics of the once proud Modernist faith some very public validation.

But if, with the help of Jane Jacobs, Robert Venturi, and the St. Louis demolition experts, American Modernism was now officially history, what was to replace it? Venturi had provided a certain intellectual permission to rebel, but even his own buildings had offered little in the way of direction to those architects who shared his irreverent views. And assuming that a new direction could be found, what would it be called? The early attempts at baptism included C. Ray Smith's "Supermannerism," and Jencks's "Ad Hocism," but the term that stuck was "Postmodernism."

The movement, if it could be called that, was by no means monolithic, at least at the beginning. On the contrary, its definition and mission were fiercely debated, and nowhere with more ferocity than at the Institute for Architecture and Urban Studies (IAUS), in New York City.

Saint Louis Housing Authority

PRUITT-IGOE APARTMENT COMPLEX, *Minoru Yamasaki, St. Louis, Missouri, 1955. Sending Modernism out with a bang.*

Conceived in 1967 by a media-savvy young architect named Peter Eisenman, the institute was a cross-breeding of the traditional artistic salon with a professional training program, to which was added a publishing arm that produced a steady stream of polemical books and periodicals that explored why Modernism had gone astray and probed the architectural territory that lay ahead.

In short order, IAUS took on the attributes of what the author Tom Wolfe, in his acerbic assault on the architectural elite, *From Bauhaus to Our House*, later termed the "art compound," whose members "formed an artistic community, met regularly, agreed on certain aesthetic and moral principles, and broadcast them to the world."[1] This was

---

[1] Tom Wolfe, *From Bauhaus to Our House* (New York: Farrar, Straus & Giroux, 1981), p. 17.

hardly a new phenomenon. As Wolfe reminded his readers, it had been going on in Europe for centuries, and one needed only to look back to the days of Daniel Burnham, Ralph Adams Cram, Richard Morris Hunt, and Stanford White to realize that professional networking, as it came to be called in the 1980s, had a long and powerful tradition in America.

Eisenman, who had done graduate work at Cambridge University after architectural studies at Cornell, imbued IAUS with a highly intellectual atmosphere, and under his direction the institute quickly became the place to be for up-and-coming young architects with a taste for indulging in what Eisenman and his colleagues liked to call the architectural "discourse."

The term is significant, because it invoked conversation rather than construction, and, with frequent infusions from such European literary theorists as Claude Lévi-Strauss and Jacques Derrida, the institute became a place where an architect could, without apology, spend much more time talking about architecture than creating it. Eisenman himself, during his IAUS period, built very little (four private houses identified by Roman numerals and notorious for their uninhabitability), and one of the institute's most vigorous theorists, Leon Krier, actually condemned the idea of construction as a betrayal of "pure" architecture.

For all its revolutionary trappings, the institute in its early years seemed to be promoting a turning back of the design clock. The most influential of its adherents—who included Eisenman, Charles Gwathmey, Richard Meier, John Hejduk (like Krier, a non-builder), and Michael Graves—came to be known as the "New York Five." But they were also dubbed the "Whites," partly because they preferred building their architectural models in white cardboard, but also to symbolize their affection for abstract forms. They especially favored those of Le Corbusier in the 1920s, when he was designing such pristine structures as the Villa Savoie, that deceptively simple stuccoed box elevated on spindly steel columns called "pilotis."

What saved the Whites from charges of mere Corbusian mimickry was their abandonment of any underlying social purpose in their work. Unlike Le Corbusier, who had insisted—however naively—that his architecture could improve the human condition, these architects were more interested in the clarity and cleanliness of his shapes. These men had grown impatient with the 1960s impulse toward architecture as a vehicle for social reform, and were intent instead upon the pursuit of an aesthetic of elegant abstraction.

Charles Gwathmey was steeped in Corbusian precedents, and as a student—first at the University of Pennsylvania under the influence of Louis Kahn, and then at Yale under Paul Rudolph—was drawn in particular to the French master's rather quixotic search for an ideal proportional system. Le Corbusier had called his system the Modulor, and it never proved to be of much practical value in guaranteeing high-quality design, but it nicely summed up his romantic urge for a "universal" method of producing beautiful buildings. The aspect of Le Corbusier's work that Gwathmey pursued most vigorously, however, was spatial manipulation, the interplay of volumes for visual delight.

That impulse became clear in 1966 with Gwathmey's first important project, a house and studio for his parents on the east end of New York's Long Island. The buildings were boldly abstract structures clad in vertical cedar siding—an innovative combination of Corbusian cerebration and the American construction vernacular. The buildings' minimalist angularity gave them a strong, if vaguely alien, presence on the flat landscape of the surrounding potato fields, and created a dramatic, almost brazen contrast with the shallow gables and white-columned porches of the shingled buildings that characterized the area. (The impact of Gwathmey's diminutive buildings was so great that it inspired scores of similarly abstract houses, the profusion of which soon stripped even the best of them of any novelty, turning the once tranquil farm and resort area into a sprawl of unrelated structures seeking to outdo one another in formal gymnastics.)

Following the success of the project for his parents, Gwathmey went on—with the help of his partner Robert Siegel—to more ambitious designs. The most characteristic were lavish vacation houses that expanded on the geometric experiments begun with his earliest buildings. Gwathmey and his partner also did a series of elegant restaurant, office, and apartment interiors, most of them marked by a skilled juxtaposition of expensive wood, glass block, and brushed steel. What became one of Gwathmey Siegel's signature buildings, however, was the enormous beach house the firm completed in 1979 for the wealthy de Menil family not far from the site of the house Gwathmey had done for his parents. With funds apparently no obstacle, the partners raised a palace

comparable to the most extravagant of McKim, Mead & White's earlier vacation retreats. Its complex interpenetration of interior and exterior spaces, and its lacy fretwork of screens and porches, summed up all the formal and conceptual work Gwathmey had done since his parents' house and studio. The de Menil residence, which was promptly dubbed "Toad Hall" by the architectural press in mock tribute to the excesses of the main character in the children's story *The Wind in the Willows*, all but exhausted the possibilities of applying Corbusian principles to high-end American patronage.

But where Le Corbusier's villas could be lyrical, Gwathmey Siegel's tended to be earnest—handsome, to be sure, but without much feeling that either uninvited guests or subtle thinking were welcome. This was an aesthetic of wealth, not necessarily of refinement. And refinement was a quality at which Gwathmey's fellow White, Richard Meier, ex-celled, even to a fault.

GWATHMEY HOUSE AND STUDIO, *Charles Gwathmey, Long Island, New York, 1966.* New forms, but they might have been anywhere.

Elements of several of Meier's early houses bore a family resemblance to those of Gwathmey's own vacation retreats, but Meier soon staked out an entirely independent identity. The most striking early example was his Bronx Developmental Center, a facility for disabled children in New York City. Completed in 1977, this crisply finished building was wrapped in innovative metal panels that became Meier's favorite cladding. His Hartford Seminary in Hartford, Connecticut (1981), reached even higher levels of elegance, bringing together a keen sense of three-dimensional composition with a sure feel for industrial materials—glass block and pipe railings in addition to the metal skin—and the way they could be used to exploit natural light.

Located in a low-rise residential neighborhood of undistinguished

RICHARD MEIER

neo-Colonial and mock-Tudor homes, the seminary is almost painfully pristine in its compositional clarity. But it proved to be a mere sketch for the High Museum of Art, in Atlanta, whose elegant finishes and precise forms consolidated Meier's identity as a purist. What distinguished the High Museum from its predecessors, including the Hartford Seminary, was the even more complex way in which Meier manipulated his masses, creating a dynamic interplay of exterior and interior shapes that at times appeared on the verge of confusion but was always redeemed by its underlying geometric order. While the High Museum tested the limits of Modernist rationalism, it did not exceed them, giving them instead a freshness and picturesqueness that was almost theatrical. The museum was an instant critical success when it was completed, in 1983, and it quickly qualified as a landmark on the American architectural landscape.

Yet that landscape might have been almost anywhere. One of the qualities that are at once intriguing and disturbing about Meier's best buildings is that they seem to have descended from the ether, like space vehicles, and threaten to levitate homeward at any moment. The Hartford Seminary is a stunning but ultimately alien presence in its archi-

HARTFORD SEMINARY, *Richard Meier, Hartford, Connecticut, 1981.* An otherworldly elegance.

tecturally mixed neighborhood. The High Museum, while more sculpturally dramatic than the seminary, shares its otherworldly, untouchable quality. The most familiar photograph of the building focuses on the entrance ramp, which leads with compelling force to the swelling, curved form of the main atrium. But seen from almost any other angle, the building seems cramped by its site, which is hemmed in by a combination of nondescript brick buildings and sleek high-rises, and awkward in its massing.

As in the case of the Hartford Seminary, the High Museum has not improved with age. The metal surfaces of both buildings hover over their bases as if to avoid contamination by the surrounding earth. (There could be no further extreme from Frank Lloyd Wright's need to embrace the site.) And because Meier's aesthetic was based so heavily upon cleanliness, even the slightest discoloration of the shimmering white surfaces by rain or rust can be jarring, like a gravy stain on a dress shirt. This was at heart an indoor architecture, conceived through models safe from the weather, and viable outdoors only under ideal conditions.

HIGH MUSEUM OF ART, *Richard Meier, Atlanta, Georgia, 1983. An icon that owed much to this photograph.*

No less fascinated by Le Corbusier than Gwathmey and Meier among the Whites was Michael Graves. Born in Indianapolis and trained at Harvard's Graduate School of Design, Graves was an accomplished painter as well as an architect. If Meier was drawn to Le Corbusier's pristine early forms, and Gwathmey concentrated on the spatial possibilities of the Corbusian tradition, Graves retrieved from the French master his sensibility as a Cubist painter, creating buildings that were largely exercises in the illusionistic interpenetration of planes. In this, Graves was spritually closer to Meier than to Gwathmey, but—perhaps because of his training as a painter—Graves came to shun Meier's monochromatic palette. His addition to the Benacerraf House in

MICHAEL GRAVES

Taylor Photographic, courtesy of Michael Graves

Princeton (1969) was a complex exercise in planar relationships, with openings in one wall glimpsed through another in a way that could be geometrically confusing, but had substantial visual energy. This was partly due to his use of muted colors to distinguish the separate elements from each other. A thick railing painted blue was, according to the architect, intended to suggest a "horizon," while a green beam was meant to "relate" to nearby hedges.

The Benacerraf House was the first tangible step toward the more refined system of color "coding" that Graves was to develop in the coming years: The parts of a building that touched the ground would be given earth tones (terra cotta, brown), while those open to the sky were blue, and so forth. It was all very cerebral, and sparked a devoted following at Princeton, where Graves was a member of the architecture faculty. But for the moment, Graves remained bound to an architecture based on the assembly of parts into vaguely Cubist constructions.

Arrayed against the Whites in the debates at the Institute for Architecture and Urban Studies and in the popular as well as the professional press were the "Grays," so named because they tended to build *their* architectural models in gray cardboard, and had an unconcealed fondness for the weathered shingled buildings of the late nineteenth century, but also because of their sympathy with the "impure" architecture endorsed by Robert Venturi.

The Gray who was closest to Venturi's sensibilities was Charles W. Moore. Like Venturi, Moore had studied at Princeton and had profited from that school's uniquely strong emphasis on architectural history. But he brought to the experience a less intellectual, more visceral, appreciation. Indeed, one of the many books Moore wrote (this one with Kent Bloomer) was called *Body, Memory, and Architecture*; it argued forcefully that buildings must be understood to be at some level anthropomorphic, and comprehensible to the everyday user.

In contrast to the Eastern intellectualism of Venturi, Moore's architecture drew upon Mexican and Asian as well as the more familiar European precedents. Of all the architects who came to be grouped under the Postmodernist banner, Moore was by far the most ecumenical—and the least concerned about consistency in his use of historical sources.

Moore became known for a rather flamboyant playfulness in his work, yet his first major building was sublimely understated. It was a condominum complex set on the rugged cost of California roughly a

CHARLES MOORE

hundred miles north of San Francisco. Named "Sea Ranch," the complex was inspired partly by the barns and other farm buildings that dotted the picturesque coastal landscape, but it also reflected the intense environmental concerns that had emerged with the ecology movement of the early 1960s. The site—5,200 acres of land along ten miles of spectacular cliffs—was planned with the collaboration of Lawrence Halprin, a San Francisco landscape architect who had done as much as anyone to make ecology an issue in American design.

The first buildings of what was called simply Condominium 1 were set delicately into the landscape, seeming almost to shelter in the folds of the cliffside meadows. Moore and his design partners (most prominently Donlyn Lyndon, William Turnbull, and Richard Whitaker) oriented the first buildings in such a way as to bring the maximum amount of sunlight into the interiors, but also to deflect the powerful winds off the Pacific. The architects went so far as to use wind tunnel tests to help them arrive at the most efficient shapes.

The resulting slanted rooflines were a dramatic departure from the norm for the time, and along with the spatial acrobatics of the interiors became enormously popular among other architects, who embraced them more for their formal novelty than for their environmental inspiration. Indeed, Sea Ranch imitations began turning up from California beaches to the Vermont woods, where they redefined the look of the tra-

SEA RANCH, *Charles Moore with MLTV Associates, north of San Francisco, 1965.* Moore imprinted a generation with his environmentally sensitive design.

ditional ski lodge. With the benefit of hindsight, it is fair to say that Sea Ranch imprinted a generation of architects. But the motives of sensitivity to nature and unpretentiousness of form were soon lost, in much the same way as the formal power of Gwathmey's early houses was lost, in the profusion of imitations.

Moore set off in a number of different directions after Sea Ranch. A peripatetic, impish man who loved travel and was fond of talking about the importance of "joy" in architecture, he had a carnivorous appetite for historical borrowing. In a book on the architect's work, Moore is quoted describing himself as something between "Litmus paper and a piranha fish."[2] He also had a highly developed sense of humor. It was Moore who could be most credited with the proclivity of Postmodernism for visual witticisms—not the intellectual and ironic form Venturi favored, but a bolder, at times almost slapstick variety. The main room of the house Moore built for himself in 1962 in Orinda, Califor-

---

2 Gerald Allen, *Charles Moore* (New York: Whitney Library of Design, 1980), p. 8.

Morley Baer

UNIVERSITY OF CALIFORNIA FACULTY CLUB, *Charles Moore, Santa Barbara, California, 1968.* A lively variation on a stuffy theme.

nia, had as its centerpiece a pavilion sheltering a sunken bathtub and framed by classical columns.

Lighthearted as Moore was in much of his design work, he was devoted to the fundamentals of design in his role as a teacher. When he became chairman of the architecture department at Yale in 1965, succeeding Paul Rudolph, Moore was instrumental in establishing a program that gave the students a chance not just to design buildings—from concert sheds to low-income housing—but also to build them. Except for the school that Wright had established at Taliesin, Yale was, thanks to Moore, one of the few in the country that actually provided its students with an opportunity to saw boards and hammer nails. Moore's interest in the student building project reflected another aspect of his design philosophy, which was rooted in an open-minded appreciation of the way people live their lives—how they work, relax, even bathe—rather than in preconceptions of how they *should* do these things.

Unlike many architects, Moore was a committed collaborator. His favored mode of operation was to establish a small office wherever his teaching assignments took him, whether to Berkeley, California; New Haven, Connecticut; or Austin, Texas. He would associate with a small group of other architects in the design process, often deferring to their views even though he was the senior partner. (With a candor uncharacteristic of his profession, Moore once told a colleague that he had "never actually designed a building by himself.") When the assignment ended, Moore would move on, leaving the firms—such as Moore Rubell Yudell, in Santa Monica, California, and Centerbrook Architects of Essex, Connecticut—to function on their own, often with impressive success.

As his career progessed, Moore adopted a steadily looser aesthetic. No doubt his penchant for movement—from place to place and firm to firm—had something to do with it, but so did the "let it all hang out" spirit of the times. His faculty club for the University of California at Santa Barbara (designed with Turnbull and Lyndon and finished in 1968) was a frontal assault on the traditional stuffiness associated with such facilities, and employed neon lighting and a pedestrian bridge passing through the central space. The club seemed to sum up the 1960s collision—most evident on the nation's campuses—of tradition and experimentation, and moved one architecture critic to perorate that its architect had "pushed simultaneity of disparate elements to the most attenuated limit of discordant togetherness."[3] Others saw a gratuitous manipulation of forms, distortion for its own sake.

Moore's sense of theater reached its high point in New Orleans with his Piazza d'Italia, completed in 1978. Intended to honor the city's Italian-American community, the project took the form of a circular open space that included an eighty-foot-long relief map of Italy submerged in a fountain. At one side was an exuberant pastiche of brightly colored, vaguely classical arcades decorated with Latin inscriptions. When critics pointed out to Moore that the capitals on his columns had no iden-

---

[3] C. Ray Smith, *Supermannerism* (New York: E. P. Dutton, 1977), p. 53.

tifiable precedent, he explained that they were of the "delicatessen order." Other decoration included medallions that spouted water from masks in the shape of Moore's face. Such "what-the-hell inclusiveness," as Moore's biographer David Littlejohn has described it,[4] cost Moore heavily in the estimation of many of his peers, and in the number of clients willing to put up money for what often threatened to be transient undertakings. But others came to acknowledge that, for all his apparent superficiality, Moore was onto something about how ordinary people— as opposed to many of his fellow architects—responded to architecture, and what they demanded of it.

It is not surprising that Moore was among the first in his profession to see beyond the carnival atmosphere of America's definitive playground, Disneyland, to its qualities as an inviting set of public spaces. Horrifying many of his readers, he had written as early as 1965 (only nine years after the theme park opened) that, "by almost any conceivable method of evaluation that does not exclude the public, Disneyland must be regarded as the most important single piece of construction in the West in the past several decades. The assumption inevitably made by people who have not yet been there—that it is some sort of physical extension of Mickey Mouse—is wildly inaccurate." Instead, he wrote, "it is engaged in replacing many of those elements of the public realm which have vanished in the featureless private floating world of southern California. . . ."[5] When Moore died, in 1993, no one was surprised when one of the memorial services for him included music performed by a New Orleans–style jazz combo.

Like humor, though, joy is not easily captured in bricks and mortar, and it rarely endures past the involvement of the creator. While Sea Ranch made a fundamental contribution to the thinking about American architecture in the early 1960s, much of the rest of Moore's work proved disappointingly lightweight. More than Venturi, whose architecture was overshadowed by his writings, Moore's legacy, despite his own long list of publications, rested largely on his buildings. Some of his later ones—particularly the Beverly Hills Civic Center (1982), the addition to the art museum at Dartmouth College (1985), and the Wal-

---

[4] David Littlejohn, *Architect: The Life and Work of Charles W. Moore* (New York: Holt, Rinehart & Winston, 1984), p. 79.
[5] Charles Moore, "You Have to Pay for the Public Life," *Perspecta* (1965), p. 65.

PIAZZA D'ITALIA, *Charles Moore, New Orleans, 1978.* The architecture of "joy" did not please everyone.

© Norman McGrath

ter Haas School of Business at the University of California at Berkeley (1995)—were convincing enough, particularly in the way Moore assembled their masses into inviting communal spaces, but as a whole they were more diverting than enduring.

Nevertheless, Moore deserved substantial credit for advancing the search for alternatives to Modernism. Perhaps a certain amount of mockery was necessary to temper the anger at the architectural past displayed by so many who had found fault with it. But if the debate over architecture's future benefited from Moore's humanistic good humor, it found its academic footing in a massive exhibition mounted in 1975 by New York's Museum of Modern Art. In a dramatic about-face, the institution that had done so much to advance Modernism in America turned its galleries over to an exhaustive exploration of Modernism's arch enemy, the architecture of the Beaux-Arts period. To an architectural community that had already begun to rummage through the aesthetic attic, the MoMA show provided a thrilling concentration of drawings, photographs, models, and renderings—tangible evidence of the power of classicism as it had been practiced before it had come into such disrepute. The sense of revelation appeared to vindicate such architects as Allan Greenberg, who had suffered the scorn of fashion for years while designing private villas of which John Russell Pope would have been proud. Suddenly, the decision by the J. Paul Getty Trust to create a museum in Malibu, California, in 1970 recalling the Roman villas at Herculaneum no longer seemed quite so retrograde. Indeed, the new museum, designed by the Los Angeles firm of Langdon & Wilson, seemed almost prescient, although the Getty would later change its own course, commissioning Richard Meier in 1984 to design a vast expansion in Los Angeles. (The addition of rough travertine to Meier's traditional metallic palette for this $1 billion complex, completed in 1997, threw his purist aesthetic into even higher relief.)

Architects like Greenberg held out for an almost literal interpretation of the classical ideal; but for most of their colleagues, such restraint was too much to bear. What emerged was rooted in the "rediscovery" of the classical, but it was an altered, nostalgic, version; less theatrical than Moore's, but nonetheless more picturesque than correct.

The most dramatic example of an architect who reverted to classicism was Michael Graves, who had originally been listed among the "Whites," but had concluded that his early, abstract work had been lost on much of his public, and began to move toward a more decorative architecture that, he hoped, would be "capable of being read by anybody." At first, however, building was the least of Graves's concerns. Having intended to become an artist before he decided on architecture as a career, Graves was drawn both by talent and inclination to the scenographic opportunities now open to him, and began to turn out delicately colored drawings of architectural fantasies. So popular were his drawings that they launched a brief collecting boom in what commentators quickly dubbed "paper architecture." (A show of Graves drawings at a New York gallery in 1980 brought in $60,000.)

The drawing that established Graves as the dominant representative of this new mini-industry was one of a cultural center in the form of a bridge over the Red River, separating the towns of Fargo, North Dakota, and Moorhead, Minnesota. Executed in 1977, the drawing is an evocative vision of vaguely classical forms abstracted in the manner of the eighteenth-century visionary French architects Etienne-Louis Boullée and Claude-Nicolas Ledoux. The bridge was to serve as a roadway, but was to accommodate an art museum above it, as well as a history museum on one side of the river and a broadcasting station on the other. At the middle of the span was a waterfall that was to be powered by a windmill drawing water from the river below.

With its muted earth tones evoking the Rome where, in the early 1960s, Graves had been a fellow of the American Academy, and its embrace of the automobile as well as culture, farm machinery (the windmill) as well as high technology (the broadcasting station), the Fargo-Moorhead drawing became an instant symbol of the architectural moment. Graves insisted that the design was intended to be built, but no one was surprised when it was not. In fact, the scheme probably had greater impact on paper than it would have in built form, because it seemed such an alluring justification for stepping yet further away from the restraints of construction into a realm of architecture as a topic of intellectual debate.

As Graves's early career made plain, debate was becoming an increasingly acceptable substitute for building in the eyes of many of the country's leading architectural institutions. By 1982, Graves's twenty-three-page curriculum vitae listed forty-one awards—but only four built designs. The awards derived mainly from Graves's activities as a teacher at Princeton and as a theorist. In discussing architecture, the words he emphasized were "anthropomorphic," "mythic," subliminal," and "symbolic." They were well suited to his designs. His drawings showed small, complex structures of a delicate scale, with an assortment of columns and pediments that might have been inspired by the architecture of Greece, Rome, or ancient Egypt. Most had a deceptively primitive look—warm, unthreatening, innocent. They were, to a large degree, buildings as children might like to make them if they had the drawing skills. Graves's Plocek House, in Warren, New Jersey (1979), was embellished with columns and capitals, keystones and moldings, but all simplified as if they had been assembled from a set of toy blocks.

The non-specific classicism Graves had developed was unlike anything his colleagues were doing. It was more accessible than Venturi's work, less labored than Gwathmey's, more humane than Meier's abstractions, and more consistent than Moore's flights of fancy. It was architecture in the mind's eye, and it made Graves—who fancied berets and long scarves—something of a matinee idol for a time, even beyond the architecture community. The headline of one consumer magazine profile asked rhetorically: "Why Is Everyone Talking About Michael Graves?"

But the limitations of Graves's essentially pictorial approach rapidly became apparent when he began to move beyond the intimacy of the domestic scale. Largely on the strength of his publicity (and the support of Philip Johnson, who was on the selection committee), Graves in 1980 won the competition to design a municipal building for the city of Portland, Oregon. Completed two years later, the Portland Public Services Building, as it was officially called, marked the first major urban high-rise commission for any of the New York avant-gardists who had congregated around the Institute for Architecture and Urban Studies in the 1970s. It also provoked one of the sharpest architectural debates on record.

The Graves design called for a fifteen-story building that in its blocky massing and basic organization could not have been more mundane. But the decoration of the box caused nothing short of a national architectural uproar. The main portions of the building were painted a creamy beige. Over the main entrance rose a pair of seven-story pilasters topped by enormous brackets. The central area of the upper stories was rendered as a huge truncated V, a gigantic keystone for a nonexistent arch. Along the sides of the building were draped pale blue ornamental swags, and over the front door was a super-scaled statue of a scantily clad woman in flight. Graves dubbed the statue "Portlandia," a Latinizing name with mythological resonance, however overblown it might have been for a city of the American Northwest. Completing the composition were rows of unusually small windows punched into the walls with unrelenting regularity.

Much of the local population—including the losing competitors— found the proposal an affront to the sober spirit of the rest of Portland's architecture, and protested noisily. But the sheer novelty of the scheme, coupled with the allure of having an East Coast architect of Graves's

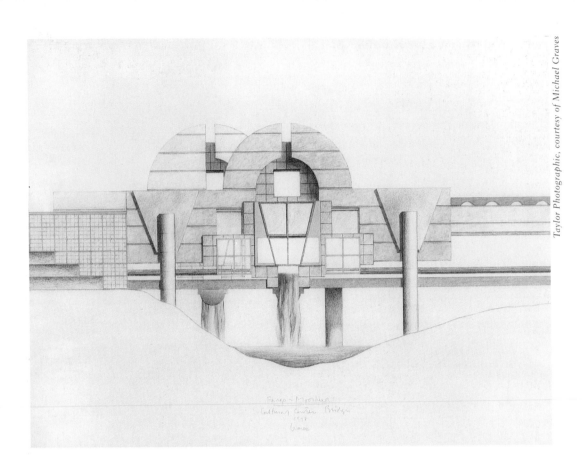

Taylor Photographic, courtesy of Michael Graves

FARGO-MOORHEAD CULTURAL CENTER, *Michael Graves, Fargo, North Dakota, 1977 (project).* The drawing helped launch a fashion for "paper architecture."

fame working in their midst, carried the day. There is no question that the building did much to put Portland on the American architectural map; but once the controversy had subsided, the impression lingered that the whole thing had been a rather condescending exercise peformed by a sophisticated academic on a culturally overeager community. The building had no inspiring interior spaces, and it was notoriously uncomfortable to work in. The exterior colors did not stand up well to the wet Oregon weather, and no promotional copy about classical precedents or literary irony could overshadow the ungainliness of Graves's ornamentation. While his simplifications of the classical orders had a certain charm at the scale of the fabric showrooms he designed for the Sunar company in Chicago and New York, they simply could not be sustained on a civic monument.

To be sure, the limited budget provided for this government project contributed to the thinness of the final effect in Portland, and Graves's more sculptural high-rise headquarters building for the wealthy Hu-

Carter Wiseman

mana Corporation in Louisville, Kentucky (1985), showed the impact of better funding. But the basic inability to translate evocative drawings into compelling spaces was not limited by size. Indeed, Graves's diminutive library in San Juan Capistrano, near San Diego (1980), was nothing short of delightful in the drawings, and in the sunshine of Southern California, Graves's Roman palette of colors was more appropriate than it was in the rainy Northwest. But the architect's exterior forms were beset by a prissy playfulness, producing a dollhouse effect that was compounded by the cramped interior spaces.

Graves's difficulty in combining his vision of idealized architecture with existing reality was put to a particularly severe test when he was commissioned in 1985 to design an addition to the Whitney Museum of American Art, in New York City. The building to which he was asked to add had been designed by Marcel Breuer, and completed in 1966. It was a brooding Modernist box of dark gray stone with a facade that stepped outward from a moat parallel to the street. A single large window stared out from the uppermost story, giving the building a Cyclopean aspect. It was not a friendly piece of architecture, but it was a monument of its time and conveyed undeniable sculptural power.

Graves proposed adding a mass of similar size at the southern end of the Madison Avenue block, linking the two with a rounded towerlike structure, and binding the three lower elements together with a Kremlinesque attic element that extended nearly the entire width of the site. The scheme met with a hail of criticism, some from preservationists who wanted to save the adjacent buildings that were to have been demolished for the addition, but most of it from those who felt that, however uninviting the original building was, it had a right to its own identity. They argued convincingly that the Graves plan would have subsumed the Breuer building and demeaned it.

Graves went through two revisions of the plan over the next years, but by 1989 funding troubles and a turnover in the Whitney's leadership combined with the continued objections from critics to doom the addition altogether. The whole episode drew much-needed attention to the challenge of adding to an existing landmark—especially a Modernist one of such power—but it also confirmed that Graves was not the architect to do it. When confronted by the single-mindedness of Breuer's geometry, Graves's picturesque aesthetic was revealed as even more superficial than it had appeared in Portland and San Juan Capistrano. Unwilling to defer to Breuer, Graves had tried to overwhelm him, but didn't have the artistic or ideological muscle to do so.

Although Graves and many of his Postmodernist colleagues went on to design several buildings for the Disney entertainment empire (see chapter Eleven), his star status began to fade after the Whitney episode. He continued to produce major buildings at a rapid rate, yet none sparked the critical attention of his earlier work. Some of his most en-

during designs proved to be for textiles and household implements, particularly a whimsical teapot, and prompted Graves to open a boutique
to complement his Princeton architecture studio.

Robert A. M. Stern was able to adapt more skillfully to the requirements of the time. As a student at Yale's school of architecture in the
early 1960s, Stern had rapidly distinguished himself, but as much
through his publishing efforts as through his design skills. He became
editor of *Perspecta*, the school's journal, and in 1965 brought out the
landmark issue that included an excerpt from Venturi's *Complexity and
Contradiction*, as well as Moore's seminal essay, "You Have to Pay for
the Public Life" (which included Moore's tribute to Disneyland). Stern
also showed a flair for scholarship, writing his thesis on George Howe,
the former chairman of the Yale department, and, as Stern pointed out
in what became a well-received book, a pivotal figure in the transition
between Eclecticism and Modernism in America.

Stern began his practice in Venturi's shadow, and his early houses,
particularly the Lang House in Washington, Connecticut (1974), were
dutiful implementations of Venturian teachings. (The appliquéd moldings on the Lang House echoed those on Venturi's house for his
mother.) But Stern quickly separated himself from the intellectualism
of Venturi, and embraced those aspects of popular taste that had a more
commercial appeal. His work was soon dominated by country and

**SAN JUAN
CAPISTRANO
LIBRARY**,
*Michael Graves,
San Juan Capis-
trano, California,
1980.* A playful
design, a frivolous
building.

suburban houses that invoked the imagery of old wealth. Many of his buildings were designed for the Hamptons, that cluster of wealthy resort communities on Long Island's east end where Gwathmey and Meier had also staked claims. But Stern soon veered away from the Corbusian tradition favored by his colleagues, and reached further back into history to the style of the shingled mansions that had proliferated in the area before the turn of the century.

Some of the buildings Stern designed in this style betrayed a certain confusion about whether he was making an architectural statement in the Venturian mode, by subtly mocking the old establishment, or earnestly trying to develop a language of his own. His 1979 renovation of a shingled cottage in East Hampton was distinguished mostly by the addition of two-dimensional mock-classical columns and a split pediment that were awkwardly, if intentionally, overscaled. A 1981 addition to a residence in Llewellyn Park, New Jersey, introduced a lumpy overlay of vaguely Egyptoid details drawing attention to the fact that the architect knew his history, but was not about to ape it.

As time went on, however, Stern chose to blur—and finally all but eliminate—the differences between the older architecture and the new on which it was based. Even the editors of a 1981 monograph on Stern's work could not resist a sly comment on his motivations. Stern, they wrote, "has an implicit understanding of the workings and desires of his urbane, elite clientele . . . he has never disappointed them or their ambitions."[6]

Although Stern continued to focus on residences for the rich, and even did a few high-rises, his most fully characteristic building was the Ohrstrom Library, a building he completed in 1991 for St. Paul's School, in Concord, New Hampshire. The library displayed historical references that spanned the spectrum of wealthy clients' architects from Edwin Lutyens to H. H. Richardson and beyond. (It was described in the architect's office brochure as "counterpointing in a dialogue across time.") Located next to a picturesque pond on the boarding school's rambling campus, the library in plan is much like that of a church, with the stacks in the nave. The two-story structure is clad in a warm red brick interrupted by decorous stripes of yellowish sandstone. At one end, a

<hr />

6 Peter Arnell, and Ted Bickford, *Robert A. M. Stern, Buildings and Projects 1965–1980* (New York: Rizzoli, 1981), p. 9.

**ROBERT
A. M. STERN**

large gable roof abuts an entertaining but rather excessive chimney. At the other end rises a turret topped by a weathervane, and, in between, the roof is punctuated by those eyebrow windows one associates with country houses of the Richardson era.

The overall impression of the building is welcoming and sheltering, but its lush appointments succeed only partly in concealing the absence of any truly fine spaces (like those in the Richardson libraries to which Stern's building bears a superficial similarity). The St. Paul's library conveyed a sense that the architect was so focused on the social implications of a building for a preparatory school that he was unable to engage the artistic opportunity.

Stern's efforts were not to be taken lightly, however. He more than any of his contemporaries seemed to have understood that Americans— at least most of those who could afford architects of stature—had never been much interested in the avant-garde. That fact was one with which Venturi had never come to terms. In his own way, Stern was assuming the mantle of George Howe while Howe was still in his pre-Lescaze period, taking architecture back to meadows sprinkled with sheep and roofs that sagged as if with the weight of centuries.

Neither Stern nor his fellow nostalgists should be judged merely by market standards. To a significant degree, they were trying to reconnect with architectural forms that most Americans understood instinctively rather than intellectually. Their buildings did not need elaborate explanations; they did not have to be "glossed," as Venturi's did. A house by Stern looked like a house, not a construction site or an artistic manifesto in built form.

However superficial or remote, Stern—along with Moore, Graves, and the more earnest Gwathmey and Meier—had achieved by the 1980s a dominance of the profession not seen since the days of the eclectics, when a small group of well-connected architects could be expected to fulfill the needs of the social and financial elite. Not the least of the reasons for the preeminence of the Postmodernists, however, was the attention lavished on them by the popular press.

The phenomenon began with the appointment in 1963 by the *New York Times* of Ada Louise Huxtable as the newspaper's first full-time architecture critic. Huxtable, who had worked briefly in the architecture department of the Museum of Modern Art, became a clear-eyed journalist with a passion for her subject, castigating in prose that was at once elegant and pugnacious what she saw as inferior design and planning, while championing the occasional architectural success (most often in the preservationist cause). As real estate development began to surge in New York and most other major cities of the country, Huxtable's insistence on intellectual rigor and high design standards made her the conscience of the national architectural community.

In 1973, Huxtable was succeeded by Paul Goldberger, a prolific, Yale-educated writer who covered the design world energetically, but stimulated resentment in some quarters by concentrating sympathetically on a small group of architects, most of whom had close ties to Goldberger's alma mater. Even on the merits, the impulse was understandable. Harvard remained closely identified with the discredited reign of Gropius and Breuer; the University of Pennsylvania had had its moment in the sun under Louis Kahn; and Graves alone could not establish Princeton as a dominant force. Cornell, which had trained Meier, was a power, but more for the theories of such faculty members as Colin Rowe than for its impact on the national design scene. Yale, however, had had both Kahn and Venturi on its faculty. Philip Johnson, although an alumnus of both Harvard College and the Graduate School of Design, had always found Yale more welcoming, and served as a visiting critic at its architecture school for twenty years. Gwathmey and Stern had both graduated from Yale, and Moore had been chairman of the architecture department.

This remarkable run of talent might never have exceeded the sum of its parts, however, without the support of Yale's most visible faculty member, Vincent Scully. Having graduated from Yale College in 1940, Scully had written an influential book on what he dubbed the Shingle Style with the support of Henry-Russell Hitchcock, Philip Johnson's collaborator in writing *The International Style*. Scully became an early and enthusiastic supporter of Johnson's architecture, but his greatest enthusiasm was reserved for Kahn and Venturi, and he made his passions known with unique energy in a series of books that were far more accessible to the average reader than most scholarship. A charismatic ex-marine, Scully was a master at the lectern, enthralling thousands of undergraduates with his colorful assertions about what he saw as the role of the subconscious in design and the universality of architectural forms. The loyalty of those students—whether architects, writers, or developers—in later life helped make of Scully nothing less than an academic celebrity, however contradictory the terms may seem. By the late 1960s, he had become unquestionably the most influential American academic in the architectural world. In 1980, he was the subject of a thirteen-page profile in *The New Yorker*, an achievement few, if any, of his art history colleagues could match.

But unlike many more traditional scholars, who limited their role to the disinterested researching, analyzing, and disseminating of historical fact, Scully became an unabashed advocate of practicing architects. Many of his aesthetic judgments were remarkably accurate, particularly those of Kahn and Venturi. But Scully also involved himself in promoting the work of those to whom he had personal loyalties.

OHRSTROM LIBRARY,
*Robert A. M. Stern,
St. Paul's School,
Concord, New
Hampshire, 1991.*
More social than
scholarly.

When Scully retired from the Yale faculty in 1991, his final lecture was covered on the front page of the *New York Times*, of which his former student Paul Goldberger was by then the cultural editor. Scully wrote introductions to monographs on the work of Stern and Graves, while Stern and Graves were unfailingly generous in their treatment of Scully in their own writings. In 1995, the Architectural League of New York, of which Stern was a past president, held a $500-a-plate dinner honoring Scully for his contributions "to the art of architecture in America." No scholar was more entitled to such public appreciation, but the list of contributors—Goldberger, Graves, Johnson, Stern, and Venturi among them— was almost as remarkable as a map of professional and personal interconnectedness as it was for artistic achievement.

Of course, if the inbreeding of the American architectural and academic communities from the 1970s through the 1990s struck some as cabalistic, there was no sin in that—as long as the result was high-quality architecture, and unless the orchestrated aspect of it all restrained the efforts of other talent. There is no question that much of the work was superior. However otherworldly Meier's High Museum, it is an architectural landmark. However transient in its influence, Sea Ranch remains a seminal work of environmental sensitivity. However derivative, Stern's Ohrstrom Library is a document of social aspiration in American architecture. But with the passage of even a few years, the Portland Public Services Building stands out more for its self-important superficiality than for the architectural advances claimed by the hype surrounding its unveiling. If that were not damage enough, one could look to the near success of Graves's crudely trendy plan for the Whitney Museum, or Gwathmey Siegel's aggressively bland addition to the Guggenheim Museum (1992), for evidence of what the influence of a small group of people with shared professional debts could accomplish.

If some observers detected an emerging sense of isolation, even corruption, among the Postmodernists, they would reply that they were simply responding to a persistent appetite among Americans for a change from the discredited ways of a previous generation. No American architect had more to do with—or was better equipped to profit from—this cyclical impulse than Philip Johnson, who had all but introduced Modernism to Main Street, and would now take major credit for having run it out of town.

High-Rise, Hard Sell

owerful as the appeal of Postmodernism had proven to be among the country's architectural avant-garde, it was slow to make major inroads with American corporations and institutions. Even their most architecturally sensitive members still shied away from Postmodernism's intellectualism, and continued to rely for their public identities on the clean lines and simplified forms of Modernism.

No architectural firm satisfied this appetite with greater skill or consistency than the one headed by I. M. Pei. After twelve years as head of the developer William Zeckendorf's in-house architecture team, Pei in 1960 left to set up his own organization, taking with him several younger men who had followed him at Harvard. After designing a number of buildings that received high critical praise but little public exposure, Pei in 1964 became the surprise choice of Jacqueline Kennedy, the widow of the assassinated president, to design a library in his memory.

The saga of the Kennedy Library was long and ultimately frustrating. The building was delayed by the difficulty of securing the desired site in Cambridge, Massachusetts, and then the local populace protested so loudly about the prospect of mobs of tourists in their midst that the library was shunted off to a landfill on the edge of Boston Harbor. However, if the executed design showed the debilitating effects of delays and disagreements (the final version was largely the work of one of Pei's collaborators), the very fact that the firm had won the commission gave it such credibility that when the John Hancock insurance company was looking for an architect to design a new headquarters building in Boston it turned to I. M. Pei & Partners.[1]

Pei put the design in the hands of Henry N. Cobb, a fellow GSD graduate who had been made a partner of the firm. Braving a storm of proper-Bostonian protest, Cobb designed a pristine glass tower that rose sixty stories over the city on a site adjacent to Richardson's Trinity Church. The outrage over what was seen by some to be a desecration of a landmark site was compounded during the building's construction when the windows began to break, sprinkling the sidewalks below with shards of glass. By the time the original glass had been replaced by a sturdier variety in 1976, the John Hancock Tower—with its crisp, V-shaped notches in the narrow ends of its parallelogram-shaped shaft—had been recognized as the most elegant corporate high-rise since the Seagram Building.

If Cobb's Hancock Tower marked what was arguably the last and best expression of the Modernist skyscraper ideal on the commercial cityscape, the building that Pei designed for the National Gallery of Art in Washington, D.C., became a comparable monument to institutional ambitions.

---

[1] For a full account of both the Kennedy Library and Hancock commissions, see Carter Wiseman, *I. M. Pei: A Profile in American Architecture* (New York: Harry N. Abrams, 1990), chapters 5 and 7.

HENRY N. COBB

The original gallery had been designed by John Russell Pope in the neoclassical style and completed in 1941. The East Building, as the addition was called, was to occupy a trapezoidal site on the Mall at the intersection of Constitution and Pennsylvania avenues. Pei exploited the awkward location by dividing the trapezoid into two triangles, providing separate spaces for exhibition galleries as well as a study center. Those triangles then became the design motif for the entire structure, which emerged as a sharp-edged sculptural composition of undeniable impact. Although the new building, which opened in 1978, was almost violently different from the original in its aesthetic, it was remarkably close in spirit, expressing a classical kinship that was amplified by the use of the same Tennessee marble as Pope had used in 1941.

As a result, the exterior of the Pei building made a powerful statement on the Mall without overwhelming its more literally classicizing neighbors. The interior, however, was unlike anything seen in museum de-

Carter Wiseman

sign since Wright's Guggenheim in New York. As in the Guggenheim, Pei's entrance has a low ceiling that contrasts dramatically with a skylit central space. But where Wright relied on the spiral for his inspiration, Pei pursued the the triangular theme spawned by the site. The result was an exhilarating piece of architectural theater, so exhilarating, in fact, that some critics complained (as they had about the Guggenheim) that the art on display took second place to the architecture. The charge was mitigated by the presence of small gallery spaces in the towers adjacent to the main space, but there was no question that the overall message of the East Building was of architectural muscle expressed with rigorous geometrical logic and extraordinary grace.

Between them, Pei and Cobb in their different architectural arenas had taken Modernist abstraction about as far as it could go. Indeed, the more picturesque attributes of Postmodernism as they had emerged in the domestic architecture of Charles Moore, Michael Graves, and Robert Stern were gradually beginning to make themselves felt among

Carter Wiseman

clients with more ambitious programs who recognized more than ever architecture's potential not just for institutional identity, but for sales. In January 1979, *Time* magazine gave Postmodernism its official endorsement as an acceptable style for late twentieth-century corporate America by putting Philip Johnson on its cover. Photographed from below, the seventy-three-year-old architect was seen in a vaguely sinister pose,

AP/World Wide Photos

his coat draped around his shoulders like a cape, holding a model of his latest building, a headquarters tower for the telecommunications giant AT&T.

Designed for a site on New York's Madison Avenue, the thirty-seven-story building was unlike anything seen in the city since the early years

© Peter Mauss/Esto

of the century. In high and deliberate contrast to the run-of-the-mill glass-and-steel Manhattan office buildings of the recent past, this headquarters was to be clad in pink granite. It was to have massive pillars at the base, which sported oculi and moldings, and an enormous arched entrance behind which hovered *Genius of Electricity,* a gold-colored sculpture of a scantily clad youth gripping a lightning bolt. (The statue had stood atop AT&T's former headquarters, and had been salvaged when the old building was sold.) Most important, however, the tower had a *top*. Rather than the flat roofs favored for tall office buildings since Mies van der Rohe had made them all but obligatory, the design for AT&T culminated in an enormous classicizing broken pediment, through which the air-handling system was to exhaust clouds of steam. In recognition of its remarkable resemblance to a traditional highboy, the building was quickly dubbed the "Chippendale" skyscraper.

The fact that the man who had been Mies van der Rohe's leading promoter could adopt such a dramatically different design language took many observers of the architectural scene by surprise. Many critics—most notably Ada Louise Huxtable of the *New York Times*, who had until then been generally sympathetic to much of Johnson's work—blasted the building as a bad joke, and a one-liner at that. But those who knew Johnson well had always appreciated his ability to anticipate changes in taste, and to adjust accordingly. Now, with the nation riding a wave of economic prosperity—and with Modernism in a terminal condition—Johnson took the Postmodernist impulse that was transforming the look of vacation houses for the wealthy and applied it to America's architectural icon, the office building. By topping it with an eye- and media-catching piece of ornament, Johnson created a unique fusion of aesthetic rebellion and corporate commerce. His building was less architecture than it was logo, less work of art than hood ornament. As such, AT&T set an example for clients and architects alike, giving them permission for a fundamental redefinition of urban architecture in America.

While the AT&T Building made headlines for its sponsor, it also catapulted Johnson into the public consciousness. He was well known to the architectural world as a curator, critic, and former assistant to Mies, but he had a mixed reputation as a designer, and had never had much of a profile beyond New York's cultural elite. Overnight, it seemed, AT&T made Johnson the subject of stories in newspapers, consumer magazines, and even on television, where he was routinely referred to as the "dean of American architecture," succeeding Richard Morris Hunt.

Johnson's eventual recognition as a celebrity might have been predicted. Born in Cleveland in 1906, he had been an accomplished social and intellectual networker since his days as an undergraduate at

Harvard, where his friends included Alfred Barr, who later founded the Museum of Modern Art and gave Johnson a job as its first director of architecture and design, and Lincoln Kirstein, the future founder of the School of American Ballet.

Johnson received his undergraduate degree *cum laude* in 1930, having concentrated in classics and philosophy, although he took seven years to do it, dropping out twice to recover from attacks of depression. After graduation, he joined his fellow alumnus Henry-Russell Hitchcock on an extended European trip, which acquainted them with the latest work of the German and French Modernists, particularly Mies van der Rohe and Le Corbusier. When they returned, Johnson served as assistant to Hitchcock organizing the now-legendary show, "Modern Architecture: International Exhibition," which opened at the fledgling Museum of Modern Art in 1932 (see chapter Four). But two years later, although he had become the first director of MoMA's department of architecture, Johnson abruptly resigned from the museum and eventually returned to Harvard to study architectural design.

In 1942, while still in architecture school, Johnson (who had already become a wealthy man through the sudden rise in the value of stock

THE GLASS HOUSE, *Philip Johnson, New Canaan, Connecticut, 1949.* A crystalline object that nonetheless has roots.

given to him by his father) designed and built a house for himself on the edge of the Harvard campus, submitting it successfully as his thesis project. The building's stark geometry and its walled forecourt showed a strong debt to Mies van der Rohe, whom Johnson had met on his European tour and whom he had encouraged to emigrate to the United States.

The Cambridge house was followed in 1949 by Johnson's most enduring architectural accomplishment. What became known as the Glass House was set on wooded property Johnson had purchased in New Canaan, Connecticut. A mere fifty-six feet long, the diminutive building was a rectangular box clad entirely in glass and supported by an elegantly crafted metal framework. Inserted toward one end was a brick cylinder that contained a fireplace and the bathroom.

For those familiar with Mies's design for the Farnsworth House, near Plano, Illinois, Johnson's building was clearly derivative, as the architect was quick to acknowledge. (Although Mies's design dated from 1946, when Johnson first studied it, it was not built until 1951.) But there were significant differences. While the Farnsworth House seemed to hover pristinely above the ground on its slim supports, its open-air porch creating a dynamically asymmetrical counterweight to the enclosed living space, Johnson's building was set firmly on its hillside site and was almost hermetically enclosed. But as a sealed volume that was at the same time transparent, Johnson's building represented a striking combination of machine age sensibility and the American romantic tradition—stretching back to Alexander Jackson Davis and Thomas Jefferson—of immersion in nature.

On the strength of the Glass House, which attracted wide critical attention, Johnson designed a series of more or less Miesian houses for other clients, and then went to work for Mies himself, serving, from 1957 to 1959, as an assistant on the Seagram Building. Johnson's major role in the Seagram design was the interior of the supremely elegant Four Seasons restaurant. But the younger man had already begun to tire of the master's rigor, and he soon set out on his own.

Johnson's eagerness to separate himself from the Miesian box began to show itself most clearly in a series of buildings for cultural institutions. The first was the Amon Carter Museum of Western Art in Fort Worth, Texas, completed in 1961. That was followed by the Sheldon Memorial Art Gallery (1963), in Lincoln, Nebraska, and the New York

Sheldon Memorial Art Gallery

State Theater (1964), which was part of Lincoln Center for the Performing Arts. All of these buildings were clad in light-colored masonry, with grand, richly appointed main spaces framed by vaguely classicizing columns and cornices. But they all shared a certain decorative fussiness that was cast into higher relief by comparison with the enduring geometric rigor of Mies's work.

Johnson's career took a dramatically new direction after he formed a partnership in 1967 with John Burgee, a Notre Dame graduate twenty-seven years his junior. Indeed, Johnson later told the architectural writer Carleton Knight III that Burgee "gave me a new lease on life."[2] The first building Johnson and Burgee designed together, the IDS Center in Minneapolis, was completed in 1973, and was a remarkably innovative achievement, combining a sleek office tower with shops, a

SHELDON MEMORIAL ART GALLERY, *Philip Johnson, Lincoln, Nebraska, 1963.* Light at first glance, lightweight at second.

---

[2] *Philip Johnson/John Burgee, Architecture 1979–1985* (New York: Rizzoli, 1985), p. 9.

hotel, and restaurants centered on a glassed-in atrium and connected to the surrounding buildings by pedestrian bridges. The success of IDS attracted the attention of a prominent Texas real estate developer named Gerald Hines, who asked Johnson and Burgee to design a high-rise for him in Houston.

Many architects with artistic ambitions had tended to shun real es-

PENNZOIL PLACE, *Philip Johnson and John Burgee, Houston, Texas, 1976. An elegant early step away from the box.*

© Houston Chronicle

tate developers, considering them a lesser breed than the enlightened individuals, universities, corporations, and other cultural institutions that made up the elite corps of American architectural patrons. But Burgee, who had spent his early professional years with the commercial Chicago firm of C. F. Murphy Associates, was less averse to such clients than was Johnson. Moreover, they both found Hines to be an unusually enlightened developer, and they decided to accept his offer. The result was Pennzoil Place, a building that became an instant landmark on the Houston skyline.

Completed in 1976, Pennzoil took the form of a pair of glass shafts separated by a narrow slot and joined at the base by a common lobby. What made the complex unlike anything that had preceded it was that Johnson and Burgee had sheared off the tops of both towers in such a way as to create an impression of trapezoidal crystals or minimalist sculptures rather than standard office-building shafts. Johnson described the effect as as "shaped modern."

But Johnson knew well that Modernism—even the shaped variety and even for high-rises—was in steep decline. Such other, younger architects as Venturi, Stern, and Graves were charting a new and different course. So Johnson once again changed his own direction and joined them. At first, his involvement was largely one of patronage. Years before, Johnson had underwritten *Perspecta*, the architecture journal that Stern edited as a graduate student, and he had helped Stern with the 1966 exhibition "40 Under 40," which gave so many of the original Postmodernists their first real professional recognition. Johnson had been a major backer of the Institute for Architecture and Urban Studies, and had been crucial to Graves's selection as architect of the Portland Public Services Building. He regularly put in a good word with clients for favored architects who were unemployed, and passed along commissions he and his partner either did not want or were too busy to accept.

Having helped so many of the younger architects launch and further their careers—and well aware that they were providing the first viable alternative to Modernism—Johnson now began to benefit handsomely from their energy and innovation. In doing so, he rapidly became his profession's most visible representative, and in turn served as its primary promoter.

With Pennzoil, Johnson and Burgee had expanded on a triad of pow-

TRANSAMERICA CORPORATION TOWER, *William Pereira, San Francisco, 1972. A maligned but bold tower-as-logo.*

erful but simple ideas. One was that real estate developers had much to offer as clients, particularly money for large-scale projects whose visibility might attract other commissions. The second was that a building with a distinctive look could be expected to do more for a company's image than a standard-issue office tower. That idea had been clear since the earliest skyscrapers in New York and Chicago, but had been diluted by the sameness of Seagram's imitators, and reemerged only in 1972 with the Transamerica Corporation's pyramid-shaped tower in San Francisco by William Pereira. The third idea was that American cities, most of which had sprung up with little historical identity of their own, could improve their images, too, if they had prominent markers visible from afar.

In an America that was increasingly concerned with imagemaking ("designer" jeans, "name-brand" Scotch, "world-class" automobiles), Johnson had understood that cities as well as corporations could profit from the impact of a skyline that was distinctly different from their competitors. "Symbolism has returned to architecture," Johnson declared some years later in assessing the impact of those insights. "The tops of buildings provide a chance for architectural expression second only to entrances. Those are the things that give a building its identity."[3] George Klein, a New York developer who became one of Johnson's main clients, addressed the issue from a less artistic direction. "Companies are always looking for an image," he said. "They spend fortunes on logos. But their most important products—their buildings—are rarely paid attention to. Architecture makes good business sense."[4]

But even Pennzoil, with its sleek glass cladding and sharp-edged simplicity, retained a basically Modernist identity, and even with shaped tops such spires had their limitations. That had been demonstrated by Citicorp Center, a fifty-nine-story Manhattan tower designed by the Boston architect Hugh Stubbins. It had gone up in 1977 to enthusiastic reviews, at least in part because its top, which was sliced off at an angle, gave it a unique presence on the New York skyline. The angled roof was originally intended to house glassed-in balconies for condominiums. That proved impractical, as did a subsequent scheme for adding solar reflectors, but the shape remained, and did much to fur-

---

[3] Interview with the author, December 3, 1981.
[4] Interview with the author, December 2, 1981.

ther Citicorp's image. In fact, although Pennzoil is usually credited with having started the trend toward recognizable tops, Transamerica and Citicorp were the true pathbreakers for the 1970s. Pennzoil's effect was amplified, however, by the doubling of the towers and their greater formal elegance.

Apart from furthering the interest in a more varied profile for the urban office building, Citicorp had been the first New York high-rise to be affected by a local zoning code change that allowed developers to build higher than normal in return for such amenities as pedestrian plazas, "vest pocket" parks, and other forms of public open space. Citicorp was permitted to go higher by including at its base a church, a public plaza, a subway entrance, and a seven-story atrium.

These zoning provisions were critical to the design of AT&T. Like Citicorp, AT&T had been granted extra height in exchange for providing pedestrian space at street level. This was done by raising the occupied floors on piers, leaving a covered plaza adjacent to the street, and adding a glazed arcade at the rear of the building. All those attributes were overshadowed by the celebrated top, for which the architects cited sources reaching back to classical Greece and ancient Egypt.

Many New Yorkers found the return to masonry and the ornamental touches a welcome relief from the repetitiveness that had dominated local skyscraper design for so long. But more thoughtful observers saw the building for what it was: an exercise in commercial promotion. John Burgee's defense of the design unwittingly confirmed the reason for the condemnation. "Not everyone likes the AT&T Building," he said during an interview, "but everyone notices it."[5]

After World War II the idea of decorating a high-rise with anything other than applied I-beams had since been so discredited by Modernism that no one had been willing to investigate alternatives for fear of arousing professional opprobrium. Clearly, if a blue-chip institution like AT&T was willing to embrace the new historicism, the rest of corporate America could safely contemplate doing the same. It had taken Johnson, with his unique combination of irreverence and influence, to act on the frustration with the Modernist forms and rehabilitate the very ideas those forms had been invented to destroy.

---

[5] Interview with M. W. Newman in *Notre Dame* (Summer 1989) p. 46.

HELMUT JAHN

Other clients were quick to follow AT&T's example, and other architects found themselves retooling rapidly in response. If New York had enjoyed a reputation for flamboyance in its early skyscrapers, Chicago was often seen as the home of sobriety in skyscraper design. But with AT&T's certification of corporate architectural display, Chicago was forced to take notice. Its most prominent player in the new skyscraper game was Helmut Jahn, a German-born architect who, like Burgee, had begun his career with the firm of C. F. Murphy Associates. Jahn plunged with abandon into the reshaping of the high-rise box, producing a series of highly recognizable towers not just for Chicago but also for New York, San Diego, and Philadelphia, among other cities. For a while Jahn became a serious competitor with Johnson and Burgee in designing the most arresting office buildings in the land. Jahn's James

R. Thompson Center in Chicago (1984)—a curved stack of three blue-glass forms centered on an atrium—was quickly dubbed "Starship Chicago" by local critics. And in New York, Jahn draped a high-rise adjacent to the Chrysler Building in a pattern of colored glass, while flaring the top in order to create, as the architect put it, "a deliberately *anti*-top building that would not compete" with its Art Deco neighbor.[6]

But virtually all of Jahn's designs were, even in the newly accepting high-rise climate, a bit too flamboyant. And, in contrast to Johnson's consistently high-budget buildings, Jahn's were almost invariably cheaply finished. Moreover, Jahn proved much less adept at presentations to clients than the elegant and articulate Johnson, who was renowned for arriving at a meeting without a single drawing, and closing the deal on the basis of wit and charm alone.

[6] Interview with the author, February 20, 1985.

The older generation did what it could to catch up with what Johnson had set in motion. Edward Larrabee Barnes, a near contemporary of Johnson's at Harvard, had remained, like Pei, devoted to the Modernist principles of basic geometry and clarity of form. Although Barnes never actually abandoned those principles, he began to inflect them with a clearly decorative intent. Barnes's 1984 headquarters building for IBM, on Madison Avenue just a block north of AT&T, was distinguished primarily by its irregular shape (which made room for a glass-enclosed public garden to the south), and the architect's use of patterned gray-green granite for the cladding. But its most powerful—some felt frightening—gesture was the way in which the forward corner

Edward Larrabee Barnes

**EDWARD
LARRABEE
BARNES**

Cervin Robinson

of the forty-three-story building was cantilevered over the entrance. Although the overhang was securely braced, the sense of instability it produced on the visitor was a deliberately theatrical act of a sort unthinkable in the era of high-rise rationalism.

Kevin Roche, the heir to Eero Saarinen's office, had made a major contribution to humanizing Modernism with his 1967 headquarters for the Ford Foundation at 320 East Forty-Third Street in New York. Its strong geometry was mitigated by an enormous atrium that contained lush plantings and was visible from the street though glass that rose almost the full height of the building. Here was a building that was as considerate of the passer-by as it was of the employee, and it set a high standard for civic architecture. After Ford, Roche became known for a much less hospitable style that relied on great expanses of reflective glass, but in the 1980s, Roche also joined the trend toward more accessible imagery. For New York's financial district, he designed a fifty-two-story tower (1985) in the form of a quasi-classical column that recalled some of the lesser entries in the 1922 *Chicago Tribune* competition. It caught the eye, but only briefly (and, given its location in the crowded

© Ezra Stoller/Esto

FORD FOUNDATION, *Kevin Roche, John Dinkeloo & Associates, New York City, 1967.* A high standard later betrayed.

Wall Street neighborhood, only from certain viewpoints). The surprisingly simple-minded image had an undeniable impact as a rendering in the client's promotional brochure, but it was simply too obvious to remain interesting for long. Its only virtue was that it was clearly not like the buildings next to it.

A few of the younger high-rise designers proved substantially more adept at creating images that were also aesthetically interesting. One of the best of these architects was Cesar Pelli, who had made a name for himself in California with the Pacific Design Center, an enormous showroom structure clad in blue glass that was completed in 1975, and while unusual in its form (which earned it the nickname "the Blue Whale"), could still be considered a late Modernist building. Pelli had moved east in 1977 to become dean of Yale's architecture school and accepted a commission from the Museum of Modern Art in New York for a residential tower and an expansion to the museum itself (1984). Rather than rely on recognizable historical devices as Johnson and Roche had, Pelli employed a rich variety of subtly colored glass to give what was little more than a standard high-rise box a sense of visual intrigue that achieved a sympathy with the older masonry buildings surrounding it, but stood entirely for a post-masonry architecture.

Skidmore, Owings & Merrill, which through its offices in New York, Chicago, San Francisco, and Portland had long dominated the world of corporate office buildings in the Miesian mode, held out against the Postmodernist phenomenon for several years. But under a young partner named David Childs it quickly found ways to catch up. His World Wide Plaza (1986) on New York's West Side drew on the masonry buildings of early twentieth-century Manhattan and attracted so much attention while still under construction that it became the subject of a television documentary.

One of the most innovative of the firms that had turned to signature high-rises as their mainstay was Kohn, Pedersen, Fox. Although based in New York, its major early success was a building in Chicago, a crystalline office tower with a curving facade that followed the bank of the Chicago River. Known as 333 Wacker Drive for its address, the 1983 building had a familial link to Modernism in its abstract geometry; but it was clearly intended to make a dramatic decorative statement, and did so with power and grace. The firm's later buildings, particularly those in New York, made more direct references to the pre–World War I

60 WALL STREET,
Kevin Roche,
New York City, 1985.
Cartoon classicism at
gargantuan scale.

© *David Anderson, photographer, J. P. Morgan & Co., Incorporated.*

generation of skyscrapers, but in ways that combined an understanding of the local architectural tradition with a striving for fresh forms. Such more established firms as Zimmer Gunsul Frasca in Portland, Oregon, also joined the move toward a more shapely brand of high-rise, which was exemplified in their case by the KOIN Center, a thirty-story brick tower completed in 1985 and intended to recall the Art Deco skyscrapers of the 1920s.

While corporations were the main proponents of the building-as-image movement, government agencies—as Jahn's James R. Thompson Center had demonstrated—were hardly immune. One of the most extraordinarily inappropriate designs of the period was by the Boston architect Moshe Safdie for a city-owned site at the southwestern end of Central Park in New York. Conceived as a pair of prismatic towers— one fifty-seven stories high and one seventy-two—sprinkled with glassed-in elements described as "hanging gardens," it was so big that it threatened to cast a significant portion of the park into shadow. Although supported by the city government, the design was defeated by a coalition of citizens' groups. Commenting on the involvement of elected representatives in a project that seemed to raise sales well above civic interests, the president of one opposition organization commented, "It's like the chaplain bayoneting the prisoners."[7]

Varied and vigorous as architects like Jahn, Pedersen, and Safdie were, Johnson maintained his lead in the pursuit of high-rise supremacy. He did it largely by turning the pages of architectural history books faster than anyone else. For the sixty-four-story Transco Tower (1983), outside Houston, Johnson and his partner turned to the setbacks of such classics by Bertram Grosvenor Goodhue as the Los Angeles Public Library and the Nebraska State Capitol (see chapter Three), but rendered them in glass and at enormous scale. The PPG Corporate Headquarters, in Pittsburgh (1984), took its inspiration from London's nineteenth-century Houses of Parliament, by Sir Charles Barry, but reinterpreted the forms in reflective glass. By wrapping the building in an irregular facade, the architects succeeded in creating a variety of reflections and re-reflections that made the surface of the tower at once ethereal and substantive. (One facet might take on the light colors of

---

7 Carter Wiseman, "Cashing in on the Coliseum," *New York*, July 29, 1985, p. 42.

the sky or the clouds, while at the same time the adjoining one might reflect the darker colors of a nearby masonry building.) But the overall effect was, in more than a technical sense, superficial.

Surely the most extreme example of the Johnson-Burgee borrowings was the RepublicBank Center, in Houston, also completed in 1984. According to the architects, one stylistic source for this pair of buildings was seventeenth-century Dutch guild halls. The lower structure served as the banking hall, while the tower contained offices. Both were clad in reddish granite and terminated in sharply pitched gables ornamented with finials. The historical references made interesting magazine copy, and the building's shape was certainly, if briefly, entertaining.

RepublicBank Center was finished in the same year as 580 California, in San Francisco, a mansarded tower topped by vaguely classical figures wrapped in togas, but without faces. A year later, Johnson and Burgee unveiled a crenellated tower for New York's Wall Street district, and a cluster of châteaulike structures known as The Crescent for Dallas. In Chicago, they produced a forty-story office tower topped with a tribute to a long-demolished building by the revered local firm of Burnham & Root, the Masonic Temple of 1892. For variety, there was even an occasional return to basic geometry, as in the garish elliptical forms of what became known as the "Lipstick Building" (1985), in New York.

Although Gerald Hines remained one of Johnson's most loyal clients, he was soon joined by other real estate developers who had come to appreciate the commercial appeal of Johnson's ability to create an image on the skyline. In New York, the most aggressive of the newly aware clients was George Klein, who made it a point to "collect" architects—Johnson, Roche, Jahn, and Pei, among them—to elevate the profile of his rapidly expanding real estate firm.

The increasing collaboration among high-profile architects and real estate developers was chronicled in company brochures and books that often approached library quality. The volume devoted to Klein's collection of towers by name-brand architects concluded with the declaration that the company "understands the attraction a certain degree of architectural style brings to prestige-minded corporations."

But no amount of promotional hype could conceal the basic lack of aesthetic sensibility—and the fundamentally hazardous potential of the tower-as-logo—presented by the Johnson-Burgee design for a quartet of office towers Klein hoped to build adjacent to New York's famed Times

© *Peter Mauss/Esto*

Square. For years, the Times Square area had been in a state of decline, the once storied "crossroads of the world" increasingly clogged with pornographic movie houses and peep shows. In 1980, a massive plan was launched by the New York State Urban Development Corporation to renovate the area. The centerpiece was to be a cluster of four office buildings ranging in height from twenty-nine to fifty-six stories. Fundamental to the plan was a set of architectural design guidelines intended to reduce the visual impact of such enormous buildings and maintain a sense of scale and continuity with the rest of the neighborhood.

Hedrich-Blessing

Johnson and Burgee were awarded the commission, and almost immediately disregarded the design guidelines. "If the guidelines were taken seriously," Johnson said not long afterwards, "you wouldn't need an architect, you'd need a technician."[8] His proposal embellished the four towers with faux-mansard roofs, monumental entrances, and assorted ornamentation evidently meant to evoke Paris on the Hudson, but at overwhelming scale.

---

[8] Interview with the author, February 9, 1984.

In this project as in no other the urban price of the promotional strategy Johnson and Burgee had undertaken with Pennzoil Place became devastatingly apparent. The Times Square proposal met with a storm of protest—much of it against the transparently inappropriate architecture—which delayed it long enough for a recession in the office market to doom it, a least in the original Johnson-Burgee form.

But by then, Johnson was so prominently established as the most mediagenic architect in America that such a setback could be absorbed without much pain. (Although Burgee continued to play a significant role in the management of the office, as well as in the design of many buildings, including those for Times Square, he was never in the sort of demand generated by Johnson's personal flair, and the partners eventually separated.) Johnson continued to delight and dismay—often simultaneously—the writers and supplicants who sought him out. At public appearances he was predictably outrageous, but almost always extracted the barbs he flung at others with what appeared to be self-deprecation. If he predicted that Louis Kahn would not be remembered as a great architect, Johnson was sure to remind the audience that he considered himself not a very good architect either. His appetite for repartee was virtually inexhaustible, but his listeners were often left wondering what it was that Philip Johnson really cared about.

One subject on which Johnson had trouble being witty was politics, about which he had once cared a great deal. Although in most cases an artist's political convictions are better left to family archives, in Johnson's case his early and persistent fascination with an especially malign political instinct provides a helpful clue to understanding the common factors underlying his apparently mercurial design career.

In the early 1930s, as the Nazis were consolidating power in Germany, Johnson had written sympathetically of the new architecture they were promoting. In 1934, shortly after resigning from the Museum of Modern Art, Johnson and a friend attempted to found a political organization called the National Party, whose proposed policies had more than a passing similarity to those of European fascism. The pair made a trip to Louisiana to see the right-wing demagogue Huey Long, and when they were turned away, Johnson went on to serve as a correspondent in Germany covering the opening phases of World War II for *Social Justice*, a publication put out by an even more rabid and

REPUBLICBANK CENTER, *Philip Johnson, Houston, Texas, 1984.* The most theatrical of the architect's one-line historical high-rises.

anti-Semitic American rightist, Father Charles Coughlin. Johnson later went to great lengths to distance himself from his youthful "enthusiasms" (in fact, not so youthful; he was in his late twenties), and such was his influence that until the 1980s few writers chose to dwell on them, if they knew of them at all. But a close look at Johnson's architecture—regardless of period or style—makes clear that it is unified by an underlying aesthetic of authoritarianism. Indeed, the fundamental relationship

42nd Street Development Project

between Johnson's mature architecture and the principles upon which his early political idols operated suggests that the apologies of his later life were less than fully sincere. And they give a sinister twist to Johnson's oft-repeated description of his ambition in life: to be *l'architecte du roi*, or architect to the king.

One can see clues to Johnson's fondness for order over art in his first important building, the Glass House, which has the rigorous clarity but not the lyricism of Mies's Farnsworth House. In an article in the September 1950 issue of *Architectural Review*, he wrote: "The cubic, 'absolute' form of my glass house and the separation of functional units into two absolute shapes rather than a major and minor massing of parts comes directly from Ledoux, the Eighteenth Century father of modern architecture."

Many of Johnson's Modernist colleagues might have used similar language in those days, but most later mellowed, while Johnson merely mutated under stylistic cover. The authoritarian impulse is no less evident in the cultural buildings Johnson designed in the 1960s, and is helpful in locating what appeared to some to be an aberration in his career on what is in fact an aesthetic continuum. For all of its apparent refinement, the Amon Carter Museum, in Fort Worth, is a fundamentally simplistic concept. One glance at the facade takes in the entire architectural idea. There is little subtlety, and no mystery. Unlike a Kahn building, this one gets no better the longer one looks at it.

The most celebrated of Johnson's buildings remains AT&T, but a close examination reveals a fundamental lack of grace. The famous top is simple without being interesting. The facade, while varied in its organization, is predictable once one has seen even a fragment of it. But it is at the base, whose gestures to urban pedestrian life were so widely publicized at the time of the design's unveiling, that the language of the architecture is clearest. The arcade is too high for its depth; the ceiling seems threatening rather than sheltering. For all the talk of Postmodernist ornamentation, the uninflected walls at the street level were not just inhospitable but offputting. (The space has since been filled in with shops, but while it remained open few pedestrians used it, and the addition of ornamental cast-iron furniture did little to increase the number of users.) The arched entry looms rather than invites. AT&T's message — reinforced by every architectural detail — is that the company is big and the employee is small. For confirmation that a different effect is possible, even in a more clearly Modernist building, one need only refer to the open space of the adjacent IBM Building, which immediately became a midday favorite, but whose corporate client was no less monolithic in its identity than AT&T.

Johnson refined his technique in the flurry of high-rises that followed AT&T. But again and again, familiar design devices recurred, particularly a relentless symmetry (Transco, PPG, 580 California), and the superscale entrance arch (Transco, RepublicBank Center, The Crescent,

190 South LaSalle, Times Square Center). The scale and details of these buildings are eerily similar to those of the Reichs Chancellery and other buildings designed by Albert Speer for Adolf Hitler.

By draping his commercial buildings in what appeared to be fanciful historical references (The Crescent) and rich materials (Transco), Johnson obscured the basic message of his architectural vocabulary rather as he masked his lack of personal commitment with wit and repartee. But the message was as evident in the 1980s as it was in the 1930s, when the stripped neoclassical became the style of choice for bureaucracies from Berlin to Washington, D.C. That even 1930s classicism could have a human face was made clear by such architects as Paul Cret and Bertram Goodhue. But without the sensibilities of such practitioners, the architecture of bureaucracy is almost always anti-artistic. No amount of historical gloss can conceal the purposeful banality of the design that flourished in Berlin and Rome before World War II, and whose sponsors Johnson would seem, on the evidence of his own designs, to have taken as mentors.

Casting back over his career, it is fair to say that, with the possible exception of the Glass House, Johnson produced not a single building that could be called great, in the sense of a University of Virginia, Boston's Trinity Church, or a Salk Institute. And the Glass House retains its allure more because of the link it provides between Mies and Johnson — and between Modernism and its legacy — than for its stature as a work of art. Yet Johnson had an indisputable effect on his profession. For one thing, his keen eye for talent and his generous financial and personal patronage were critical to many younger architects; and for another, he made architecture a subject of public debate in America as it had never been before.

What is remarkable is that so many of those engaged in that debate were willing to ignore or rationalize Johnson's lack of design talent and the damage he did to architecture and its reputation as an artistic undertaking. One of the reasons is that Johnson dominated the social and journalistic scenes on which the profession had come to depend, and he had put many of its major figures in his personal debt, financial or otherwise.

The tragedy is that in acquiring his star status Johnson had infected architecture — almost single-handedly — with a greater sense of cynicism than it had ever had in America. By making architecture largely for promotional effect, he had demeaned its standing as an art. When the economic boom of the 1980s began to fade, the architects of the logo-ism Johnson had done so much to create came to be associated in the public mind with greed and venality.

In a speech given at Harvard in 1954 entitled "The Seven Crutches of Architecture," Johnson had said, "My interest is the art of architecture, not the technics or the sociology, not whether we do anything good, but whether we do anything beautiful." Johnson's own ability to create beauty was uneven, and in any case his commitment to it even in the abstract was far less important than his commitment to power. "I am a whore," Johnson cheerfully declared at a conference of architects in 1982, perhaps expecting everyone to brush the statement off as a typical Johnson provocation.[9] It was, however, very close to a statement of fact. Johnson, of course, had turned his back on Modernism, returning to the eclectic fold with a vigor that might have impressed even Cram. The difference is that Cram believed in the power of architecture to do good, while Johnson and his followers believed no less fervently in architecture's power to sell. "I do not believe in principles, in case you haven't noticed," he told a colleague at the 1982 conference.[10]

That sort of pronouncement moved an officer of New York's venerable Architectural League (and formerly a beneficiary of Johnson's support) to lament publicly, "Except for some institutional work, virtually the entire province of new design has been left to corporations indulging their wealth in headquarter monuments of little perceivable social utility or to developers chasing wealth by meeting demands for products at the outside margins of the market. The result is profoundly debilitating for a profession that is ethical at its core."[11]

Despised or admired, though, Philip Johnson could stake a powerful claim to have been at the center of every major American architectural

---

[9] *The Charlottesville Tapes, Transcript of the Conference at the University of Virginia School of Architecture, Charlottesville, Virginia, November 12 and 13, 1982* (New York: Rizzoli, 1985), p. 19.

[10] Ibid., p. 15.

[11] Paul S. Byard, "Disquieting Times for New York Architects," *New York Times*, February 7, 1987.

development from 1932 onward. As a Modernist, he had been the most vigorous force behind the landmark "International Exhibition," and he had been instrumental in bringing Mies van der Rohe to the United States. As a preservationist, he had contributed his own money to help save numerous endangered buildings (most notably Richardson's 1887 Glessner House in Chicago). As a Postmodernist, he had promoted Venturi, and had supported the Institute for Architecture and Urban Studies. Now, still easily bored, and ever attuned to the changing ways of taste, Philip Johnson would position himself at the center of yet another architectural debate.

CHAPTER 10

The Flight from the Real

For all its apparent success in bringing architecture more force-fully before the American public, the eagerness to use high-rise design as a marketing tool had some disturbing consequences for both the art and the profession. By the early 1990s architects themselves seemed to sense a growing distaste with the unbridled commercialism of the previous decade, whether it was the corporate version as practiced by Johnson and Jahn, or the smaller-scale brand favored by such Post-modernists as Graves and Stern. Articulating this sense of malaise, the influential professional journal *Progressive Architecture* in 1994 warned of a shift in the public perception of architects: "We are too often seen, particularly since the 1980s, to be promoting the interests of wealthy clients—fat-cat developers, big corporations, rich institutions or individuals—over those of the general public."[1]

The disenchantment with an architecture of excess was not entirely a matter of principle, or even choice. Many of the nation's most powerful corporations were suffering major contractions—or "downsizing," to use the euphemism of the day. AT&T, to mention only the most prominent, announced in 1996 that it was cutting its workforce by forty thousand. (It had already been forced to sell its New York City headquarters to Sony, the Japanese electronics firm.) At the same time, many of the developers who had been the primary clients of the building-as-logo phenomenon saw their properties standing unrented for months, if not years.

But quite apart from economics, architecture was suffering a downsizing of another sort. Lawsuits over architects' liability had begun to mount, and the cost of insurance was rising accordingly. One response was for firms gradually to turn over much of the responsibility for construction to builders and contractors. While this followed a certain defensive logic, it made the architect substantially less important than before in the overall building process. "When architects declined to provide high-risk services, such as the discovery and remediation of hazardous materials," observed a writer for *Architectural Record* in 1996, "others seized the opportunity."[2]

Under financial pressure, some developers were quite capable of retaining an architect to prepare conceptual drawings for a project, then severing the relationship and turning over the development of the design and its execution to a builder or construction manager. In many cases, clients simply bypassed the architect altogether, enlisting an experienced builder who could also deliver an architectural "look" without the expense and time involved in the real thing.

In the absence of opportunities to build, and burdened by a sense that serious design was growing increasingly marginal to the building

---

[1] Thomas Fisher, "Can This Profession Be Saved?" *Progressive Architecture* (February 1994) p. 47.

[2] Robert Spencer Barnett, "Redesigning the Architect," *Architectural Record* (February 1996) p. 110.

process, it was perhaps not surprising that the architectural conversation became increasingly abstract. After all, it had been during the construction downturn of the 1970s that the thinking behind Postmodernism had flourished. But two decades later the thinking was driven not so much by a sense of rebellion against an existing orthodoxy or a longing for a lost architectural past as by a palpable sense of unease.

The corporate restructuring highlighted by the cutbacks at AT&T and such other major companies as IBM was becoming a disturbingly common phenomenon, and Americans as a society began to feel that, this time, the employment situation might not necessarily prove cyclical. The use of computers had done much to eliminate jobs in many occupations, but the situation was especially acute among architects. Between 1989 and 1994, non-residential construction in the United States declined by 31 percent, and architectural employment by 24 percent. One of the main reasons was that computers had eliminated many of the entry-level drafting jobs in which young architects usually finished their technical training.

All of these influences contributed to a sense among many avant-garde architects that they had to find a new approach, one that would be appropriate to its time, however unsettling that time might be.

Without a coherent ideology—but, thanks to Postmodernism, aware that the past was a rich resource for stylistic inspiration—some younger architects began to cast back over the unsung talents of recent history. One of them was R. Buckminster Fuller (1895–1983), the visionary inventor who had conceived the geodesic dome. During his long career, Fuller became an extraordinarily influential man, but his theories of a society unified by technology had never attracted much attention among architects. Although his enormous dome for the U. S. Pavilion at the 1967 Exposition in Montreal attracted wide public attention, the most widespread use of the invention was made by the military, which found smaller versions of the structure well suited to radar installations.

A more recent clue to a new direction had been provided by SITE (for "Sculpture In the Environment"), a group founded in 1970 in New York City. Although its lead partner, James Wines, was not an architect by training, the firm was commissioned in 1971 by the Best Products company to design a series of showrooms. Since these had to include enormous spaces that had no form implicit in their function, Wines and his colleagues produced a series of simple brick boxes, but then altered

BEST PRODUCTS STORE ("NOTCH PROJECT"), *SITE, Sacramento, California, 1977. Lighthearted, but with a question about what architecture is for.*

them with such disconcerting elements as a wall that appeared to be peeling away toward the adjacent parking lot, and one that seemed to be crumbling onto the awning over the front door. The SITE building for Best that attracted the most attention was one the firm called "Notch Project," in Sacramento, California (1977), in which the main mass of the structure seemed to have been wrenched from its foundations, leaving an entire corner of the building exposed and ragged as if it had been sitting on a geological fault. (The detached fragment was mounted on a mechanical track and could be moved at will.) Architecture, Wines said, "is not just about form anymore; it's a matter of what it makes you think about."[3]

Wines and his collaborators described their work as "De-architecture," and it had an undeniable visual appeal. But that appeal was based more on surprise and humor than on original forms, and the ideas could not be easily adapted to other building types.

More earnest attempts at new directions had been under way for

[3] Interview with the author, May 26, 1981.

some time in the studios of several solitary practitioners. O'Neil Ford (1905–1982), a Texas-based architect, had made a name for himself by promoting the integration of the products of modern technology, especially precast concrete, with regional architectural styles. Bruce Goff (1904–1982) had also been employing a variety of industrial materials, and for a church in Edmond, Oklahoma (1953), used pipes originally intended for the rigging of oil wells. Paolo Soleri had been working on Arcosanti, his experimental city in the Arizona desert, since 1970. The aim of this ambitious project, in which Soleri hoped to house seven thousand people, was "to improve urban conditions and lessen our destructive impact on the earth" by providing "a model for how the world builds its cities." All of these architects had to some degree rejected the mainstream and were arguing in their different ways for an architecture that responded to the forms or principles of nature. But apart from small groups of loyal apprentices and former students, the influence of these men remained limited to their own separate worlds.

HOPEWELL BAPTIST CHURCH, *Bruce Goff, Edmond, Oklahoma, 1953.* Industrial materials proved both practical and decorative.

The unifying influence would come from another quarter altogether. During the 1960s and 1970s, a group of philosophers and literary scholars had been advancing a theory they called "deconstruction." Led by Jacques Derrida in France, this group argued that past modes of criticism had erred in assuming that there was a fixed, accessible truth within a given work—that there was a "right answer" to the analysis of a poem, a play, or a novel. In Derrida's view, there was no absolute interpretation of a work of art. Indeed, because the artist drew on so many levels of personal experience—recognized and unrecognized—and because each reader or beholder brought such different experiences to the beholding, many interpretations could be considered equally valid.

Complicating matters was the inherent limitation of language to describe any apparent "truth" with precision. Language, Derrida and his followers insisted, was fundamentally metaphorical, and therefore inherently imprecise. By "deconstructing" a work of literature, these scholars argued, they could uncover its hidden inconsistencies, prejudices, and contradictory meanings. The result was that the apparent order imposed by the author would be revealed for what it was: camouflage for chaos, an attempt to paper over uncertainty.

The deconstruction idea swept literary departments in several prominent American universities in the 1970s, but had begun to lose favor by the 1980s, especially after a young scholar unearthed pro-Nazi articles that had been written by Paul de Man, a leading Yale deconstructionist, in the 1940s.

Even though deconstruction was fading in literary circles, it was picked up by a number of architects. Most prominent among them was Peter Eisenman, the founder of the now-defunct Institute for Architecture and Urban Studies. Transferring the literary line of thinking to architecture, Eisenman—and what soon became a growing band of followers—argued that a building should be made up of differing "texts" that need not, indeed *should* not, be resolved into a unified whole.

For all its literary sources, the architectural trend had a distinctly technological dimension. If computers were putting some architects out of business, they were also allowing others to perform extraordinary manipulations of their designs. Drawings could be disassembled, inverted, colored, or changed in scale with unprecedented flexibility and speed. Whether they could ever be executed in built form became less an issue than how complex they were on the screen. One critic described the colorful computer-aided drawings produced by the most talented practitioners as "hallucinatory," using the term as a compliment.

The growing fascination with the graphic capabilities of the computer extended the drift toward "paper" architecture that had been launched with such power by Michael Graves with his drawing of the Fargo-Moorhead Cultural Center. But now an architect didn't need Graves's substantial skill with pencils and pens; infinite graphic variations were far more easily available with a computer and a "mouse."

Although technology may have provided the underpinning for Modernism, computers alone were not enough to create a new movement. By turning their backs on technology, the Postmodernists had granted permission to rediscover history, but most of that history had been more or less classical. One period of architectural history that had been overlooked had remarkable affinities for the computers' capabilities: Russian Constructivism. Centered on such figures as Vladimir Tatlin and Kazimir Malevich, the Constructivist movement had flourished during the period just after the Revolution of 1917, and came to be identified with visionary buildings that displayed their structural members with sculptural verve. Few of them were ever built, but on paper they had considerable power, and in many cases showed a graphic sensibility that was remarkably close to what the avant-garde of the 1990s was doing on computer screens. There was an added allure in Constructivism's opposition to the "bourgeois" society against which it was rebelling, especially since Postmodernism had become so closely associated with the modern equivalents of revanchist capitalism.

Indeed, by this time, Graves, Gwathmey, and Meier had become so set in their architectural ways, and so commercially successful, that they offered little to seekers after architectural innovation. Of the original New York "Five," only Peter Eisenman and John Hejduk had remained steadfastly outside the mainstream, devoted as they were to pure form and opposed to compromising it through construction. Although Eisenman maintained a certain public persona through his publications, Hejduk had been shunted aside during the building boom of the 1980s, and was left to cultivate a small coterie of admirers as head of the architecture school at New York's Cooper Union. Now that fantasy was in vogue, Hejduk was rediscovered as something of a visionary, bizarre as some of his visions might be. At a show of his work in 1988 in New York, Hejduk exhibited schemes for what were entitled "The Useless House," "The House of the Suicide," and "The House of the Suicide's Mother."

The most prominent representative of the emerging sensibility turned out to be someone who had developed independently of the New York orbit. Frank Gehry had been born in Canada in 1929, studied at the University of Southern California and, briefly, at Harvard, but had spent nearly two decades doing unremarkable commercial buildings. Gehry eventually came to be counted by Philip Johnson among the acolytes he described as his "kids," but he had never shown much interest in the Postmodernist preoccupation with history and witticism.

FRANK GEHRY

Frank O. Gehry & Associates

Rather than look to historical precedent—as Stern, Graves, Moore, and the other Postmodernists had done—Gehry approached architecture more as sculpture, turning particularly to collage for inspiration. In the tradition of Maybeck, Greene & Greene, and other California forebears, Gehry began to chart a course far different from that of the Eastern architectural establishment.

Gehry came suddenly to prominence in 1978 when he unveiled a remodeling of his own house—an unexceptional pink-shingled suburban dwelling built in the 1920s in Santa Monica, just west of Los Angeles. When he bought it, the building was, in the architect's words, "a dumb little house with charm." But instead of abiding by its original identity or demolishing it altogether, Gehry proceeded to punch through walls and peel away part of the roof. He then expanded the building with unexpected shapes protruding at unexpected angles and executed them in an unorthodox array of materials—corrugated metal, unfinished plywood, chain-link fencing. The floor of the new dining room and kitchen area was paved with asphalt. The architect dubbed the ensemble an example of "cheapskate architecture."

One of Gehry's neighbors was so upset by what the architect had

GEHRY HOUSE, *Frank Gehry, Los Angeles, 1978.* A "dumb little house with charm" that fueled a design revolt.

done to the neighborhood that she tried to sue him. But the house was seized upon by some more sophisticated critics as a seminal example of a new sensibility, one that recognized the confused nature of contemporary life and expressed it with unmistakable energy.

Gehry's brand of architecture could be seen as particularly appropriate to California, which was regularly wracked by earthquakes, floods, mudslides, and fires. Moreover, the state's major city was renowned for its lack of coherent form, something Gehry was quick to acknowledge as a direct influence on his architecture. "I tried to see L.A. for what it was," he told an interviewer in 1991. "If you look out the window, you could see everything as a mess—or you could begin to compose things, find relationships between shapes."[4]

Primary among Gehry's techniques was the fragmentation of a building's form into discrete, largely sculptural shapes, which seemed to be colliding rather than interpenetrating in the Gwathmey or Meier mode. When a complex of buildings was involved, the collisions took on even greater complexity. Gehry's Loyola Law School in Los Angeles (1984) departed from the traditional regularity of campus plans to become an assemblage of independent forms suggesting a village that had grown up over time. But these were not nostalgic sorties back into the aesthetic of the Italian hill town, or even turn-of-the-century American summer homes—images that had been so attractive to the Postmodernists—but to the haphazard, unplanned accretion that characterized much of American urban growth, especially in Southern California.

Gehry's architecture might well have been dismissed as merely regionalist and random, but his search for formal relationships elevated it beyond those charges. However unorthodox the massing of his Loyola Law School, or his California Aerospace Museum (1984), also in Los Angeles, these early buildings manifested an underlying sense of compositional coherence, even if it was not conventionally architectural. They were interesting to look at, and grew more interesting the longer one looked. For all the sharp edges on the exteriors, the buildings' interiors were remarkably inviting. Moreover, despite the architect's insistence that his primary concerns were "cheapness, destruction, distortion, illusion, layering, and Surrealism," his buildings were also

---

[4] Cathleen McGuigan, "Maverick Master," *Newsweek*, June 17, 1991, p. 54.

enlivened by a sense of humor.[5] (The aerospace museum had an F-104 fighter plane bolted to the facade.) And his 1997 Guggenheim Museum in Bilbao, Spain, would rival Wright's original in sculptural boldness.

Gehry was hardly alone in his pursuit of alternatives to Postmodernism, but his appeal was augmented by the superficial similarity of his work to that being done by a number of Europeans who had become popular as visiting lecturers at the Ivy League architecture schools. Rem Koolhaas, a Dutch architect and writer, had made a name for himself in 1978 with a book entitled *Delirious New York*, which celebrated his romantically European image of the chaotic nature of America's dominant city in ebullient prose and irreverent caricatures of its buildings. Another name that appeared with increasing frequency on the lecture circuit was that of Zaha Hadid, an Iraqi architect based in London whose prominence was based largely on her computer-aided renderings of splintered architectural fantasies. The Viennese firm of Coop Himmelblau had attracted attention in the architecture journals for its unorthodox additions to existing buildings. The best known was an unexceptional Beaux-Arts block that, when Coop Himmelblau had finished with it, looked as if another building had been demolished and then deposited on the roof of the original.

Of course, the bourgeois regularity of Vienna, against which Coop Himmelblau was rebelling, was a far cry from the ad hoc texture of Los Angeles, which Gehry was celebrating. And the predominantly low-rise character of London had little in common with the spikey profile of New York. Nevertheless, there were formal similarities in the work of all of these architects, particularly in its aggressive diagonals and profusion of sharply pointed forms.

Ever alert to changes in the winds of architectural fashion, the durable Philip Johnson at this point emerged again to distill a formal essence from what Gehry and his contemporaries, both foreign and domestic, were doing. And with the help of several younger, like-minded architects, Johnson arranged in 1988 to mount a show at the Museum of Modern Art, perhaps hoping to do for "Deconstructivism" what he had done for Modernism in 1932.

---

[5] See Martin Filler, "Eccentric Space: Frank Gehry," *Art in America* (June 1980), p. 114.

In an effort to suggest that despite the architects' disparate origins and contexts there was indeed a movement under way, Johnson and his collaborators on the MoMA show minimized the more whimsical aspects of Gehry's work, focusing instead on its formal irregularity and its purported kinship with that of the Europeans, regardless of their fundamentally different views of the world. The show included the work of seven firms—Coop Himmelblau, Eisenman, Gehry, Hadid, and Koolhaas, as well as a Milan-based architect named Daniel Libeskind, and a Swiss-born French architect, Bernard Tschumi.

Like the 1932 show and the anointing of the New York Five in 1972, this exhibition signaled the instantaneous creation of another club. Johnson himself acknowledged the manipulatory dimension of the exercise by referring to the remark by the most publicity-conscious of all

LOYOLA LAW SCHOOL, *Frank Gehry, Los Angeles, 1984. The irregularities of an ancient village all at once.*

Michael Moran

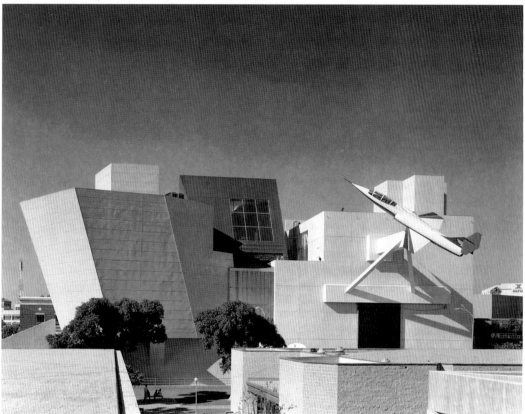

Pop artists, Andy Warhol. Everyone, Warhol had famously declared, is entitled to fifteen minutes of fame. Speaking to a reporter from *HG* magazine after the Deconstructivist show opened, Johnson, who had done so much to establish Michael Graves as the dominant Postmodernist, declared: "Michael Graves's fifteen minutes are up."[6]

Most of the architects in the MoMA show had built little of substance, and except for Gehry and, later, Eisenman, they did not seem particularly interested in doing so. Their main concentration was on imagery and language, particularly the language of anger. Their writings—and much of the writing about them—were laced with such verbs as "violate," "tear," "dislocate," "infect," "reject," "destabilize," "confuse," and "scar." The wit that had been one of Postmodernism's more attractive qualities had been replaced with an extraordinary

CALIFORNIA AERO-SPACE MUSEUM, *Frank Gehry, Los Angeles, 1984.* A sculptor's skill steadied the apparent whimsy.

---

[6] Charles Gandee, "The Revolution of '88?" *HG* (May 1988) p. 37.

amount of vitriol. One of Hadid's clients explained that he had hired her because her work expressed "danger." Writing in the catalogue to the MoMA show, the associate curator, Mark Wigley, attempted to sum up the meaning of it all. The Modernist dream, he concluded, had become "a nightmare."

The reasons were not altogether clear. Was it because jobs in architecture firms were suddenly so scarce, and commissions even scarcer? Or because the lingering hope that architecture could be a force for positive social change had been discredited by the commercialism of the previous decades? Such explanations must be left to the realm of speculation, but the symbols of animosity were unmistakable.

However complex the sources of the turn toward Deconstructivism, the message was, at heart, simplistic, suggesting that because the world is chaotic, architecture should be, too. Nonetheless, it captivated many of the architecture schools in much the same way as it had the literature departments. Eisenman, who had spent two years as an adjunct professor at Harvard's Graduate School of Design, later published accounts of the work done by his studio. A description of one of those studios by an instructor suggests both the cerebral and the combative nature of the undertaking:

> The seminar was a crash course in the martial art of intellectual doubt, for Eisenman insisted that only an informed, skilled and motivated infantry would have a chance in the impending confrontation. Writings by Freud, Derrida, and Nietzsche were studied to keen the senses to various ulterior centrisms. . . . Finally, analyses and discussions of works by Valéry and De Man and various isolated topics focussed the attack on the metaphysical and psychoanalytic implications of architecture's role as the centering experience.[7]

If the tone of the Deconstructivist "discourse" was aggressive, the content was often impenetrable. In 1991, Eisenman responded to an interviewer's question about the role of the national media in architecture by declaring: "Architecture posits the question of aura in regard to both iconic and indexical signs." He went on to assert: "I believe that we are

---

[7] Jeffrey Kipnis, "Star Wars III: The Battle at the Center of the Universe," in *Investigations in Architecture, Eisenman Studios at the GSD: 1983–85* (Cambridge, MA: Harvard University Press, 1986), p. 43.

New York Times

always going to have an auratic condition, meaning some kind of presence in architecture, because there is always some *being-in* as opposed
to the condition of language *being-as*. It is the being-in of architecture
that is questioned in the media today."[8]

The most distinguishing aspect of this kind of commentary is that it

[8] Interview with Eisenman by Robert E. Somol, *Newsline*, Columbia University
(March 1991) p. 2.

cannot be understood without access to the private language of the participants. Eisenman and his associates had rediscovered the hoary technique of appearing to be profound by using material with which their listeners were not familiar, and which they were not likely to challenge while willingly under the sway of a teacher to whom they had granted guru status. The exercise was extended to the realm of design by developing projects from physical precedents that were usually unknown to any but the initiated. Thus, a project for a site in Ohio was "based" on archeological evidence of a long-vanished cluster of Indian burial mounds, which were invisible to the occupants. Such exercises may have intellectual appeal, but they had virtually no applicability to architecture as a building art. As such, they represented an even longer stride into the in-group realm of "code" than had been taken by the Postmodernists with their often obscure quotations of historical details.

Apart from appearing to have literary and mathematical authenticity, Deconstructivism had another level of appeal. By casting itself simultaneously as architecture *and* philosophy, it could avoid judgment by the standards of either discipline. It suspended all the traditional measurements of quality. Just as university departments of literature could argue that Shakespeare was not necessarily superior to an obscure tribal bard from a previously underappreciated culture, the advocates of architectural Deconstructivism could say that one design was as good as the next because standards had no meaning in a world that was by definition irrational.

The descent of architectural discussion into the literary and abstract was given added momentum in 1988, when Bernard Tschumi became dean of the school of architecture at Columbia. "For centuries, architecture was about coherence," said Tschumi shortly after taking up his position. "Architects tried to make everything fit together neatly. But the world has changed so much that making things fit doesn't make sense anymore."[9]

The defiant libertarianism of such views had an almost irresistible appeal to some students, at least in part because it relieved them of any obligation to design buildings that might be tested by such traditional standards as buildability or maintenance. The eventual necessity of painting or repairing a Deconstructivist building was clearly not an

---

[9] Interview with the author May 12, 1988.

© Jeff Goldberg/Esto

WEXNER CENTER FOR THE VISUAL ARTS, *Peter Eisenman, Ohio State University, Columbus, Ohio,* 1989. Just because life is confusing, should architecture be?

issue in the design process. The introduction to a book entitled *Violated Perfection* attempted a summation of the Deconstructivist sensibility by declaring: "Architecture, along with accepted manners of behavior such as 'legible' language, politics, and most other cultural constructs, acts as the artificial consciousness of the modern world, as that which attempts to present an aura of stability and continuity in order to per-petuate relative relationships of economic and social power."[10] Behind

---

[10] Aaron Betsky, *Violated Perfection* (New York: Rizzoli, 1990), p. 12.

the polemical posturing, however, there was rarely more than a confluence of vaguely Surrealist juxtapositions and a romantic exploitation of mechanical forms for visual effect.

Peter Eisenman, who had popularized Deconstuctivist theory at the outset, was however no longer content with his original role, and set about remaking himself as a practicing architect. Eisenman's first major building at once embodied much of what he had been talking about, and provided proof of its lack of substance. The building was the Wexner Center for the Visual Arts at Ohio State University, in Columbus, Ohio. Completed in 1989, it was located on the edge of an oval green at the heart of the university campus and inserted between two existing structures. Its major exterior features were the partially reconstructed towers of an armory that had occupied the site, but had been demolished. At the heart of the structure was a steel trellis, described by the architect as "scaffolding," covering a pedestrian pathway.

Visitors could be forgiven for finding the building confusing. According to Eisenman, the orientation of the Wexner Center paid homage to a confluence of two grids, one by which the campus had been laid out, and another by which surveyors had laid out the city of Columbus. The building was also intended to line up with the university's football stadium, even though it lay a considerable distance across the campus.

While these points of reference made colorful subjects for conversation, they remained elusive to anyone approaching the building; the surroundings gave no clues about a preexisting grid to visitors without a map, and the football stadium could not even be seen from the site. In fact, the intensely rational explanation for the siting of the building seemed to be little more than an afterthought to justify a manifestly random combination of forms.

The exterior of the Wexner did provide a certain relief from the formality of the neighboring neoclassical buildings; the interior, however, presented a more disturbing prospect. The galleries were large or small for no apparent reason. The progression from one to another was deliberately confusing; a visitor was often not sure which way to go. The staircases were oppressively narrow; here and there a column dropped from the ceiling, stopping short of the floor; beams failed to meet the walls, and the wire cages housing the light fixtures were off-axis. The effect was disorienting, if not actually threatening.

The Wexner had a certain spatial energy, but it raised the question whether a work of architecture intended for public use—and especially the display of works of art—is the appropriate vehicle for the imposition of an architect's personal worldview. Was it fair to ask a gallery-goer or a university student interested in the art on exhibition to subject him- or herself to an architect's conviction that discomfort is central to the experience? Significantly, when the Wexner opened, no works of art were on display; the main exhibit was the building itself. When works of art were subsequently put on view, they suffered so much from the intrusion of the architecture as to make Wright's Guggenheim or Pei's East Building seem far more hospitable to their contents than their worst critics had claimed.

With the Wexner Center, Eisenman had become the first of the Deconstructivist architects to design a major building. The city of Columbus was sufficiently impressed by both the building and the publicity it attracted to commission him to design another one, this time a convention center. Completed in 1993, the 580,000-square-foot building is located on the edge of the city, adjacent to a curving stretch of highway. One facade faces the highway, to accommodate deliveries; another faces an avenue connecting downtown to the Ohio State University campus.

By definition, convention centers are almost always tedious buildings. They must house enormous amounts of neutral space that can be subdivided at will to match the needs of exhibitors who might include jewelers one week and arms dealers the next. In Columbus, Eisenman provided all the necessary space, but camouflaged it with what had by then become his signature formal distortions. Seen from above (a view possible only from airplanes or helicopters), the roof was a compendium of sinuous forms that effectively broke up what would otherwise have been a single mass. Along the street facade, the architect rendered the surface in a series of angled shapes that were embellished with suggestions of blank windows and painted a variety of pastel colors.

There is much to be said for taking formal liberties with such a potentially boring building type, but once the novelty has receded, one looks for more. Why a horizontal mullion here, a tilted one there? Why this color rather than that? The architect would have his clients believe that there were artistic answers to such questions, among them that the irregular forms were intended to relate to the collection of shabby old buildings across the street. But most of those structures were likely to be demolished at some future date. Without them, would there still be an explanation for Eisenman's treatment of the street facade? The doomed structures seemed hardly worthy of a memorial.

Of course, it is not entirely fair to demand that abstract art have an underlying rationale. But if the criteria for judgment are to be sculptural rather than architectural, it is surely fair to ask whether the visual impact is compelling. The answer to that question lies in the realm of taste, and by locating it there, Eisenman was able to escape accountability on yet another conventional scale.

The interior of the Columbus Convention Center seemed a more appropriate place to play such games, if only because the unarticulated space of the exhibition hall invited some counterbalancing vivacity. And in the concourse that abutted the exhibition area, Eiseman produced a genuinely lively experience by raising and lowering the roof level at unexpected intervals, canting the walls, and painting the entire enclosure in a variety of inviting colors. Unlike the Wexner, the Convention Center interior broadcast entertainment rather than menace. But the buildings shared a gratuitous quality: They left no clue to why the architectural decisions had been made, or why they could not have been made differently.

Eisenman extended his efforts at deliberate confusion in 1996 with the Aronoff Center for Design and Art at the University of Cincinnati. The opening of the building was accompanied by a symposium attended by a now-familiar cast of characters, among them Michael Graves, Charles Gwathmey, and Richard Meier. The angular forms, tilted walls, and overall sense of instability were celebrated not just by Eisenman's fellow architects, but by the school's officials, who were eager to point out how much attention the building would attract to a little-known institution. "We knew we can't turn this place into the University of Virginia," said the president, "but at least this way we could get people wanting to come here just to see what we have."[11] The fact that

---

11 See Paul Goldberger, "Saluting a Building by a Man Who Stirs Things Up," *New York Times*, October 14, 1996.

the university president's comment on the building's appeal sounded eerily like a 1980s real estate developer boosting sales with a high-rise logo only confirmed the triumph of notoriety over aesthetics as a measure of architectural quality.

Ironically, one of the most compelling uses of Deconstructivism's illusionistic techniques was demonstrated in a building by the architecturally conservative James Ingo Freed, a partner of I. M. Pei's who had studied under Mies van der Rohe at IIT. Freed's 1993 U.S. Holocaust Memorial Museum in Washington, D.C., employed many of the distortions of perspective and unexpected juxtapositions of materials favored by the Deconstructivists, but Freed's goal was to create an architectural evocation of the century's most heinous crimes. Here was a nightmare worthy of the name.

As had been the case during his days at the Institute for Architecture and Urban Studies, which gave birth to the journal *Oppositions*, Eisenman broadcast his new work through a publication of his own, ANYONE (for Architecture, New York, Vol. 1). The tabloid quarterly was distinguished primarily by its incestuous introspection, and caried almost exclusively transcripts of conversations among a small group of familiar participants, most prominent among them Derrida, Eisenman himself, Hadid, Koolhaas, Tschumi, and, occasionally, Gehry. Apart from the almost illegible graphics, the main visual feature of the publication was the enormous size of the photographs showing the architects at work or in conversation with their colleagues. The magazine embodied the disturbing phenomenon of having the most famous members of a public profession speaking almost entirely to each other. The conversation was unintelligible to the uninitiated, but it demonstrated that no amount of shared jargon could guarantee a work of aesthetic achievement. Indeed, when the pronouncements were measured against the extremely few built expressions of them, the architecture fell grievously short. The most powerful message broadcast by this *architecture parlante* was that cerebration past a certain point was almost always fatal to a process that had traditionally depended on some level of intuition to be considered art.

Philip Johnson, who had served as the godfather of the Deconstructivist trend, was apparently determined not to be left behind by his offspring, and he earnestly tried to remake the faux-French designs he and

U.S. HOLOCAUST
MEMORIAL MUSEUM,
*James Ingo Freed
(Pei Cobb Freed &
Partners),
Washington, D.C.,
1993.* Freed's tech-
nique was similar,
but with a deadly
earnest purpose.

John Burgee had originally created for New York's Times Square as
monuments to the new sensibility by stripping off the old decor and
adding some angular protrusions. But this time, even Johnson, weighed
down by his lingering fondness for authoritarian order, could not deliver. His awkward attempt to stay current was widely derided, even by
his most loyal followers, and a lack of funding left the tower complex
unrealized.

A more interesting—and far fresher—entry in the Times Square saga was one by Arquitectonica, a youthful firm based in Miami. It had established its reputation by embracing the racy—even vulgar—resort style of its home city. And it had come up with some entertaining results. The building that first gained it national attention was the "Atlantis," a twelve-story Miami condominium tower that was sheathed in reflective glass in sturdy Modernist fashion, but was pierced near the center by a four-story opening that passed from one side of the building to the other. Inside this "sky court" was a bright red spiral staircase, a blue whirlpool, and a swaying palm tree.

Although the members of Arquitectonica had been trained at Ivy League architecture schools, their practice had flourished outside the northeastern architectural mainstream. Nevertheless, their independent interest in the Russian Constructivists and their willingness to experiment qualified them for inclusion with the more academically based New York group, and they succeeded in winning the competition for the Times Square tower over Michael Graves and Zaha Hadid. Arquitectonica's entry—a forty-seven-story tower clad in colored glass with a curving strip of light splitting it from top to bottom—was described as looking like a meteor at the moment of impact. In this setting, such a fantastic image seemed not at all inappropriate. Times Square was, after all, based on entertainment, racy and otherwise.

But the continuing preoccupation of the more orthodox Deconstructivists with theory took them steadily further from such commercial opportunities. It seemed telling that *Progressive Architecture*, which had championed experimental design for decades, and in February 1994 had run the story posing the question: "Can This Profession Be Saved?" was, by January 1996, out of business.

With some of its most prominent representatives at the helm, American architecture as an art was drifting perilously close to irrelevance. In retrospect, there was a cruel if unintentional irony in the title of the MoMA show that had provided a name for the art's most recent incarnation. Without an ideology, with fewer clients, in search of a mission, and without charismatic leadership, the very profession seemed to be deconstructing itself. Whether it would regain its stature would depend heavily on its response to the accelerating tendency of Americans to redefine the traditional meaning of "community."

ATLANTIS CONDOMINIUM, *Arquitectonica, Miami, 1982.* An architectural sensibility that matched the mission, without cynicism.

Refuge vs. Community

John Portman didn't go to an Ivy League architecture school. And he didn't belong to any of the New York clubs where the American architectural establishment did so much of its business during the 1970s and 1980s. He certainly didn't consider himself one of Philip Johnson's "kids." And he had no use for theory. John Portman liked to think of himself as "the people's architect." And he had good reason.

Born in South Carolina in 1924 and educated at the Georgia Institute of Technology, Portman in 1963 embarked on the first phase of

JOHN PORTMAN what came to be called Peachtree Center, in Atlanta. The complex of buildings eventually included a merchandise mart, several hotels, stores, garages, and two office towers, all linked by pedestrian bridges. But the cornerstone was the Hyatt Regency Hotel, which was finished in 1967.

It was an ambitious building, providing eight hundred guest rooms and topped by a revolving restaurant that provided sweeping views of the surrounding city. But the heart of the architectural idea was the central atrium, which rose almost the entire height of the hotel. The open space was furnished with plants, fountains, and gleaming metal sculptures, and up one side sped elevators with glass walls that allowed the guests to take in the entire space as they zoomed to their rooms.

One of the reasons Portman was able to bring the Hyatt to fruition was that he was not only an architect but also a developer. He eventually became head, simultaneously, of a conglomerate of twelve different companies. Unlike Philip Johnson, who had caused a minor sensation within the architectural establishment by doing so much work for developers, but remained on the architectural side of the aisle, Portman was as much businessman as designer. And this made him nothing less than an outcast in his profession. Indeed, the American Institute of Architects at one point saw fit to question Portman's business ethics, suggesting that it was inappropriate for him to have a long-term financial interest in his designs, since it might compromise his attention to the client's needs. Portman explained that, since he was his own client, there was no conflict of interest.

The negative reaction to Portman's work within the architectural leadership was not limited to his role as a developer. The details of his first building were crude, the proportions ungainly, and the materials often cheap. But black sheep as he may have been among the elite, Portman was a hit with the customers, who packed his hotel in record numbers. With the success of the Hyatt Regency behind him, he went on to design a host of similar—and considerably more refined—complexes across the country, most notably the Embarcadero Center in San Francisco (1974), the Renaissance Center in Detroit (1976), the Bonaventure Hotel in Los Angeles (1977), and the Marriott Marquis Hotel in New York's Times Square (1985).

Portman was onto something more than making a stay at a hotel convenient and entertaining. It was fear. Many of America's major urban areas in the 1960s and 1970s were under such assault from social unrest and racial strife that *Newsweek* magazine went so far as to institute a regular department called "Cities" to complement its existing national affairs and international desks. Downtowns had become increasingly vulnerable to crime, and few people who could afford to avoid them were eager to visit them after dark. Portman understood this, and so did his public. In a monograph on his work, Portman is quoted as proclaiming: "We must provide architecture and environments that soothe the spirit and reduce anxiety and uncertainty."[1] A promotional volume on Atlanta published in 1995 noted with pride that Portman's Peachtree Center was "not a claustrophobic container but a gigantic playground, a space where you can live, eat, work and have fun without ever coming 'down to earth'."[2]

----

[1] Paolo Riani, *John Portman* (Washington, D.C.: American Institute of Architects Press, undated), p. 237.

[2] Isabella Brega, *Atlanta: Appointment with History* (New York: Smithmark, 1995), p. 99.

John Portman & Associates

Although Portman was the most flamboyant architect to adopt this otherworldly, defensive posture, others of much higher aesthetic rank were also sensitive to the problem he was addressing. The "brutalist" aesthetic embodied by Paul Rudolph in his Art and Architecture Building at Yale and by the firm of Kallmann, McKinnell & Knowles in their Boston City Hall (1968) had set the tone. I. M. Pei's 1968 Everson Art

Museum, in Syracuse, New York, was one of the more successful such buildings of the period, but it was located in an increasingly bleak downtown, and Pei gave it an appropriately impregnable look. His 1973 Johnson Museum for Cornell University included a sculpture court that was raised several stories off the ground. One reason, Pei said, was to make sure that student demonstrators would not use the works of art as targets for graffiti. Gordon Bunshaft's Hirshhorn Museum, in Washington, D.C., completed in 1974, had many of the attributes of a German gun emplacement on the Normandy coast. What had been justified artistically by the Modernists as an interest in pure forms was becoming, however subliminally, the expression of a far deeper concern for safety.

That concern contributed to the shaping of an entirely new building type: the enclosed suburban mall. The formula usually included a multistory covered atrium ringed with balconies that provided access to a wide variety of retail stores. There were almost always fountains to create soothing background noise, as well as restaurants, movie theaters, occasionally a "food court," and sometimes a stage for lunchtime performances. A few even had skating rinks. Temperature and light levels were controlled by computers.

Not the least of the reasons for the success of these malls was that they were, like Portman hotels, both convenient *and* safe. Patrolled by their own security guards, they suffered from a predictable amount of shoplifting, and the occasional car break-in in the parking lots, but the sort of street crime that had become such an issue in the inner cities was all but unknown. At the 1.3-million-square-foot Danbury Fair Mall, which opened in 1987 in Danbury, Connecticut, and quickly found itself serving as many as one hundred thousand people a day, officials reported in 1992 that there had been only two muggings and no violent crimes on the property in the previous three years.

Although the malls were often designed by architects rather than contractors, the names of even the most prolific among them—Victor Gruen, who in 1954 had designed a sprawling precursor to the mall phenomenon, the Northland shopping center in Detroit; Marc Weissman, a New York architect of more than eighty malls across the country; and Jon Adams Jerde, designer of the Mall of America, a 4.2-million-square-foot complex outside Minneapolis—rarely appeared in the high-design magazines, and their work was almost never discussed in architecture schools except as an object of derision.

UNION CARBIDE HEADQUARTERS, *Kevin Roche, Danbury, Connecticut, 1982.* Anti-urban enclaves developed problems of their own.

The same combination of appetites—primarily for convenience and security—that gave birth to the suburban mall contributed to the emergence of another architectural phenomenon as major corporations began to look beyond the big cities to locate their headquarters. These buildings often did attract architects of stature. One of the most notable examples was for Union Carbide, which between 1976 and 1982 developed 645 wooded acres in Connecticut's Fairfield County centered on an enormous structure designed by Kevin Roche, the architect of the elegant Ford Foundation headquarters in New York City. Intended to accommodate 3,500 employees, the building was made up of a quarter-mile-long block that also contained parking facilities, along with a cafeteria, a bank, and shops.

Within five years of its completion, however, Roche's building was 30 percent vacant. Union Carbide had suffered a host of setbacks, financial and otherwise, and found that it could no longer fill its rural enclave. A similar fate befell other companies as a result of hostile takeovers and leveraged buyouts. Many found that what they had promoted as a "corporate campus" was no longer suited to their changed needs, and when they decamped, they left the host towns wondering why they had agreed to change their zoning to allow the intrusions in the first place. Some of the buildings eventually found replacement tenants, but the newcomers often discovered that the spaces that had been customized for the original organization were hard to adjust for their own use. And without the unifying presence of a single company, one of the initial appeals of these buildings—their remoteness from congested downtowns—proved a deterrent to new tenants who had nothing in common with their neighbors down the hall.

One of the reasons for the growth of the suburban headquarters—and their ultimate abandonment—had been the dramatic advancements in communications technology. It was increasingly possible, through telephone, fax, computer, and modem, to do work at great distances. Not only did workers no longer need to be in the downtown office, they no longer needed to be in any one place, wherever that place might be. What came to be called "telecommuting" gave office workers dramatically greater flexibility in choosing where they lived.

Traditional suburbs had long been the location of choice for those who wanted to live outside a city but remain in touch with it, but technology-induced flexibility created an opportunity for more far-flung options. A model for such options had existed since the 1960s in the planned communities for retirees. The pioneer in this category was Sun City, which sprouted in 1960 out of what had been a cotton field on the outskirts of Phoenix, Arizona. Designed as a self-sufficient refuge for people over fifty-five years of age, it included a golf course, recreation center, shopping center, and five model homes. More than 100,000 people toured the development over the three days of its opening ceremonies (237 of them put down deposits), and its continued growth over the subsequent years led to several expansions. The promotional brochure for one of the offspring, Sun City West, described its appeal this way: "Here you'll find everything is planned and designed around the needs and wants of mature adults. You'll find a community that is kept clean and meticulously maintained."

Cleanliness—and of course security—tended to overwhelm architecture as the attractions of Sun City and the hundreds of similar communities that imitated it from California to Florida; but by the 1980s, the popularity of such communities had extended well beyond retirees.

At the upper social and financial end, the newer developments engaged some prominent designers. St. Andrews, begun in 1982 in Hastings-on-Hudson, north of New York City, was designed by Robert A. M. Stern. It was set on the grounds of the nation's oldest golf course and was made up of town houses intended to evoke a mood of turn-of-the-century elegance. According to the architect, it was "designed to bring the amenities and image of a luxurious detached single-family dwelling to the more constrained spatial context of cluster row houses."[3]

Most of the newer communities, however, had few architectural pretensions, and for all their amenities, they often had a rather sinister dimension. Klahanie, Washington, a development of nearly ten thousand east of Seattle founded in 1985, was typical. It was populated largely by middle-class people who had turned their backs on Seattle, even though that city was widely considered among the most livable in the nation. Such enclaves were exempt from local government, and had their own systems of regulation, which normally dictated such things as the colors residents could use to paint their houses, and forbade the hanging of basketball hoops on garages. Klahanie's planners expected to need twenty years to develop the property; by 1995, it was nearly full.

According to the Community Associations Institute, the number of community associations, excluding condominiums and cooperatives, increased from 4,000 in 1970 to 66,000 in 1990. Ominously, real estate agents in Southern California estimated in 1995 that one-third of all new developments built in the area over the preceding five years were not only regulated by private, or "shadow," governments, but were also enclosed by walls and gates.

Closely related in spirit to the growth of the corporate parks and the gated residential communities were the agglomerations described by *Washington Post* writer Joel Garreau in a 1991 book as "edge cities." These were massive undertakings that grew rapidly but without much advance planning near major freeway intersections—within reach of major cities, but usually beyond the reach of zoning restrictions. Among them were the Galleria area west of Houston (developed by Gerald Hines, and larger than downtown Denver); the area around Route 128 and the Massachusetts Turnpike near Boston; Irvine, in Orange County

---

[3] *Robert A. M. Stern: Buildings and Projects, 1981–1986* (New York: Rizzoli, 1986), p. 86.

south of Los Angeles; the Tysons Corner area outside Washington, D.C.; and the Perimeter Center area at the northern end of Atlanta's beltway.

According to Garreau, an edge city had at least 5 million square feet of leasable office space, 0.5 million square feet of retail space, and "more jobs than bedrooms." He estimated that by 1991, two-thirds of American office facilities were to be found in such concentrations, and 80 percent of them had grown up since 1970. Garreau argued that "By moving the world of work and commerce out near the homes of the middle and upper-middle class, [edge cities have] knocked the pins out from under suburbia as a place apart."[4] These communities, he predicted, would be the "crucible of America's urban future."

One of the main reasons for such a forecast was that edge cities did at a much larger scale what John Portman had done in his hotels. Garreau described Bridgewater Commons, an edge city in northern New Jersey, as paying "overwhelming homage to one principle: making women—specifically women—feel safe."[5] The efforts paid off. Some 9 million people a year passed through Bridgewater Commons. In the development's first two years, the local police received reports of only two assaults.

The builders of these communities developed a design language of their own. An "active water feature" described an artificial fountain or waterfall that masked traffic noise. But, as was the case for malls, rarely did the edge city developers engage architects from the design establishment. In general, development and high design maintained their traditional distance, even as this major new building opportunity was evolving. Garreau reported that "Architects were lucky if they got to choose the skin of the building." The reason, he argued, was that "They viewed themselves as having a higher calling—trying to find someone to pay them to define space in ways that relate man to his environment with fresh insight and artistic visions, perhaps. It was not so much that these designers had been banished from playing a role in the major decisions about Edge City. As often as not, they had exiled themselves."[6] The developers, meanwhile, "had spent lifetimes laboring to uncover

[4] Joel Garreau, *Edge City* (New York: Doubleday, 1991), p. 399.
[5] Ibid., p. 49.
[6] Ibid., p. 221.

what they regarded as the verifiable, nontheoretical realities that govern human behavior. They had then gone out and built an entire world around their understanding of what Americans demonstrably and reliably valued."[7]

As a result, some building types actually seemed to be dying out. With such exceptions as the expansion of the J. Paul Getty Museum, by Richard Meier, and the 1994 San Francisco Museum of Modern Art, by the Swiss architect Mario Botta, there were fewer major musems under construction, partly because so many had been built in recent years, but also because financial support for the arts was dwindling, and many of the cities in which they were located were increasingly unattractive to visit. There was slim likelihood that there would be many more calls for large civic buildings of the sort Michael Graves had designed for Portland. Entertainment was so easily and cheaply available through television and videos that conventional performance halls were threatened with obsolescence (although baseball stadiums were enjoying a resurgence, in part because of the links they offered to an idealized American past that predated football). And so many downtown skyscrapers had been left partially empty by corporate downsizing that the prospect of many more high-rises on the scale of New York's AT&T or IBM buildings was questionable, at least in the near term. (According to a survey of office construction conducted in 1994, office buildings of more than four stories, a category that represented roughly half the market in the 1980s, had shrunk to about 30 percent.)

While many of the most prominent leaders of the architectural establishment were concentrating on theory, the sorts of buildings they might otherwise have designed were being replaced by building types in which they had minimal interest, and for which they had scant training—most notably malls, planned residential communities, and chain-owned hotels. The most common new form was the "big box" store, a totally utilitarian enclosure for the display and sale of hundreds of thousands of products. It was not much different from an airplane hangar, and the addition of a sign reading "HOME DEPOT" or "WAL-MART" fulfilled all too literally the requirements of Robert Venturi's "decorated shed." But they were proliferating without a trace of elevated architectural involvement.

---

[7] Ibid., p. 222.

The spread of these stores added measurably to the economic decline of the older city centers, in turn reducing the opportunity for the sort of architectural activity that had always been concentrated in them. But the urban centers were hardly giving up. With the help of the preservation movement, many city officials began to see that one of the major advantages they had over the sprawl beyond their borders was the distinctive architecture of their collective pasts. And they made belated haste to exploit it.

One urban architectural expression of the sentiment was a vaguely defined movement known as Contextualism. Increasingly aware of the damage done by the indiscriminate demolitions of the 1950s and 1960s, many architects had begun to look for ways to reassemble the urban mosaic. At one extreme was an addition to New York City's Jewish Museum, which had been designed as a residence in 1908 by C. P. H. Gilbert in the high-château mode so popular at the time. Kevin Roche, whose reputation was based largely on his sleek Modernist abstractions and corporate headquarters, such as the one for Union Carbide, demolished an earlier, Modernist addition to the museum and replaced it with a building that seamlessly replicated the style of the Gilbert original.

A more evolutionary approach to urban augmentation was demonstrated by a building completed in 1983, on New York City's Park Avenue, by James Stewart Polshek. The challenge of 500 Park, as the building was known, involved working with a building already on the site. This was the admirable 1960 glass-and-aluminum headquarters by Gordon Bunshaft of Skidmore, Owings & Merrill for the Pepsi-Cola Corporation, which later sold it to Olivetti. The eleven-story structure was a gem of corporate Modernism. Nevertheless, it occupied far less room than the local zoning allowed.

When the Olivetti site and that of a nondescript hotel behind it were bought in 1980, Polshek was asked to renovate the Skidmore, Owings & Merrill building and come up with a design for an adjoining tower to replace the hotel. His forty-two-story addition was a model of sensitive architectural cooperation across time and style. The architect wrapped the new tower in textured gray-green granite, but fused the two structures by bringing a portion of the tower forward on one side, and cladding it in materials similar to those of Olivetti. He used the same cladding for a cantilevered strip of the tower, creating a dramatically interlocking set of forms. Olivetti was not merely preserved; it was given

**JAMES
STEWART
POLSHEK**

the sympathetic environment without which its pristine Modernist geometry had always seemed slightly alien. By New York construction standards, 500 Park Avenue was not a major undertaking. But by the standards of sensitive urban architecture, it set a high mark for any city.

A similar impulse was demonstrated with comparable success but at far greater scale in another New York project just a few miles to the south. The site of Battery Park City was a ninety-two-acre parcel of land-fill in the Hudson River created largely with the dirt excavated for the adjacent World Trade Center. Several plans had been advanced for the land over a period of twenty years, but in the early 1980s a collaboration

500 PARK AVENUE, *James Stewart Polshek & Partners, New York City, 1985.* A singular example of an addition that makes the combination better than either part.

Timothy Hursley

Henk Morgan

CESAR PELLI

of unusual talents under the guidance of Richard Kahan, the head of the New York State Urban Development Corporation, produced a landmark of modern urban development.

The goal was to create a mixed-use community of offices and residences not unlike some of the edge city developments, but anchor it stylistically to the nearby buildings. The centerpiece of the development was a quartet of office towers by Cesar Pelli & Associates, architects of the Museum of Modern Art's expansion. Ranging in height from thirty-three to fifty-one stories, the stone-and-glass office buildings, which served as the economic "engine" of the entire development, were given distinctly different tops and situated in a staggered pattern to mitigate the overwhelming effect of the flat-topped Trade Center towers.

Impressive as the commercial core of the project was, it was a one-time undertaking, at least in New York City. More instructive for efforts to rehabilitate an aging city was the residential complex to the south. It was made up of ten buildings, all of them based on New York's characteristic domestic architecture, especially the buildings of the 1920s and 1930s along Central Park West and Park Avenue. The buildings were centered on a small park, and the entire grouping benefited from a broad esplanade along the Hudson. Lest the development appear cut off from the rest of the city, the planners aligned the streets in Battery Park City with the existing Manhattan grid.

What made Battery Park City so instructive was not just its reliance on the urban vernacular of its city's past, but a set of strict design guidelines based on a distillation of New York's most durable architectural successes—the romantic office towers of lower Manhattan, and the finely textured buildings of the city's older neighborhoods. Worked out by the architecture and planning firm of Cooper, Eckstut (whose partners, Alexander Cooper and Stanton Eckstut, later established separate firms), the guidelines required that all the buildings be clad in stone for the first two floors; they had to have prominent cornice lines to link the new buildings visually to the older ones nearby, and were required to vary the rooflines to echo the sculpted spires of the adjoining financial district. The rules went so far as to prescribe the size of bricks and the color of the mortar. Beyond those rules, architects were left to their own devices. "We decided to let a bunch of different designers loose in a competitive environment and see what they would come up with," said Richard Kahan. "It wasn't a question of how many great buildings we could create. If the whole works, each component can be less than great."[8]

Although such restrictions might in years past have seemed oppressive, the architects who agreed to design the residential towers (Charles Moore, Ulrich Franzen, and the firms of Davis, Brody & Associates, and James Stewart Polshek & Partners among them) came up with a re-

---

[8] Interview with the author, quoted in "The Next Great Place," *New York*, June 16, 1986.

BATTERY PARK CITY, *Cesar Pelli and others, New York City, 1985.* Planning and design triumphant in the service of urban habitability.

© Peter Aaron/Esto

markably satisfying variety of designs. The guidelines, said Ulrich Franzen, "brought about a level of sensitive design that was probably impossible otherwise. In fact, they tended to liberate creativity."[9]

---

[9] Ibid.

The impact of Battery Park City was immediate and wide-reaching. Under pressure from an aroused community, the flamboyant New York real estate developer Donald Trump, who had been planning a luxurious development on Manhattan's Upper West Side, eventually abandoned his original plans for six 70-plus-story towers flanking a central spire of 150 stories (intended to be the world's tallest) designed by Helmut Jahn, and turned first to Alexander Cooper and then to Richard Kahan to help reconfigure it along Battery Park City lines. A consummate salesman, Trump retained Philip Johnson as architect of the revised scheme, but only on the condition that he abide by a set of design guidelines, something Johnson had refused to do in Times Square, where the guidelines had also been worked out with Kahan's support.

Battery Park City had still other effects in New York. Although the original plan to redevelop the seedy Times Square area according to the guidelines drawn up by Kahan and Cooper had been overridden by Johnson and then stalled by recession, commitments by the Walt Disney Company in 1995 helped bring it back to life. And although the overall strategy was substantially different (focusing on family entertainment rather than office development), the scale was dramatically reduced.

While America's older cities were struggling to regain their vitality, the suburbs to which so many urban dwellers had fled were beginning to exhibit some age-related problems of their own. Primary among them was traffic, which grew more congested as the suburban population increased and the dependence on jobs in nearby cities remained. Other problems included a steadily rising cost of housing in the more desirable suburbs, which tended to force out the grown children of local residents, breaking down family bonds. The suburbs also lacked apartments or other low-income housing options for the teachers, firefighters, and other support personnel on whom these areas depended. Added to that was the scarcity of entertainment and work for young people, and the difficulty in finding day care for the increasing number of children with two working parents. Although retirement communities like Sun City were understandably well equipped to care for the elderly, most suburbs were not. Gradually, too, the sort of criminal activity from which many of the residents had fled began to infiltrate their new refuges.

Beyond all that, however, was a growing sense that the newer suburbs, and especially the ones with extensive restrictions on their residents, were socially deadening. The sorts of associations and relation-ships that can be developed only through an interaction with a variety of people over time, but which create a successful social environment, were being designed out of the new "communities" by the very exclu-siveness of the codes that made them attractive.

Alarmed by the deterioration of the suburban ideal, and mindful of the successes of such historically inspired urban initiatives as Battery Park City, a group of young architects and planners in the mid-1980s embarked on the development of a new form of community design. What made the idea especially appealing was that it was based, not on the conventional American suburb—or even on the "new-town" for-mula developed by James Rouse at Columbia, Maryland, in the late 1960s—but on the model of small towns of the past.

The first and best-known of these developments was on the Gulf coast of Florida, not far from Panama City. It was called "Seaside," and it launched a movement that came to be known variously as "neo-tra-ditionalism" or the "new urbanism."

Seaside was developed by Robert S. Davis, an Alabama native who had inherited his eighty-acre site on Florida's "Redneck Riviera" from his grandfather. Davis had been put off by the standard forms of resort development in the state, and wanted something that would evoke the spirit of the small Gulf coast communities where he and his family had spent vacations when he was a child.

To accomplish that, Davis retained Andres Duany and Elizabeth Plater-Zyberk, a husband-and-wife team with backgrounds in both ar-chitecture and city planning. Educated at Princeton as undergraduates and at the Yale architecture school, the couple had been intrigued by the vernacular housing in the neighborhoods of New Haven, and had set about studying it in detail. Together, Duany and Plater-Zyberk had gone on to become founding members of Arquitectonica, the Miami firm that later won the competition for a Times Square skyscraper, but they eventually soured on such large products, and were drawn back to the smaller scale of their earlier studies.

Duany had been encouraged in these studies while working in the offices of Robert A. M. Stern, who, in addition to his own design work, had become an authority on early American suburbs. Their other main source of inspiration was Leon Krier, a London-based urban theorist who had long argued for a return to cities laid out according to pedestrian rather than automotive needs. Their conclusion, as Duany told the *Wall Street Journal* in 1993, was that "You really cannot have a good society unless a portion of the population can live without the car as a tool."[10]

Of course, this was hardly a new idea. Architects and planners had been lamenting the damage done to American life by the automobile for decades; but no one had come up with a systematic and convincing way to repair it. Seaside, although primarily a resort, was designed in part to be a prototype for larger, self-sustaining communities across the country. And unlike the run-of-the-mill gated community or edge city, it represented the apparent confluence of high-quality architecture and all-American small-town values. Here, purportedly, was the meeting of the high and low cultures that had so long eluded American architecture.

Like the planners of Battery Park City, DPZ, as Duany and Plater-Zyberk's firm became known, chose not to design individual buildings, but concentrated on a code that would determine almost as much as the covenants common to gated communities. In this case, however, the restrictions were informed by a much higher level of design quality, specifying, for example, not just the location and height of buildings but also roof pitches and window proportions, and such details as what sort of siding could be used, and how far the mandated picket fences could be from the mandated front porches.

At the heart of the DPZ philosophy of the "revival town" was Krier's idea that housing, shopping, and work should be close enough together so that residents could get to all of them without driving. The planners operated from a theory that people will hesitate to spend more than five minutes walking on an errand, and that therefore the ideal size of a neighborhood—which should include basic services and shops—should be somewhere between forty and two hundred acres, so that residents could live within a quarter-mile of a green, a square, a meeting hall, a convenience store, or a transit stop.

Duany and Plater-Zyberk were not alone in such thinking. They were joined by other architect-planners such as Peter Calthorpe in San Francisco. But they were by far the most energetic and ambitious, turning out designs for numerous planned communities across the country.

---

[10] Eric Morgenthaler, "Old-Style Towns Where People Walk Have Modern Backers," *Wall Street Journal*, February 1, 1993.

In an effort to make their theories available beyond the reach of their own offices, they eventually published something called a Traditional Neighborhood Development ordinance, a generic document that could be used by existing towns and cities as well as by new developments.

Seaside captured the imagination of the academic design community, all but supplanting what was left of Deconstructivism as a topic of debate in the leading schools, and provoking a flurry of articles and books. Lots in DPZ developments sold briskly, and although Seaside itself eventually became primarily a high-priced time-sharing community for wealthy absentee owners (most of the year-round population was made up of property managers and maintenance crews), the concept it had launched soon attracted the attention of other developers. Most notable among them was the Disney Company, which in 1995 announced plans to create a residential community of its own near its Walt Disney World amusement park in Orlando, Florida.

Alert to the underlying theatricality of much 1980s architecture, the nation's preeminent entertainment company had already come to the professional aid of some of the best-known Postmodernists, whose prominence on the national architectural stage was beginning to fade, and signed them up to create buildings for its theme parks. Michael

**ANDRES DUANY
AND ELIZABETH
PLATER-ZYBERK**

Pelham Photo

Graves had designed two hotels for Disney World, as well as the company's headquarters building in Burbank, California, using nineteen-foot-high cast-concrete models of the Seven Dwarfs to support the pediment. Robert A. M. Stern had also designed two hotels for Disney World, basing them on the grand resort structures of the turn of the century. Having passed along his own interest in suburbs to Duany while he was an employee in Stern's firm, it was no surprise that when Disney exhibited an interest in residential development, Stern should turn to the successful example set by Seaside. Stern's close collaborator in the design phase was Jaquelin Robertson, a veteran city planner and architect who shared Stern's fondness for vintage resort architecture.

Quoting almost verbatim from the writings of DPZ and their followers, the promotional materials for Celebration, as the project was called,

SEASIDE, *Andres Duany, Elizabeth Plater-Zyberk, and others, near Panama City, Florida, 1985.* The high quality of the architecture concealed the limitations of "neo-traditionalism."

explained that the 5,000-acre development—intended to accommodate 20,000 residents—would be "designed as a pedestrian-friendly place to live, work, and play." The downtown, the promoters went on, "is planned to be a traditional retail and business district modeled after those found in small American towns." It would include a school, town hall, bank, post office, a "cinema," and a "health campus" providing something only Disney could have called "healthcare edu-tainment." In contrast to most of Seaside, the downtown would be accessible to automobiles as well as pedestrians.

The list of architects selected for Celebration included such familiar figures as Graves, Johnson, Moore, and Venturi. But it also included such seasoned practitioners of large-scale residential design as Cesar Pelli and Alexander Cooper, who had collaborated on Battery Park City, and William Rawn, whose 1988 rehabilitation of the old Boston Navy Yard had won him a reputation as a designer of some of the most sensitive new housing in the country.

Powerful as this group appeared to be, it was shadowed by the pervasive Disney proclivity for tidiness and order. And here Celebration departed in a fundamental way from the original spirit of Seaside, which had provided design guidelines but allowed architects almost total freedom to operate within them. The range of design in the Celebration residential offerings was strictly limited to six basic types, outlined in the *Celebration Pattern Book*: Classical, Coastal, Mediterranean, Victorian, Colonial Revival, and French. Significantly, there was no provision for Modern, Postmodern, Deconstructivist, or any other creative variation on the approved themes.

Of course, the list was merely confirming what dispassionate observers—and developers—had known since the days of the pattern books against which Frank Lloyd Wright had rebelled: that most Americans are far more interested in comfort than aesthetic statements in their houses. A more recent reminder of that was a study conducted in 1980 by a researcher at the State University of New York at Buffalo, who attempted to determine if builders of tract homes were giving buyers what they wanted. He presented 129 homeowners with generic drawings of houses in eight different styles and found that the overwhelming favorites were "Farm House" and "Tudor." "Modern" was rated last. The finding that the developers of Celebration made canny use of was that suburbanites preferred a *variety* of styles over a neighborhood done in only one. But they made sure that there would be no discordance among the choices.

While Celebration's architecture was promoted as an aesthetic matter, it also carried an increasingly familiar message in American design and planning: that residents would be safe from crime, or at least the fear of it. One had only to look at Celebration's official logotype, which displayed a silhouette of a pig-tailed girl on a bicycle pursued by a puppy as she pedaled past a picket fence shaded by a leafy tree of the sort real estate agents refer to as a "mature planting."

Attempts like those at Seaside and Celebration to rehumanize the American suburb through architecture might be construed as a refreshing return to the philosophy of the turn-of-the-century eclectics, who had no qualms about creating the illusion of pedigree and permanence. But what distinguished those architects had been their confident expansiveness. Their heirs in Disney's employ reflected a packaged fearfulness.

A longer look suggested that the very assumptions on which neo-traditionalist planning was based were nearly as flawed as those that had supported urban renewal in the 1950s. There has never been any compelling evidence that Americans, given the choice, would abandon their automobiles. Nor is there much to suggest that people will pay more at a full-price store they can walk to than they will at a discount mall they can drive to, unless, of course, they are wealthy. And if wealth is the determinant of a successful new "revival town," then nothing has been done to advance the argument for reanimating a genuine sense of community through design.

Even at the level of architectural detail, these projects embodied more wishful thinking than fact. The narrow alleys mandated by DPZ and the designers of Celebration to encourage pedestrian flow through the towns may have had a sentimental appeal, but they had long ago become synonymous in the American consciousness with trash and muggings. Front porches may be a staple of the Norman Rockwell vision of America, but they emerged before the advent of television and air conditioning, and in communities where people developed relationships over time and were still willing to chat with passers-by. By the very nature of modern American society, the potential residents of Seaside and

Carter Wiseman

CELEBRATION,
*Robert A. M. Stern,
Jaquelin Robertson,
and others, Orlando,
Florida, 1996.*
A "themed" suburb
whose restrictions
subvert true
community,
social and
architectural.

Celebration tended to be far more transient than their forebears. And the more people move, the harder it is to establish the sort of interdependency that builds neighborliness—and supports the reasons for neighborly architecture. Turnover breeds, if not suspicion, at least withdrawal into the backyard. (Celebration's front lawns, while overlooked by porches furnished with old-timey rockers, more often than not sprouted signs warning of protection by a local security firm.)

By arguing that an architecture based on an idealized view of the past would improve the present, the neo-traditionalists were altering only slightly the Modernists' attempt to sweep away the perceived shortcomings of the immediate past with an idealized view of the future: "clean" machines-for-living-in would purge the corrupt society represented by the neoclassical.

Theory aside, the neo-traditionalist trend raised the question why, if the principles on which its advocates were operating were valid, so many of the small towns from which they had derived their design guidelines were suffering.

The reasons lay in a complex array of social and economic forces, ranging from the decline in manufacturing jobs to the proliferation of inexpensive merchandise outlets that undercut the prices at mom-and-pop stores, to the growing phenomenon of single-parent families. But these were well beyond the control of architects and planners. In the end, what the neo-traditionalists were pursuing (and selling) was a facsimile—not just of a bygone architecture, but of a way of life that had largely vanished by the time their projects began construction.

The customers who signed up for Mediterranean or Victorian houses in Celebration no doubt thought that these tidy new enclaves would provide them with an improvement on shopping malls and cul-de-sacs. But while the concentrations of apparently like-minded people who valued this way of life might have suggested a rebirth of community spirit in the America of the 1990s, the opposite actually seemed to be the case. In a seminal essay entitled "Bowling Alone," published in January 1995 in the *Journal of Democracy*, a Harvard professor of government named Robert D. Putnam argued forcefully that a fundamental change had gradually taken place in the way Americans related to each other. He contended that the generations that had come of age before World War II were being replaced by people who were less likely to join organizations—including bowling leagues—vote in elections, or even trust their neighbors.

Putnam and others suggested that the usual suspect—television—was at the heart of the problem, but that the increasing use of computers was replacing the sort of face-to-face interaction that traditionally creates interpersonal ties. Added to the rising level of anxiety about personal safety, this trend toward an almost antisocial autonomy was bound to reduce the call for a life of neighborhood interaction, let alone the sort of civic monuments groups traditionally erected to celebrate their common goals and interests.

If architects should have learned anything from the death of Modernism, it was that even the highest quality design can have only a limited impact on social problems, and may in fact aggravate them. The sort of architectural thinking that produced Pruitt-Igoe and those ubiquitous office towers surrounded by plazas was rooted in the best of social intentions—improving the lot of the working class and reordering the cities to provide their residents with more light, air, and open space. By the 1990s, the shortcomings of those solutions had become overwhelmingly clear, and the retreat into merely stylistic or theoretical pursuits proved no more useful.

Reflecting a humbled awareness of that fact, the October 1994 issue of *Architectural Record* looked forward to an architecture in which "the personality of the architect is likely to bow to local tastes and local issues; an architecture where technology is more likely to be merely refined and used in service of the architecture than as a dominant force—in other words, a framework dominated by local influences and expressed content."[11]

Faced with a bleak landscape of opportunities, many younger architects began to limit their ambitions and concentrate more on the craft and details of building than on the size or scope of the project. A smaller number were able to rely on that staple of American architectural stardom, country houses for the wealthy. That market would appear to be a constant for architects, even in times that are bad economically and confusing ideologically, and there should be no shame in serving it. But as corporations in the 1990s husbanded resources that a decade earlier might have been spent on signature buildings, they and other organizations turned increasingly to the renovation of existing structures, taking their architects with them. Statistics compiled by the U.S. Department of Commerce in 1995 showed that the dollar volume of renovation work had already pulled almost even with that of new construction.

Taken together, the influences that were confronting architecture as the century neared its close were forcing a fundamental reexamination of the traditional assumptions about why—indeed *if*—people needed it at all, and what it stood for.

In the United States, at least, those assumptions have always rested heavily on waste. Whether the commodity at hand was land, natural resources, raw materials, or money, the opportunity to use it up, throw it away, and find more has always been an article of the America faith. It is a cliché to state that implicit in the American pioneer ideal was the knowledge that one could always move on to new territory. Implicit in the industrial growth of the eighteenth and nineteenth centuries was the belief that individualism and entrepreneurship would ultimately contribute to a greater good. Implicit in the move to the suburbs in the

---

11 Stephen A. Kliment, "Paradox," *Architectural Record* (October 1994), p. 9.

1950s was the confidence that the urban problems the exurbanites were fleeing would stay where they had been left. But such thinking has its negative consequences for the built environment.

By the end of the century, there were fewer and fewer places to which to move, and many of those places—whether a conventional suburb, a gated community, an edge city, or a Celebration—were not always fulfilling their promotional claims.

Just as waste and flight proved to be inadequate responses for a maturing society, so was the abdication of responsibility for its surroundings. Judging by the steady centrist drift of American politics in the 1990s, it was clear that feelings of frustration with the status quo were provoking a determination by people across the country to take back some measure of control over their environments. At one level, that meant making not just cities but also towns and suburbs attractive again as places of commerce, education, and culture.

If a community cares about itself, good architecture—both what already exists and what is yet to be built—may again become a powerful component of that community. But on the eve of the millennium, the future of community in the United States is far from certain. Every indicator suggests that the country will continue to fragment along lines of income, ethnicity, politics, and race. And diversity is not a condition with which architecture has dealt well in the twentieth century. Indeed, diversity had been anathema to the design community ever since Modernism institutionalized the idea of a universal architectural ideology. The Postmodernists claimed to have overturned the orthodoxy of their predecessors, but what they did *not* overturn was the emphasis on the architect as the source of ideas, the form-giver. The dominance of celebrity architects in the 1980s merely extended the practice for a media age. And the next wave of "rebellion," launched by the Deconstructivists, only reinforced the idea of the architect as a stand-apart *artiste*—with self-destructive results.

One of the most basic problems with architecture in twentieth-century America has been that many of its most famous representatives gradually came to believe that their proper role was not to ask questions, but to dictate answers. It should have come as no surprise that their audience was gradually reduced largely to wealthy patrons, educational and cultural institutions craving notoriety, and credulous students.

If the art and profession of architecture is to flourish in the next century, its members will have to come to terms with the lessons of Portman and Disney, of gated communities and edge cities, without allowing themselves—or their clients—to be seduced yet again by style or ideology, and by participating in the public process to raise the level of artistic expectation and execution. In a stunning acknowledgment of the changed rules, the editor of *Architectural Record* asserted in 1994 that "a new stereotype [of the architect] is emerging," one "not conceived narrowly as designer of buildings (although this will always be a core service), but one who serves across a far wider range in the building marketplace." He went on to say that "All who operate under the umbrella of building design are essentially performing functions of this broader-based architect. Perhaps the title itself must be changed, so that pride doesn't get in the way of reality."[12]

To be sure, some of the traditional building types that in the past represented the highest architectural achievement may be rendered all but irrelevant in an age when technology can deliver information and culture to the consumer virtually anywhere. But new types will emerge. There was a time when office buildings were left to builders and engineers, at least in Chicago. But that building type reached its highest expression in the hands of Mies van der Rohe. For years, few architects of high esteem (except the independent-minded Eero Saarinen) paid much attention to airports. They are now among the most heavily designed complexes in the world, and can be very beautiful indeed. Is the superstore the next major challenge? Probably not. But hospitals and health-care facilties have rarely benefited from the best architectural talent. (A small but symbolic example of the way in which that can change was the conversion in 1995 of a banal 1960s Los Angeles office building to a center for cancer care by the avant-garde firm Morphosis.) Only a notable few of the country's leading architects have involved themselves over the years in the design of public schools, but those buildings are clearly more likely to be "the crucible of the future" than edge cities. And should the older cities regain the trust of the citizenry as places to live and work in security, the rehabilitation of their neglected architectural legacy—as some of the "new urbanists" have begun to realize—

---

12 Stephen A. Kliment, "Architect Bashing: Enough Already!" *Architectural Record* (June 1994), p. 7.

will be a monumental challenge. Surely, there will be no lack of opportunity in the future.

Clues to the changing nature of the profession are already evident in the way it honors its own. A glance at the awards given by the American Institute of Architects from the early 1990s onward suggests that previously underappreciated building types are increasingly acceptable as worthy of high design—but of a chastened sort. Gone are the blank street walls and the sheer surfaces of Skidmore, Owings & Merrill's early high-rises. The AIA's 1992 gold medal went to Benjamin C. Thompson, who began his career working with Walter Gropius, but at the age of seventy-three was prouder of the waterfront revitalization projects he and his firm had designed from Boston to Chicago to Jacksonville, Florida. A profile of Thompson in *Architecture*, the official AIA publication, said of him: "Quiet background buildings, he believes, usually work best, and should be carefully conceived settings for spontaneous human exchange."[13] I. M. Pei, who had all but exhausted the possibilities of sculptural Modernism in architecture with his East Building of the National Gallery, completed in 1989 a symphony hall for Dallas that had moments of gossamer lyricism. Pei's colleague Henry N. Cobb, who had designed the icily elegant Hancock Tower in Boston, a building that still represents one of the highest achievements of the Modernist aesthetic, in 1995 finished a business school for UCLA that verged on the sensuous in its use of curving brick walls. Scores of younger architects yet to make national names for themselves are embracing an aesthetic and a level of societal sensitivity unknown in decades past.

At the close of the century, the fate of American architecture is no longer a matter of vision, ideology, or even style. It lies in a final farewell to the preoccupation with heroes and form-givers, in a terminal discrediting of the idea of architecture as the making of objects in isolation. The architecture of the future demands a day-by-day involvement in the rapidly changing conditions of the society which it serves. It can no longer be only about monuments that reflect a social, commercial, or political consensus—such as the Boston Public Library, Pennsylvania Station, the Seagram Building, or even the Portland Public Services

---

13 Mildred F. Schmertz, "Power of Joy," *Architecture* (March 1992), p. 56.

Building—but must be about the aesthetically skilled satisfaction of the needs of a society that bears little resemblance to the one that produced those monuments. For architects willing to confront those facts, the role of the profession in the future seems increasingly to lie in the knitting together of the torn urban and suburban fabric, the binding up of physical wounds inflicted by previous generations. In this, many of the practitioners who were never lionized in the press but labored diligently to make buildings of high quality—even *beautiful* buildings—within the limits of their resources may emerge as better role models for the future than the "hottest" architects of the recent past.

But there should be no illusions about the prospects for success. American architecture, like all architecture, has always served the dominant culture. As the culture went, so went architecture—from the shaping of a young nation in the image of its cultural and political origins, to the promotion and marketing of a prosperous one, to the defense of a fearfully fragmented one. And along the way, it has been influenced with increasing effect by a steadily shrinking number of practitioners whose primary distinction was their growing distance from the great majority of their potential clients.

Without vigilance and effort, American society is likely to become even more fragmented, its members seeking ever more hardened refuges. If so, architecture will follow, attempting to make the physical expressions of that trend as aesthetically pleasing as possible. But there is hope that the nation may yet find ways to celebrate its changing self in built form, transcending the anxieties and divisions wrought by its passage into maturity. If they are not the ways or the forms of the past, no matter. The architectural challenge for America is to reflect a society of increasing variation, and still give physical shape to its highest aspirations.

Acknowledgments

I would like to thank the following people for their generous help and support in the preparation of this book:

At W. W. Norton, Donald Lamm, who initiated the project; Gerald Howard, who served as editor; Ruth Mandel, who conducted the bulk of the picture research; and Sean Desmond. At Sterling Lord Literistic, Sterling Lord and Barbara Ryan. For their comments on all or parts of the manuscript, I am indebted to Laurie Beckelman, Paul S. Byard, Peter Clement, Mary Farrell, Robert Kliment, James O'Gorman, Alexander Purves, Franz Schulze, Thomas Wittrock, and especially Carole Herselle Krinsky.

Further thanks to: Ann Adelman, John Ashley, Jr., Jane Atkinson, Richard Babcock, Kent Bloomer, Christine Born, Ronald Brenne, James Marston Fitch, James Ingo Freed, Pedro Guerrero, Frances Halsband, William Hansen, Eloise Hirsch, Christopher Monkhouse, Ieoh Ming Pei, Cesar Pelli, Bruce Brooks Pfeiffer, Adolf Placzek, Alan Plattus, Cervin Robinson, James G. Rogers III, Eduard Sekler, Suzanne Stephens, Erica Stoller, and the staff of the *Yale Alumni Magazine*.

Index

aesthetics (*continued*)

  practical requirements vs., 165, 208

  principles of, 270

  as suspect, 19, 75

  see also specific styles and movements

African-Americans, 243

agricultural economy, 17

airports, 384

air rights, 237–38

air travel, 229

Akron, Ohio, 240

Aladdin Company, 79

Allegheny County Courthouse and Jail, 40

Allen, Gerald, 280*n*

aluminum, 179, 249, 367

American Academy in Rome, 206, 214, 248, 260,
  286

American Architect and Building News, 42, 80, 81

American Architects and the Mechanics of Fame
  (Williamson), 248*n*

American architecture:

  aesthetics and originality vs. construction and tra-
    dition in, 13

  and American desire for stability, 117

  American identity in, 267

  American values in, 382–83

  as art, 330, 355

  art integrated with, 85, 138, 186, 209, 287, 305–6

  commercialism of, 331–32, 346, 382

  and context, 234, 241–42, 243, 244–45, 267–72

  and crime, 359, 361, 365, 373, 379

  cynicism in, 331

  East Coast establishment of, *see* establishment,
    architectural

  eclecticism of, 18, 42, 45, 83, 88, 91, 115–48,
    183–84, 254, 258, 291, 331

  European architects influenced by, 109–12, 114,
    119, 159, 160, 165, 172

  European influence on, *see* European influence

  future of, 14, 384–86

  government as sponsor of, 322

humanism in, 216, 284, 330

humor in, 248, 249, 257, 261, 280–81, 283, 284,
  336, 336, 340, 342–43, 345

individual structures vs. neighborhoods in,
  243–45

"joy" in, 280, 283, 284

libertarianism in, 348

maturing cultural judgments on, 13, 222

morals in, 19, 31, 100, 146, 163–64, 254, 263,
  270

multiple meanings in, 248, 250, 251, 252–54,
  267

pioneer ideal in, 382

public preferences in, 80, 117, 260, 263, 267,
  283, 294, 297, 366, 378–79, 386

simplicity in, 38, 101, 186, 252, 269

social change and, 13, 29, 149, 169, 179, 259,
  269, 271–72, 331, 335, 346, 380–86

as subject of public debate, 330

symbolism of, 313–16, 331, 333, 334

theory in, 154, 162, 173, 250, 262, 271, 286, 335,
  338, 346, 353, 355, 357, 366, 382

twentieth-century, *see* Modernism, Modernists;
  Postmodernism, Postmodernists; skyscrapers;
  specific individuals and styles

American Architecture (Kimball), 138*n*

American Architecture of To-day, The (Edgell), 131*n*

American Builder's Companion (Benjamin), 24

*American Building: The Historical Forces That
  Shaped It* (Fitch), 115

American Buildings and Their Architects (Pierson),
  20*n*

American Institute of Architects, 34, 74, 90, 145,
  168, 229, 359, 385

American Radiator Building, 142

American Revolution, 19, 20

America's Favorite Homes (Schweitzer and Davis),
  80*n*

Andrews, Wayne, 23*n*, 118*n*, 168*n*

anti-Semitism, 328

Antiquities Act of 1906, 224

Antiquities of Athens (Stuart and Revett), 24

ANYONE, 353

Renaissance Center, 359

Renaissance Revival, 118

Renwick, James, 30, 31, 32, 58, 121

RepublicBank Center, 324–25, 327, 329

residential design, *see* domestic architecture

resorts, 25, 83–84, 221, 355, 374–75, 376, 377

retail shops, 211

retirement communities, 363, 373

Revett, Nicholas, 24

"revival towns," 374–80

"Revolution of '88, The" (Gandee), 345*n*

Revolution of 1917, Russian, 339

Rhine Valley, 186

Riani, Paolo, 359*n*

Richard Neutra (McCoy), 160*n*

Richardson, Henry Hobson, 37–42, 38, 39, 40, 41, 58, 65, 67–72 69, 71, 83, 86, 106, 120, 121, 228, 292–93, 299, 332

"Richardsonian Romanesque," 37, 39, 120

Robert A. M. Stern, Buildings and Projects, 292*n*, 364*n*

Robertson, Jaquelin, 377, 380

Robie, Frederick C., 104–5, 109, 191

Robie House, 104–5, 106, 106, 193, 195

Roche, Kevin, 318–20, 320, 321, 323, 362, 362, 367

Roche, Martin, 62, 160

Rockefeller, John D., Jr., 226, 227

Rockefeller Center, 142, 143, 171

Rockwell, Norman, 379

Roebling, John, 41–42, 48

Roebling, Washington, 41–42, 48

Rogers, James Gamble, 131, 132, 133–34, 133, 135, 170, 199

Roman architecture, 21, 25, 26, 74, 126, 208, 232
    ruins, 210, 214, 248, 259
    villas at Herculaneum, 285

Romanesque architecture, 35, 37, 68, 120, 121, 220, 238

romanticism, 182, 183–218, 258, 308
    Modernist materials used in, 197–98, 199

Rome, 32, 179, 206, 208, 248, 256, 286, 330

"Romeo and Juliet" (windmill), 184, 185, 197

Rome Prize, 248

Rookery, The, 58

Root, John Wellborn, 58, 62, 156

Roth, Leland, 116*n*

Rouse, James, 374

Rouse Corporation, 242

Route 91 (Las Vegas), 255

Route 128 (Boston), 364

Rowe, Colin, 295

Rudolph, Paul, 202–4, 205, 211, 215, 249, 253, 254, 256–58, 267, 272, 281, 360

Rural Residences (Davis), 28

Ruskin, John, 27, 31, 32, 35, 96, 106

Russian Constructivism, 339, 355

S

Saarinen, Aline B., 200*n*

Saarinen, Eero, 139, 198–201, 200, 202, 203, 215, 247–48, 253, 254, 258, 318, 384

Saarinen, Eliel, 139, 198

Safdie, Moshe, 322

safety:
    creating sense of, 359, 360, 361
    edge cities and, 365
    planned communities and, 363

St. Andrews, 364

St. Bartholomew's Episcopal Church, 238–39, 239

Saint-Gaudens, Augustus, 85

St. Louis, Mo., 234, 269

St. Louis Arch (Jefferson National Expansion Monument), 199, 247

St. Mark's (Venice), 27

St. Mary's Roman Catholic Cathedral, 23

St. Patrick's Cathedral, 30, 58

St. Paul's school:
    chapel of, 120
    Ohrstrom Library of, 292–93, 296, 297

Saint Thomas Episcopal Church, 117, 123–25, 124, 138

Terminal Station, 240

terracotta, 142

Thomas, George E., 249*n*

Thompson, Benjamin C., 242, 385

James R. Thompson Center, 315–16, 3*16*, 321

333 Wacker Drive (Chicago), 321, *325*

Time magazine, 303

Times Square, 325–26, 354, 355, 373, 374

Times Square Center (project), 323–26, 328, 330, 354–55, 373

"Toad Hall," 273

tobacco culture, 17

Towards a New Architecture (Le Corbusier), 146, 155, 164, 247

Town, Ithiel, 28

town houses, 364

tract homes, 378

Traditional Neighborhood Development ordinance, 376

training, architectural, *see* architectural training

train stations, 24

Transamerica Corporation Tower, 3*12*, 313–14

transcendentalism, 95

Transco Tower, 322, 329

Transportation Building (World's Columbian Exposition), 44–45, *44*, 74, 91

Trenton Bath Houses, 248

Tribune Building, 49, *50*, 70

Trinity Church (Boston), 37, 39, 83, 120, 299, 330

Trinity Church (New York), 30, *31*

Trubeck house, 258–59

Trumbauer, Horace, 116, 132

Trump, Donald, 373

Tschumi, Bernard, 344, 348, 353

Tudor style, 98, 117, 132, 275, 378

Turnbull, William, 279, 282

Turner, Paul Venable, 131*n*

Tuscany, 186, 208, *209*, 215

TWA Building, 201, *202*, 215

Tysons Corner, Va., 365

U

Union Carbide, 362

Union Carbide headquarters, 362, *362*, 367

United Nations Headquarters, 170, *170*

Unity Temple, 107, *108*, 111

universities, *see* colleges and universities

Upjohn, Richard, 30, 31, *31*, 32, 34, 120

urban decline, 359, 367, 383

urbanization, 25, 26, 80, 128, 164, 179, 191, 197, 211

anxiety about crime and, 359

social unrest and, 359

"urban pioneers," 242

urban planners, 231

urban renewal, 164, 169, 220, 230, 242, 379

urban revitalization, 367–73, 384

"Useless House, The," 340

"Usonian" houses, 191

utilitarian construction, 19

V

vacation houses, 272–74, 306, 342

Valéry, Paul, 346

Van Alen, William, 142–45, *144*

Van Brunt, Henry, 34

Vanderbilt, George W., 33

Vaughan, Henry, 120–21

Vaux, Calvert, 43

Venice, 27, 32, 135

Venturi, Robert, 246–67, 249*n*, *250* 251*n*, *251*, 252, 256*n*, 264*n*, *264*, 265, 269, 283, 287, 291, 294, 295, 296, 311, 332, 366, 378

common sense in the architecture of, 267

essential elitism of, 259–61

influence of, 278, 280, 291

irony of, 248, 249, 261–62, 266

populism in architectural theories of, 255–56, 259–60

value judgments eschewed by, 254, 255–56, 263

Vanna Venturi House, 250–51, *251*

vernacular architecture, 129, 371, 374